Integrated Korean

High Intermediate 2

KLEAR Textbooks in Korean Language

Integrated Korean

High Intermediate 2

Sumi Chang

Hee-Jeong Jeong

Ho-min Sohn

Sang-Seok Yoon

University of Hawai'i Press

Honolulu

© 2019 University of Hawaiʻi Press
All rights reserved
Printed in the United States of America

25 24 23 22 21 20   7 6 5 4 3 2

This textbook series has been developed by the Korean Language Education and
Research Center (KLEAR) with the support of the Korea Foundation.

Library of Congress Cataloging-in-Publication Data

The Library of Congress has cataloged the one-volume edition as follows:
Names: Chang, Sumi, author. | Jeong, Hee-Jeong, author. | Sohn, Ho-min,
    author. | Yoon, Sang-Seok, author.
Title: Integrated Korean. High intermediate / Sumi Chang, Hee-Jeong Jeong,
    Ho-min Sohn, Sang-Seok Yoon.
Other titles: KLEAR textbooks in Korean language.
Description: Honolulu : University of Hawaiʻi Press, [2018] | Series: KLEAR
    textbooks in Korean language
Identifiers: LCCN 2018033513 | ISBN 9780824877927 (volume 1; pbk. ; alk.
    paper)
Subjects: LCSH: Korean language—Textbooks for foreign speakers—English.
Classification: LCC PL913 .C453 2018 | DDC 495.782/421—dc23
LC record available at https://lccn.loc.gov/2018033513

ISBN 978-0-8248-8276-1 (volume 2)

Illustrations by Seijin Han

Audio files for *High Intermediate* may be downloaded in MP3 format
at https://kleartextbook.com.

Printer-ready copy has been provided by the authors.

University of Hawaiʻi Press books are printed on acid-free paper and meet the guidelines for
permanence and durability of the Council on Library Resources.

Contents

대한민국의 수도 서울

Lesson 8 Seoul, Capital City of Korea

학습 목표

내용
- 서울에 대해서 이야기할 때 자주 쓰이는 단어와 표현들을 알아본다.
- 도시나 지역에 대해서 이야기할 때 필요한 단어와 표현들을 연습해 본다.

문화
- 서울의 역사, 지리, 인구, 기후 등 여러 가지 사실들을 알아본다.
- 서울과 다른 나라의 수도들을 비교해 본다.

서울특별시
SEOUL METROPOLITAN GOVERNMENT

수도 capital city of a country 도시 city 지역 area, region 지리 geography
인구 population 기후 climate

■ 생각해 봅시다

가 ▸ 서울은 어떤 도시입니까? 서울에 대해서 아는 것들을 이야기해 봅시다.
(예: 역사, 인구, 지리, 문화, 교통, 기후, 물가)

나 ▸ 서울에 가 본 적이 있습니까?

1. 어디에 가 봤습니까?

2. 거기에서 무엇을 했습니까?

다 ▸ 서울에 가 본 적이 없습니까?

1. 어디에 가 보고 싶습니까?

2. 거기서 무엇을 해 보고 싶습니까?

라 ‣ 여러분 나라의 수도는 어디입니까? 어떤 도시인지 간단히
　　소개해 봅시다.

마 ‣ 대도시에 사는 장점과 단점은 어떤 것들이 있는지 이야기해 봅시다.

바 ‣ 여러분은 어떤 곳에서 살고 싶은지 이야기해 봅시다.

대화 서울 소개

마크하고 민지가 서울 여행에 대해서 이야기하고 있다.

마크: 민지 씨는 한국의 어디에서 오셨어요?

민지: 저는 서울에서 왔어요.

마크: 민지 씨도 서울에서 오셨어요? 제가 만난 한국 사람들은 대부분 서울에서 오셨**더라구요.**^{G8.1}

민지: 그래요? 서울이 제일 큰 도시이고 인구도 많으니까 서울에서 온 사람들이 가장 많을 거예요.

마크: 서울은 인구가 얼마나 되지요?

민지: 서울 인구는 1,000만 명 정도 돼요. 그런데 서울 주변 도시에 사는 사람들을 다 더하면 아마 2,500만 명쯤 될 거예요.

마크: 한국 인구가 5,000만 명이라고 들었는데… 그럼 한국 사람 중 반 정도가 수도권에 사는 거네요.

민지: 그런 **셈이지요.**^{G8.2}

마크: 왜 다들 서울에서 살고 싶어 하지요?

민지: 서울이 교육 환경도 좋고 직장도 많고 문화 시설도 다양하니까 서울에서 살고 싶어 하는 사람들이 많을 **수밖에요.**^{G8.3}

마크: 그럼 서울은 물가가 많이 비싸겠네요?

대부분 mostly (=거의) 주변 surroundings, vicinity 더하다 to add 수도권 metropolitan area 교육 환경 educational environment 문화 시설 cultural facilities 물가 cost of living

민지: 그럼요. 서울 물가는 뉴욕이나 도쿄하고 비슷하다고 해요.

마크: 밤에 다녀도 위험하지는 않은가요?

민지: 뭐 대도시니까 조심해야겠지만 서울은 여행하기에 안전한 편이에요.

마크: 그렇군요… 저도 내년쯤에 서울에 여행을 가 볼까 하는데 언제 가면 좋을까요?

민지: 다 좋지만 가을이 날씨가 좋으니까 시간 되시면 10월경에 가는 게 제일 좋아요.

마크: 여름에는 어때요?

민지: 여름에 가시려면 6월 초가 좋아요. **한여름**은^{G8.4} 너무 무덥고 비가 자주 와서 여행하기 좀 힘들 거예요.

마크: 그렇군요. 서울에서 **볼 만한**^{G8.5} 것들은 뭐가 있을까요?

민지: 글쎄요. 어떤 것들을 좋아하세요?

마크: 제가 역사에 관심이 많아요. 얼마 전에 경복궁에 관해서 들어봤는데 꼭 가 보고 싶어요.

민지: 경복궁 좋지요! 경복궁 근처에 덕수궁이나 창덕궁 같은 다른 고궁들도 좋으니까 꼭 가 보세요.

마크: 아, 그래야겠네요. 그리고 서울에는 산이 많다고 들었는데 등산할 만한 산이 많이 있나요?

민지: 네, 서울 중심에는 남산이 있고 주변에 북한산, 도봉산, 관악산 등이 있는데 등산하는 사람들이 많이 있어요. 그 서울타워 아시지요? 드라마에 자주 나오잖아요.

마크: 아, 네! 본 적이 있어요.

시간(이) 되다 to have time –경 around…, about… 초 beginning (of) 한여름 midsummer 무덥다 to be muggy 볼 만하다 to be worth seeing 고궁 ancient palace 중심 center

민지: 그게 남산에 있는 거예요. 서울타워에 올라가면 서울을 **한눈에**G8.6 볼 수 있어요.

마크: 아! 서울타워에도 한번 가 보고 싶었어요.

민지: 그리고 서울에는 박물관이나 미술관도 많으니까 골라서 가 보세요. 얼마 전에 제 미국 친구 하나가 전쟁기념관에 가 봤는데 볼 것도 많고 배울 것도 많다고 하더라고요.

마크: 서울에서는 정말 할 것이 많은 것 같아요. 제가 한국 여행 계획을 세울 때 더 자세히 물어볼게요.

한눈에 at one sight 고르다 to choose, select 전쟁기념관 The War Memorial of Korea
계획을 세우다 to make a plan

이해 문제

가... 다음 내용이 대화의 내용과 같으면 ○, 다르면 X에 표시하세요.

　　　1. 서울 수도권에는 1,000만 명 정도의 사람들이 산다.　　　　○　　　X

　　　2. 서울은 세계에서 제일 큰 도시이다.　　　　　　　　　　　○　　　X

　　　3. 서울에 살면 돈이 많이 든다.　　　　　　　　　　　　　　○　　　X

　　　4. 서울 중심에서는 등산을 할 수 없다.　　　　　　　　　　○　　　X

　　　5. 서울타워는 서울 중심에 있다.　　　　　　　　　　　　　○　　　X

나... 다음 질문에 대답해 보세요.

　　　1. 서울 수도권의 인구는 얼마나 됩니까?

　　　2. 한국의 많은 사람들이 서울에서 살고 싶어 하는 이유는 무엇입니까?

　　　3. 한국 역사에 관심이 많은 사람들이 갈 만한 곳들은 어떤 곳들이 있습니까?

　　　4. 서울을 전체적으로 보고 싶으면 어디에 가면 됩니까?

　　　5. 서울에서 할 수 있는 활동으로는 어떤 것들이 있습니까?

문법과 용법

~더라고 'I saw/found/witnessed/felt that; you know'

가: 너 우산 찾았니?

   Did you find your umbrella?

나: 있을 만한 곳은 다 찾아보았는데 없**더라고**.

   I looked in all the likely places, but couldn't find it, you know.

가: 그 식당 음식은 어땠어요?

   How was the food at that restaurant?

나: 음식이 아주 맛있**더라고**요.

   I found the food to be very delicious.

▶ The sentence ending ~더라고 and its spoken variant ~더라구 are one of the most frequently used sentence endings in conversation. This ending is used when the speaker casually reports, often in a polite manner, one's past observation of an event or past experience of an emotional or sensory state. The suffix –더 carries the meaning of the speaker's past observation or experience, while the statement suffix –라 and the quotative particles –고/구 convey the concept of casual reporting. This pattern can be changed into the polite style with the addition of –요.

~는/(으)ㄴ 셈이다
'it is (almost) as though; I would say'

이 일을 10년 동안 했으니 저도 이제 전문가**인 셈이**에요.

Since I have been doing this kind of work for 10 years, I would say I am basically an expert in it now.

이번 시험만 보면 이번 학기는 다 끝**난 셈이**에요.

After taking this test, the semester will be pretty much over.

▶ The pattern ~는/(으)ㄴ 셈이다 is composed of the modifier ending –는/(으)ㄴ + the noun 셈 'the situation, the case, computation' + 이다 'is', literally meaning 'it is the situation/case that …'. Its derived, more commonly used meaning is: 'it is (almost) as though …' or 'I would say …'. It is used after an adjective, a copula, or a verb to express that the subject referent of the sentence is practically or almost in the situation indicated by the co-occurring adjective/copula/verb construction. A clause indicating a reason or a condition usually precedes the ~는/(으)ㄴ 셈이다 clause.

~(으)ㄹ 수밖에
'can't help … –ing; have no other way but to'

다른 옷이 없으니 이 옷을 또 입**을 수밖에**.

Since I don't have any other clothes, I'll have to wear these again.

죽느냐 사느냐의 문제가 걸려 있으니 그럴 **수밖에요**.

Because it's a matter of life or death, there is no other alternative.

운동을 많이 하기 때문에 건강**할 수밖에요**.

Because they exercise a lot, of course they are healthy.

▶ The pattern ~(으)ㄹ 수밖에(요), which occurs at the end of a sentence, is a contraction of ~(으)ㄹ 수밖에 없어(요) 'there is no way other than to (do/be)'. 수 is a noun meaning 'way, method' and 밖에 a particle meaning 'except, but, other than, besides'. This pattern usually appears with a clause with –(으)니, –(으)니까, –기 때문에, or –어서 that indicates a reason or cause.

GU8.4

한~   'mid…; the very'

광화문 광장은 서울 **한가운데**에 위치하고 있다.

Gwanghwamun Square is located right in the middle of Seoul.

나는 요즘 시험이 많아서 매일 **한밤중**까지 공부를 한다.

Since I have a lot of tests these days,

I've been studying until the middle of the night every day.

▶ 한– is a prefix attached to a noun to mean 'precisely' or '(exactly) in the middle, at the height, the most, the very'. Common expressions containing 한– are:

한여름	midsummer
한겨울	midwinter
한가운데	the very middle
한밤중	in the middle of the night

GU8.5

~(으)ㄹ 만하다   'to be worth ...–ing'

이 영화는 역사를 좋아하는 사람들이 **볼 만한** 영화예요.

This movie is worth seeing for anyone who likes history.

국립현대미술관은 정말 가 **볼 만해**요.

The National Museum of Modern and Contemporary Art is really worth visiting.

이 텔레비전은 낡았지만 아직 **쓸 만해**요.

This television is old, but it is still useable.

▶ This pattern is used after a verb to mean that an action is worth doing. Depending on the context, it can also mean that 'something is (still) possible to do …' as in 쓸 만하다 'to be still possible to use (useable)'.

먹을 만하다   to be worth eating
주목할 만하다   to be worth paying attention
칭찬할 만하다   to be worth praising

GU8.6

한~에   'at one ...'

저는 그 여자에게 **한눈에** 반했어요.

I fell in love with her at first sight.

뱀이 쥐를 잡아 **한입에** 먹어 버렸다.

The snake caught the rat and ate it all in one gulp.

저는 숙제가 많았는데 **한숨에** 다 했어요.

I had a lot of homework, but I did it in one go (breath).

▶ This pattern, in which 한 means 'one', is idiomatically used with some nouns to mean 'at one ~'. Be careful not to confuse the 한– in this pattern with the prefix 한–, which means 'in the middle (of)' (GU8.4).

   한번에   in one go, all at once (*lit.* at one time)
   한숨에   in one breath, without stopping (=단숨에)
   한걸음에 without stopping (*lit.* in one step)

활동

가... 밑줄 친 단어와 반대의 뜻을 가진 단어를 고르세요.

1. 이 도시는 교통이 좀 불편하다.

   ㄱ. 편리하다   ㄴ. 편안하다   ㄷ. 복잡하다   ㄹ. 시끄럽다

2. 서울의 중심에는 광화문 광장이 있어요.

   ㄱ. 아래   ㄴ. 주변   ㄷ. 중간   ㄹ. 사이

3. 서울의 물가는 뉴욕하고 비슷해요.

   ㄱ. 비싸요   ㄴ. 같아요   ㄷ. 달라요   ㄹ. 비교해요

4. 여름에 여행하는 것은 참 힘들어요.

   ㄱ. 어려워요   ㄴ. 쉬워요   ㄷ. 복잡해요   ㄹ. 볼 만해요

5. 밤에 혼자 다니면 위험해요. 일찍 집에 들어가세요.

   ㄱ. 안전해요   ㄴ. 어려워요   ㄷ. 즐거워요   ㄹ. 복잡해요

나... 영어 문장을 참고해 문장을 완성해 보세요.

1. 저는 10살 때부터 서울에서 살았으니까

   _____.

   Because I have lived in Seoul since I was 10, I would say Seoul is my hometown.

2. 이렇게 좋은 자동차를 1,000달러에 샀으면 차를

_____.

If one bought such a great car for 1,000 dollars, it is almost as though s/he got it for free.

3. 다음 주가 크리스마스니까 올해는

_____.

Since Christmas is next week, it is almost as though this year has already passed.

4. 스티브는 일주일에 5일이나 술을 마신다니

_____.

Since (you say) Steve drinks 5 days a week, it is almost as though he drinks every day.

5. 이 영화를 한국에서 천만 명이 봤다는데 한국 사람의 5분의 1이

_____.

I heard that 10 million people have watched this movie in Korea; it is almost as though one fifth of Korean people have watched the movie.

다... '~(으)ㄹ 만하다'를 사용해 다음 한국어 문장을 완성해 보세요.

1. ㄱ: 요즘 _____ 영화가 없어요.

　　ㄴ: 그러게요. 지금 하는 영화들은 다 재미도 없고 감동도 없는 영화들이네요.

2. ㄱ: 이번 주말에 파티가 있는데 _____ 옷이 없어요.

　　ㄴ: 저도 그래요. 같이 쇼핑이나 갈까요?

3. ㄱ: 이 식당은 비빔밥이 ＿＿＿＿＿＿＿ . 재료도 좋고 맛도 있어요.

   ㄴ: 그래요? 그럼 비빔밥을 시켜야겠네요.

4. ㄱ: 이번에 새로 시작한 아르바이트 ＿＿＿＿＿＿＿?

   ㄴ: 네, 아직은요. 그런데 돈을 많이 안 줘요.

5. ㄱ: 아빠, 제가 오늘 집 청소도 다 하고 설거지도 다 했어요.

   ㄴ: 그것 정말 아빠가 칭찬 ＿＿＿＿＿＿＿ 일을 네가 했구나.

라... 아래에서 적당한 표현을 골라서 다음 문장을 완성하세요.

> 한가운데, 한눈에, 한밤중에, 한번에, 한여름에, 한입에

1. 너무 배가 고파서 큰 떡을 ＿＿＿＿＿＿ 다 먹었다.

2. 이 표를 보면 일의 흐름을 ＿＿＿＿＿＿ 이해할 수 있다.

3. 어떤 사람이 ＿＿＿＿＿＿ 전화를 해서 잠을 잘 못 잤어요.

4. ＿＿＿＿＿＿ 서울에 가면 더워서 좀 힘들 거예요.

5. 서울타워는 서울 ＿＿＿＿＿＿ 위치해 있다.

마... 여러분이 가 본 도시 중에서 좋아하는 도시 하나를 골라 다음 질문에 대답해 보세요.

1. 인구가 얼마나 됩니까?

2. 날씨가 어떻습니까?

3. 유명한 특산물은 어떤 것들이 있습니까?

4. 물가가 어떻습니까?

5. 교통은 어떻습니까?

6. 문화 시설은 어떤 것들이 있습니까?

7. 어떤 역사적 유적지가 있습니까?

8. 자연이 아름다운 곳이 있습니까?

9. 여행할 때 조심해야 될 점은 어떤 것들이 있습니까?

10. 그 도시를 좋아하는 이유는 무엇입니까?

바... 위의 대답을 바탕으로 그 도시를 소개하는 글을 써 봅시다.

_____

_____

_____

_____

_____

_____

_____

사... 서울을 일주일 동안 여행한다고 생각하고 여행 정보를 찾아서 일정을 만들어
보세요. 어떤 곳에 가 보고 싶습니까? 그리고 거기에서 무엇을 해 보고 싶습니까?

	서울에서 가 보고 싶은 곳과 해 보고 싶은 일들
첫째 날	
둘째 날	
셋째 날	
넷째 날	
다섯째 날	
여섯째 날	
일곱째 날	

읽기

서울의 사대문

서울은 대한민국의 수도**이자**[GU8.7] 대한민국 최대의 도시로 정치, 경제, 교육, 문화의 중심지이고 인구는 1,000만 명**에 달한다.**[GU8.8] 서울은 과거 백제(18BC~660AD)의 수도였는데 그 당시에는 위례성**이라고 불렸다.**[GU8.9] 그 후 고려 시대 때는 남경이라고 불렸고 조선의 수도가 되면서는 한양 또는 한성이라 불렸다. 1394년 조선의 수도가 된 후 현재에 이르기까지 600년 이상 서울은 한반도에서 가장 중요한 **역할**[GU8.10]을 하는 도시이다.

　　조선 시대에는 서울 주변이 성으로 둘러싸여 있었고 동, 서, 남, 북에 큰 문이 하나씩 있었다. 이 네 개의 문을 사대문이라고 하는데 지금은 성은 없어졌고 문들만 남아 있다.

　　그중 남쪽에 있는 문의 이름은 숭례문 또는 남대문이라고 한다. 1396년에 지어진 남대문은 예술적으로 뛰어나 지금까지 서울을 대표하는 건축물이다. 지난 2008년에는 화재로 나무로 만든 부분이 타 버렸는데 현재는 다시 복원되어 있다. 동쪽에 있는 문은 흥인지문 또는 동대문이라고 한다. 동대문도 남대문 **못지않게**[GU8.11] 서울을 대표하는 아름다운 건축물이다. 동대문은 다행히 조선 시대 때의 모습 그대로 남아 있다. 서쪽의 문은 돈의문 또는 서대문이라고 했는데 일제

사대문 the four main gates of old Seoul 최대 biggest 중심지 center, hub 과거 past 당시 then, in those days 불리다 to be called 현재 present 이르다 to reach 성 castle 둘러싸이다 to be surrounded 지어지다 to be built 예술적 artistic 뛰어나다 to be outstanding 건축물 building, structure 화재 fire (disaster) 타다 to burn 복원되다 to be restored 못지않다 to be just as good as 모습 looks, figure 그대로 as it is

강점기 때인 1915년에 도시 개발을 이유로 철거되었다. 북쪽의 문은 숙정문 또는 북대문이라고 하는데 다른 문과는 다르게 산에 있어서 사람들이 많이 드나드는 문은 아니었다고 한다.

남대문과 동대문 근처에는 각각 한국 최대 규모의 남대문시장과 동대문시장이 있다. 남대문시장에는 10,000개가량의 상점이 있으며 각종 토산**품**, ^{GU8.12} 생활용품, 식료품, 의약품 등을 취급하고 있다. 동대문시장에는 26개의 쇼핑몰에 30,000개쯤의 상점이 있는데 특히 다양한 옷과 액세서리 등을 살 수 있는 곳으로 유명하다.

조선 시대 때에는 이 사대문의 안쪽만 서울이었지만 지금의 서울은 그때보다 훨씬 커졌기 때문에 남대문과 동대문은 지금의 서울의 중심에 위치하고 있다. 남대문과 동대문은 화려하고 높은 현대식 건물들 속에서 예전의 모습을 지키고 있으면서 서울을 특별한 곳으로 만들어 주고 있다.

일제 강점기 Japanese occupation period 철거되다 to be torn down 드나들다 to come in and go out 규모 scale, size ―가량 about, almost 상점 store, shop 각종 various kinds 토산품 local product 생활용품 daily necessities 식료품 groceries 의약품 medicine and medical supplies 취급하다 to handle 위치하고 있다 to be located 화려하다 to be fancy 현대식 modern style 특별하다 to be special

이해 문제

가... 다음 내용이 대화의 내용과 같으면 ○, 다르면 X에 표시하세요.

1. 서울은 조선 시대 이전에는 별로 중요하지 않은 작은 도시였다. ○ X

2. 조선 시대에는 서울이 성으로 둘러싸여 있었다. ○ X

3. 조선 시대 때 서울의 크기는 지금의 서울과 비슷하다. ○ X

4. 남대문은 불이 나서 지금은 없어졌다. ○ X

5. 북대문으로는 많은 사람들이 드나들지 않았다. ○ X

나... 다음 질문에 대답해 보세요.

1. 서울의 옛날 이름으로는 어떤 것이 있습니까?

2. 사대문의 이름은 각각 무엇입니까?

3. 사대문 중에서 지금은 없어진 문은 어떤 문입니까?

4. 남대문시장과 동대문시장에서 살 수 있는 것들로는 무엇이 있습니까?

문법과 용법

GU8.7

~이자 'both . . . and...; at the same time'

사람의 이름은 최초의 선물**이자** 최고의 선물이다.

A person's name is both their first and their greatest gift.

민지는 나의 첫사랑**이자** 친구다.

Minji is both my first love and my friend.

▶ The expression ~이자 consists of the copula stem 이 'to be' and the suffix –자 'as soon as'. While the suffix –자 means 'as soon as' after a verb stem, 이자 means simultaneity. Thus, '그분은 용감한 군인이자 유명한 학자예요' means 'He is both a brave soldier and a noted scholar (at the same time)'.

GU8.8

~에 달하다 'to amount to; to come to, to total'

그 책은 길이가 300쪽**에 달한**다.

The length of that book is a total of 300 pages.

그 도시의 인구는 수백만 명**에 달했**다.

The population of that city totaled to several million.

▶ The expression ~에 달하다 derives from a combination of the particle 에 'to/in/at' and the verb 달하다 'to reach, to come to'. The expression is frequently used when referring to a degree, level, or quantity of things (e.g., money, population), and goals (e.g., destination, peak, extreme, etc.). A similar expression is ~에 이르다, also meaning 'to amount to, arrive, reach'.

GU8.9

~(이)라고 불리다 'to be called'

마크는 어렸을 때부터 수학 천재**라고 불렸**다.

Mark has been called a math genius since he was little.

한국은 동방예의지국**이라고 불린**다.

Korea is called "the well-mannered country of the East".

▶ The expression ~(이)라고 불리다 derives from a combination of the indirect quotation (or reported speech) pattern (이)라고 and 불리다 'to be called', the passive verb form of 부르다 'to call'. (이)라고 is a combination of the copula stem (이) 'to be', the statement ending –라, and the quotative particle –고 'that'. Thus, 그 아이는 천재라고 불린다 means 'that child is called a genius'.

GU8.10

역할 'role'

각자 자기에게 주어진 **역할**을 다해야 합니다.

Each person should play the role they were given to the fullest.

이 배우는 이번 드라마에서 주인공 **역할**을 맡았어요.

This actor took the leading role in this drama.

▶ In addition to the 하다 verb, other common collocational verbs used with the noun 역할 'role' include 맡다 'to take on', ~에 충실하다 'to be devoted to' as follows.

역할을 하다   to play a role
역할을 맡다   to take a role
역할에 충실하다   to be faithful to one's role

Other related meanings of 역할 include 'function, part, duty'. Be careful not to spell this word incorrectly as 역활, which is a common mistake.

GU8.11

못지않게 'no less (than); equally'

요즘 회사에서는 능력 **못지않게** 첫인상도 중요하다.

Nowadays corporations value first impressions no less than abilities.

오늘도 어제 **못지않게** 추워요.

Today is just as cold as yesterday was.

내 남동생은 나 **못지않게** 힘이 세요.

My younger brother is just as strong as I am.

▶ The pattern 못지않게 is an adverbial form of 못지않다 (contraction of 못하지 아니하다) 'not to be inferior (to); to be just as good (as); to be no less (than)'. In speaking, the expression 못지않게 can be contracted to 못잖게.

~품 'product'

한국 **제품**들이 미국 시장에서도 많이 팔리고 있다.

Korean products sell just as well in the American market.

이 카탈로그에는 저희 가게 **상품**의 사진들이 있습니다.

This catalog has the pictures of our store merchandise.

▶ The bound Sino–Korean noun 품 'product' follows another noun as follows.

기념품	souvenirs
상품	merchandise, (commercial) products
생필품	daily necessities
식(료)품	groceries
의약품	medicine and medical supplies
제품	goods, (manufactured) products
신제품	new product
지방 특산품	special local products
토산품	local products
학용품	stationery
화장품	cosmetics

활동

가... 밑줄 친 단어와 비슷한 뜻을 가진 단어를 고르세요.

1. 남대문시장에는 여러 종류의 물건을 파는 <u>상점</u>들이 많이 있다.

　　ㄱ. 상품　　　　　ㄴ. 제품　　　　　ㄷ. 가게　　　　　ㄹ. 백화점

2. 이 가게는 <u>다양한</u> 액세서리를 팔고 있다.

　　ㄱ. 많은　　　　　ㄴ. 큰　　　　　ㄷ. 각종　　　　　ㄹ. 좋은

3. 서울 인구는 1,000만 명<u>쯤</u> 됩니다.

　　ㄱ. 만큼　　　　　ㄴ. 가량　　　　　ㄷ. 이나　　　　　ㄹ. 도

4. 서울은 대한민국 <u>최대의</u> 도시이다.

　　ㄱ. 제일 큰　　　　ㄴ. 중심의　　　　ㄷ. 최초의　　　　ㄹ. 한가운데의

5. 남대문과 동대문은 예술적으로 <u>뛰어난</u> 건축물이다.

　　ㄱ. 아름다운　　　　ㄴ. 훌륭한　　　　ㄷ. 중요한　　　　ㄹ. 못지않은

나... 다음 빈 칸에 제일 적당한 단어를 고르세요.

1. 수미는 제가 제일 좋아하는 친구 _____ 제 한국어 선생님이에요.

　　ㄱ. 하고　　　　　ㄴ. 이자　　　　　ㄷ. 라서　　　　　ㄹ. 못지않게

2. 저희 언니는 부모님 _____ 저한테 중요한 사람이에요.

　　ㄱ. 못지않게　　　　ㄴ. 가량　　　　ㄷ. 이라서　　　　ㄹ. 까지

3. 이 영화에서 누가 왕 _____을/를 맡을 거예요?

   ㄱ. 일　　　　　ㄴ. 일부분　　　　ㄷ. 쪽　　　　　ㄹ. 역할

4. 저는 키가 큰 편인데 제 동생도 벌써 저 _____ 키가 큽니다.

   ㄱ. 함께　　　　ㄴ. 하고　　　　ㄷ. 못지않게　　ㄹ. 한테

5. 저는 노래를 잘 해서 친구들 사이에서 가수라고 _____.

   ㄱ. 불러요　　　ㄴ. 불려요　　　ㄷ. 들려요　　　ㄹ. 불어요

다... 다음 장소들에 대해서 조사해 보고 어떤 곳인지 이야기해 봅시다.

1. 국립중앙박물관

2. 명동

3. 북한산 국립공원

4. 서대문형무소 역사관

5. 여의도 공원

6. 인사동

7. 전쟁기념관

8. 청계천

9. 한옥마을

10. 홍대 앞 거리

라... 동대문과 남대문 근처에 큰 시장이 생긴 이유는 무엇이라고 생각합니까?

마... 여러분 나라의 도시들은 무엇으로 유명한지 써 보세요. (예: 부산은 아름다운 바닷가로 유명해요.)

_____

_____

_____

_____

_____

_____

_____

_____

_____

바... 여러분 나라의 수도와 서울을 비교하는 글을 써 봅시다.

_____

_____

_____

_____

_____

_____

_____

_____

사... 다음은 서울이 들어가는 속담이나 표현입니다. 어떤 경우에 쓰는지 알아보세요.

1. 서울에 가서 김 서방 찾는다.

2. 모로 가도 서울만 가면 된다.

3. 서울에서는 눈 감으면 코 베어 간다.

4. 서울 깍쟁이

5. 말은 나면 제주도로 보내고 사람은 나면 서울로 보내라.

추가 읽기

서울의 이모저모

서울의 기후

서울은 사계절이 뚜렷하게 나타나며 여름과 겨울은 길고 봄, 가을은 짧은 편이다. 3월 중순부터 시작하는 봄에는 날씨가 따뜻해지고 꽃이 피기 시작하지만 가끔 황사가 불어 오기도 한다. 여름에는 비가 많이 오는데 6월 중순에서 7월 하순까지는 장마가 계속되어 흐리고 비가 오는 날들이 많다. 가끔은 비가 너무 많이 와서 홍수가 나기도 하고 가장 더운 7월과 8월에는 섭씨 30도(30℃)가 넘는 무더운 날들이 계속된다. 그리고 밤에도 기온이 떨어지지 않는 열대야 현상으로 잠들기 어려운 날들도 자주 있다. 가을은 보통 9월부터 11월까지로 맑고 선선한 날씨가 계속되어서 여행하기에 좋은 계절이다. 특히 단풍이 아름다워서 산으로 여행을 가는 사람들이 많다. 겨울은 12월부터 시작하는데 아주 춥고 건조한 날씨가 계속되며 가끔 많은 눈이 오기도 한다. 보통 1월이 평균 기온 섭씨 영하 2.4도(-2.4℃)로 일 년 중에 가장 추운 달이다.

이모저모 various sides 중순 middle ten days of a month 황사 yellow dust 하순 last ten days of a month 장마 rainy season 홍수 flood 섭씨 Celsius 무덥다 to be humid and hot 기온 air temperature 떨어지다 to drop 열대야 tropical night 선선하다 (weather) to be cool and refreshing 단풍 autumn foliage 건조하다 to be dry 평균 average

한강

한강은 서울을 동쪽에서 서쪽으로 가로지르는 강이다. 역사적으로 서울은 이 한강을 중심으로 발전한 도시이다. 한강의 "한"은 크다는 뜻으로 "한강"이라는 이름은 큰 강이라는 뜻이다. 서울에서 한강 북쪽 지역을 강북, 남쪽 지역을 강남이라고 부르기도 한다. 한강에는 강북과 강남을 연결해 주는 다리들이 30개 가까이 있다. 한강 옆에는 공원들과 운동 시설들이 있어서 서울 시민들의 휴식 공간으로 이용되고 있다.

서울의 지하철

서울 지하철은 편리하고 깨끗하고 많은 노선이 있어서 세계 최고 수준의 지하철이라고 평가된다. 서울의 거리들은 차가 막히는 곳이 많기 때문에 버스나 택시보다 지하철로 더 빠르게 이동할 수 있다. 지하철 노선들은 각각 다른 색깔로 구분되어 있어서 갈아탈 때 편리하고 모든 역의 표지판은 한글, 영어, 한자로 씌어 있어서 외국인들도 쉽게 이용할 수 있다.

가로지르다 to cross 발전하다 to develop 연결하다 to connect 휴식 공간 rest area 노선 line,
route 수준 level, standard 평가되다 to be evaluated 이동하다 to move, travel
구분되다 to be categorized 표지판 sign, notice 쓰이다(씌다) to be written

서울의 행정구역

서울은 다른 지역과 분리된 도시라는 뜻으로 특별시(Special City)라고 불린다. 서울은 한국의 유일한 특별시이다. 서울특별시는 25개 구로 나뉘는데, 한강 남쪽에 11개의 구가 있고 북쪽에 14개의 구가 있다. 인구가 제일 많은 구는 송파구(27만 명), 제일 적은 구는 중구(6만 명)이다. 각각의 구는 동으로 나뉘어 있는데 서울에는 총 424개 동이 있다.

행정구역 administrative district 분리되다 to be separated 유일한 only, sole 구 district (of a city) 동 neighborhood 나뉘다 to be divided 각각 each

■■ 번역문 ■■

CONVERSATION: Introducing Seoul

Mark and Minji are talking about visiting Seoul.

Mark: Minji, where in Korea are you from?

Minji: I'm from Seoul.

Mark: You are from Seoul, too? Most of the Korean people I've met are from Seoul.

Minji: Is that so? Seoul is the largest city and it has a large population. That's probably why most the people you meet are from Seoul.

Mark: What's the population of Seoul?

Minji: Seoul's population is about 10 million. But if you add all the people who live in the cities around Seoul, it would be about 25 million maybe.

Mark: I heard that Korea's population is 50 million ... So, about half of Koreans live in the metropolitan area.

Minji: I would say so.

Mark: But why does everyone want to live in Seoul?

Minji: There are naturally many people who want to live in Seoul because Seoul has a good education system, many jobs, and a variety of cultural facilities.

Mark: Then, the price of goods must be very high in Seoul.

Minji: Of course. The cost of living in Seoul is said to be similar to that of New York or Tokyo.

Mark: Isn't it dangerous to go out at night?

Minji: Well, I guess you should be careful since it's a big city, but Seoul is relatively a safe place to travel in.

Mark: I see ... I too am thinking of making a trip to Seoul sometime around next year. When would be a good time to go?

Minji: Any time is good but since the weather is nice in the fall, it would be best to go around October, if you have the time.

Mark: How about during the summer?

Minji: If you want to go in the summer, it's good to go in early June. It's very muggy and rains often in the middle of summer, so it will be a little hard to travel.

Mark:　　I see. What are some things to see in Seoul?

Minji:　　Well, what kind of things do you like?

Mark:　　I am very interested in history. I heard about Gyeongbok Palace a while ago, and I really want to go.

Minji:　　Gyeongbok Palace is great! Other palaces, such as Deoksu Palace and Changdeok Palace, are also good, so make sure to go there too.

Mark:　　Oh, I should. And I heard that there are many mountains in Seoul. Are there a lot worth hiking?

Minji:　　Yes, there is Namsan in central Seoul, and around Seoul are Bukhansan, Dobongsan, and Gwanaksan, and there are many hikers. You know the N Seoul Tower, right? It often appears in dramas, you know.

Mark:　　Ah, yes, I have seen it.

Minji:　　That's on Namsan. If you go to the N Seoul Tower, you can see all of Seoul at once.

Mark:　　Ah, I wanted to try going to the N Seoul Tower.

Minji:　　And there are also many museums and art galleries in Seoul, so choose some and go. Not long ago, an American friend visited the War Memorial of Korea and said that there are many things to see and learn.

Mark:　　It seems there are really so many things to do in Seoul. I will ask you in more detail when I make plans for my trip to Korea.

READING: Four Great Gates of Seoul

Seoul is both the capital of the Republic of Korea, and the largest city in Korea. It is the center of politics, the economy, education, and culture, and the population amounts to 10 million. Seoul was the capital of Paekche (18 BC–600 AD) in the past and was called Wiryesŏng at the time. Later, during the Koryŏ Dynasty (918–1392), it was called Namgyŏng, and when it became the capital of Chosŏn, it was called Hanyang or Hansŏng. Since becoming the capital of Chosŏn in 1394, Seoul has become the most important city on the Korean Peninsula for more than 600 years now.

During the Chosŏn Dynasty, Seoul was surrounded by fortresses and had one big gate in each direction of east, west, south, and north. These four gates are called *sadaemun*, or the four main gates, but now the fortresses are gone and only the gates remain.

Among them, the name of the gate to the south is Sungnyemun or Namdaemun. Built in 1396, Namdaemun is artistically outstanding and is a structure that represents Seoul to this date. Back in 2008, a fire burned the wooden parts, but they are now restored. The gate to the east is called Heunginjimun or Dongdaemun. Dongdaemun, along with Namdaemun, is a beautiful structure that represents Seoul. Fortunately, Dongdaemun remains the way it looked during the Chosŏn Dynasty. The gate on the west side was called Donuimun, or Seodaemun. In 1915 during the Japanese occupation, it was demolished under the premise of urban development. The gate on the northern side is called Sukjeongmun or Bukdaemun. However, unlike the other gates, it was not a gate that many people frequented.

Near Namdaemun and Dongdaemun are the largest Korean markets, Namdaemun and Dongdaemun Markets, respectively. There are about 10,000 shops at Namdaemun Market, and it carries a wide range of local products, daily necessities, groceries, medical supplies, etc. There are approximately 30,000 stores in 26 shopping malls at Dongdaemun, and it is especially famous for a variety of clothing, accessories, etc.

During the Chosŏn Dynasty, Seoul used to only consist of the areas inside of the four main gates. However, Seoul has become much larger since, and Namdaemun and Dongdaemun are now located in the center of Seoul. Namdaemun and Dongdaemun are making Seoul a special place by maintaining how they looked in the past, even amongst the fancy and tall modern buildings.

FURTHER READING: Various Aspects of Seoul

Seoul's Weather

Seoul has four clear seasons with long summers and winters, and relatively short springs and falls. In spring, which starts in mid-March, the weather gets warmer and flowers begin to bloom, but sometimes the yellow dust blows in. It rains a lot in summer. As the rainy season continues from mid-June to late July, there are many cloudy and rainy days. At times, it rains so much that floods occur. In the hottest months of July and August, hot humid days of over 30 degrees Celsius continue. Frequently, there are nights when it is difficult to fall asleep because of the tropical phenomenon when the temperature does not fall even during the night. Fall is a good season to travel because clear and cool weather continues usually from September to November. Many people travel to the mountains because the autumn foliage is especially beautiful. Winter begins in December, when very cold and dry weather continues, sometimes with heavy snowfall. Normally January is the coldest month of the year with an average temperature of -2.4°C.

Han'gang

The Han River cuts across Seoul from east to west. Historically, Seoul is a city that developed around the Han River. The Han, in Han River means big, so Han River means 'big river.' The area north of the Han River in Seoul is called Gangbuk and south of the river, Gangnam. There are close to 30 bridges connecting Gangbuk and Gangnam. Next to the Han River, there are parks and sports facilities that serve as relaxation areas for Seoulites.

Seoul Subway

The Seoul subway system is considered to be one of the best in the world because it is convenient, clean, and has many lines. Because of the many areas of traffic congestions among the streets of Seoul, one can travel faster by subway than by bus or taxi. It is convenient to transfer between different lines because they are marked in different colors. Signs at all stations are written in Korean, English, and Chinese characters so foreigners can easily use the subway

CULTURE: Seoul's Administrative Districts

Seoul is called T'ŭkpyŏl-si, or the Special City, meaning the city is separated from other areas of Korea. It is the only Special City in Korea. Seoul Special City can be divided into 25 districts, with 11 districts south of Han'gang, and 14 districts north of it.

The most populated district is Songp'a-gu (270,000) and the least populated district is Jung-gu (60,000). Each district is divided into *dong*s or neighborhoods, with a total of 424 neighborhoods in Seoul.

📖 단어 📖

– 가량	about, almost	뛰어나다	to be outstanding
가로지르다	to cross	모습	looks, figure
각각	each	못지않다	to be just as good as
각종	various kinds	무덥다	to be humid and hot;
건조하다	to be dry		to be muggy
건축물	building, structure	문화 시설	ultural facilities
– 경	around…, about…	물가	cost of living
계획을 세우다	to make a plan	발전하다	to develop
고궁	ancient palace	복원되다	to be restored
고르다	to choose, select	볼 만하다	to be worth seeing
과거	past	분리되다	to be separated
교육 환경	educational	불리다	to be called
	environment	사대문	the four main gates
구	district (of a city)		of old Seoul
구분되다	to be categorized	상점	store, shop
규모	scale, size	생활용품	daily necessities
그대로	as it is	선선하다	(weather) to be cool and
기온	air temperature		refreshing
기후	climate	섭씨	Celsius
나뉘다	to be divided	성	castle
노선	line, route	수도	capital city of a country
단풍	autumn foliage	수도권	metropolitan area
당시	then, in those days	수준	level, standard
대부분	mostly (=거의)	시간(이) 되다	to have time
더하다	to add	식료품	groceries
도시	city	쓰이다	to be written
동	neighborhood	연결하다	to connect
둘러싸이다	to be surrounded	열대야	tropical night
드나들다	to come in and go out	예술적	artistic
떨어지다	to drop	위치하고 있다	to be located

유일한	only, sole	초	beginning (of)
의약품	medicine and medical supplies	최대	biggest
		취급하다	to handle
이동하다	to move, travel	타다	to burn
이르다	to reach	토산품	local product
인구	population	특별하다	to be special
일제 강점기	Japanese occupation period	평가되다	to be evaluated
		평균	average
장마	rainy season	표지판	sign, notice
전쟁기념관	The War Memorial of Korea	하순	last ten days of a month
		한눈에	at one sight
주변	surroundings, vicinity	한여름	midsummer
중순	middle ten days of a month	행정구역	administrative district
		현대식	modern style
중심	center	현재	present
중심지	center, hub	홍수	flood
지리	geography	화려하다	to be fancy
지어지다	to be built	화재	fire (disaster)
지역	area, region	황사	yellow dust
철거되다	to be torn down	휴식 공간	rest area

남한과 북한

학습 목표

내용
- 한국 전쟁과 남북 관계의 역사에 대해 훑어본다.
- 남북한의 언어 차이에 대해 알아본다.

문화
- 북한 사회의 특징에 대해 알아본다.
- 한반도의 분단 후 남북한의 문화가 어떻게 서로 달라졌는지 알아본다.

한국 전쟁 the Korean War 남북 관계 South Korea–North Korea relations 차이 difference
한반도 Korean Peninsula 분단 division

■ 생각해 봅시다

가 ▸ 다음에 대해 같이 얘기해 봅시다.

1. 최근에 들은 북한에 대한 뉴스는 어떤 것들이 있습니까?

2. 한반도는 왜 남한과 북한으로 나뉘어 있는지 이야기해 보고
   분단의 배경에 대해 알아봅시다.

3. 북한은 어떤 나라입니까? 북한에 대해서 아는 사실들을 이야기해
   봅시다.

4. 한국 전쟁(6·25 전쟁)에 대해서 아는 사실들을 이야기해 봅시다.

5. 남한과 북한의 언어 사용은 어떻게 다른지 이야기해 봅시다.

6. 여러분 나라에는 전쟁이 있었습니까? 여러분이 아는 전쟁에 대해서
   이야기해 봅시다.

나 ‣ 다음 내용이 북한의 상황에 맞는지 ○, X로 표시해 봅시다.

　1. 반찬으로 김치를 즐겨 먹는다. (　　)

　2. 북한에서 쓰는 말을 "북한어"라고 부른다. (　　)

　3. 설날이나 추석에는 고향에 가서 가족들을 만난다. (　　)

　4. 노래방이 있다. (　　)

　5. 평양에는 지하철이 있다. (　　)

　6. 대학생들은 청바지를 즐겨 입는다. (　　)

　7. 학생들은 영어를 안 배운다. (　　)

　8. 연애를 하는 것이 제한되고 당에서 정해 준 사람과 결혼해야
　　 한다. (　　)

　9. 쌀이 비싸서 라면을 먹는 사람들이 많다. (　　)

　10. 성형 수술을 한 사람을 볼 수 없다. (　　)

　11. 한자를 안 배운다. (　　)

　12. 교회가 많이 있다. (　　)

즐겨 먹다 to enjoy eating (frequently) 청바지 jeans 제한되다 to be limited 당 political
party 정해 주다 to decide (something for someone) 성형 수술 plastic surgery
한자 Chinese character

북한의 젊은 세대

텔레비전 토크쇼에서

사회자: 오늘은 북한을 탈출해서 한국에서 살고 계시는 분들을 모시
고 북한의 젊은 세대에 대해서 함께 이야기를 나누어 보겠습
니다.

김은희: 안녕하세요. 저는 22살이고요, 2년 전에 탈북한 김은희라고
합니다.

이영철: 안녕하세요. 저는 남한에 온 지 10년 됐습니다. 올해 46살이
고 이름은 이영철입니다.

사회자: 네, 반갑습니다. **아시다시피**G9.1 북한이 요즘 중국과 한류의 **영
향으로**G9.2 급속하게 변화하고 있다고 하는데요. 특히 요즘 젊
은 세대들은 적극적이고 대담하다고 합니다. 북한 젊은이들
은 어떻게 연애를 하는지 궁금한데요. 북한에서도 연인들이
손을 잡고 다니고 그러는지요?

이영철: 그렇습니다. 사실 1990년대**만 해도**G9.3 연인들이 낮에 손잡고
다니는 것을 많이 볼 수 없었는데 요즘은 많이 달라져서 연인
들이 자유롭게 연애를 한다고 하더라구요.

김은희: 네, 최근에는 길에서 손을 잡고 다니거나 팔짱을 끼고 다니는

세대 generation 사회자 emcee 탈출하다 to escape 이야기를 나누다 to talk (with)
탈북하다 to escape from North Korea 급속하게 rapidly 변화하다 to change
적극적이다 to be active 대담하다 to be bold, daring 궁금하다 to be curious
자유롭게 freely 팔짱을 끼다 to link arms

연인들이 많이 있어요. 평양에서는 연인들**끼리**[G9.4] 같이 맥주도 마시고 볼링도 치는 모습을 흔히 볼 수 있어요.

사회자: 아… 북한에서도 자유롭게 연애를 하는군요. 그리고 요즘은 북한에서도 한국 드라마를 많이 본다고 하던데, 정말 그렇습니까?

김은희: 네, 한국 드라마는 물론이고 다들 몰래 한국 영화도 보고 K-pop도 듣고 그래요. 한국 대중문화 영상들이 중국을 통해 DVD나 플래시 드라이브로 바로 북한으로 들어가거든요. 저도 그렇게 매일 한국 드라마를 몰래 보면서 들킬까 봐 조마조마했어요.

사회자: 아, 그런 것들을 보다가 걸리면 어떻게 되나요?

김은희: 네, 학생들의 경우 걸리면 학교에서 퇴학당할 수도 있어요.

사회자: 학생들이 많이 보는군요.

이영철: 한국 드라마나 음악 때문에 북한에서 젊은이들 사이에서 남한의 연예인들의 헤어스타일이나 패션을 따라하는 등 한류 바람이 분다고 해요. 심지어 서울말을 많이 따라하기도 한대요. 서울말을 하면 더 세련된 사람으로 여겨진다고 하더라구요.

사회자: 아, 그렇군요. 재미있네요. **그건 그렇고**,[G9.5] 여러분들이 어렵게 탈북을 해서 남한으로 오셨는데 남한에 사시면서 어려운 점은 없으신지요?

이영철: 처음에는 많이 힘들었어요. 제가 처음에 한국에 와서 알바를 하려고 했는데 저**더러**[G9.6] 말투가 이상하다고 하면서 아무도

–끼리 among or by ourselves or themselves 모습 appearance 흔히 commonly, often 다들 everyone 몰래 secretly 대중문화 popular culture 영상 video 들키다 to get caught 조마조마하다 to be anxious 걸리다 to be caught 퇴학당하다 to be expelled from a school 패션 fashion 심지어 even, what is more 세련되다 to be sophisticated 여겨지다 to be considered, regarded 말투 one's way of speaking

일을 안 **시켜 줬어요**.^G9.7 그래서 제가 너무 상처를 받았어요. 아르바이트마저 시켜 주는 데가 없어서 그때는 살길이 정말 막막했습니다. 그런데 차차 살면서 노력을 많이 **하다 보니**^G9.8 어떻게 살게 되더라구요.

김은희: 저도 말투를 고치는 것이 아주 어려웠어요. 아시다시피 남한 에서는 영어 단어를 많이 써서 처음에는 알아듣지 못해서 힘 들었어요. 엘리베이터를 북한에서는 승강기라고 하거든요. 처음에는 엘리베이터도 무슨 말인지 못 알아들었고 스크린 도어, 냅킨, 볼펜, 프라이팬, 스테이플러 등도 무슨 말인지 잘 몰랐어요. 지금은 많이 익숙해졌고 좋은 분들이 많이 도와주 셔서 잘 지내고 있습니다.

사회자: 뉴스에서도 보니까 탈북하신 많은 분들이 한국 사회에 적응 하는 것이 쉽지가 않다고 하더라고요. 하루빨리 남북한 사람 들이 자유롭게 왕래할 수 있게 되기를 바랍니다.

-마저 even, as well 시켜 주다 to let or allow someone/something 막막하다 to feel lost and gloomy 차차 gradually 고치다 to fix 익숙하다 to be familiar 적응하다 to adjust
하루빨리 as soon as possible 왕래하다 to come and go

이해 문제

가... 대화의 내용과 맞으면 ○, 틀리면 X에 표시하세요.

1. 북한에서는 거리에서 데이트하는 모습을 흔히 볼 수 없다. ○ X

2. 몇몇 한국 드라마들이 북한 텔레비전에서 방송되어서 인기를 끌었다. ○ X

3. 북한에서 남한 말투가 유행이다. ○ X

4. 북한의 젊은 세대는 남한의 문화에 관심이 많다. ○ X

5. 많은 탈북자들이 큰 어려움 없이 남한 사회에 잘 적응하고 있다. ○ X

나... 다음 질문에 대답해 보세요.

1. 북한에서 젊은 연인들은 어떤 식으로 데이트를 즐깁니까?

2. 북한 사람들은 어떻게 남한의 텔레비전 프로그램들을 봅니까?

3. 북한에서 볼 수 있는 한류의 영향으로는 어떤 것들이 있습니까?

4. 북한의 젊은 세대의 특징은 어떤 것들이 있습니까?

5. 탈북자들이 남한에 살면서 경험하는 어려운 점들은 어떤 것들이 있습니까?

문법과 용법

GU9.1

~다시피 '(just) as'

아시**다시피** 저는 돈이 없어요.

As you already know, I don't have any money.

네가 보**다시피** 나는 지금 정신없이 바빠.

As you can see, I am extremely busy.

선생님께서 말씀하셨**다시피** 저는 아무 잘못이 없습니다.

As our teacher said, I didn't do anything wrong.

▶ The connective suffix –다시피 '(just) as' is frequently used after a verb of perception such as: 알다 'to know', 보다 'to see', 듣다 'to hear', and 말하다 'to say', –다시피 is similar in meaning and usage to –듯이 and –는/(으)ㄴ 것처럼, as in 아시다시피 = 아시듯이 = 아시는 것처럼; 보셨다시피 = 보셨듯이 = 보신 것처럼.

▶ –다시피 is also used with non-perception verbs. In these cases, its meaning becomes 'practically, almost, or nearly', as in 그 아이는 죽다시피 되었다 'The child was as good as dead' and 나는 이 책을 외우다시피 읽었다 'I read this book to the point where I practically had it memorized'. –다시피 frequently occurs with the verb 하다 'to do', as in 저 사람들은 술집에서 살다시피 한다 'Those people practically live at the pub' and 오늘 너무 바빠서 밥 먹을 시간도 없이 굶다시피 했어 '(I) was so busy today that I practically starved and didn't have any time to eat'.

GU9.2

~의 영향으로 'due to; under the influence of'

고기압**의 영향으로** 오늘은 맑은 날씨가 계속되겠습니다.
Due to the high air pressure today, the weather will remain sunny.

요즘 한류**의 영향으로** 한국에 대한 관심이 높아지고 있습니다.
The influence of the Korean Wave these days is raising interest in Korea.

▶ 영향 means 'influence, impact, effect'. In the pattern, 영향 preceded by the possessive particle 의 'of' and followed by the instrument particle 으로 'with', literally meaning 'with the influence of'. Some other frequently used expressions with 영향 include (건강)에 영향을 주다/미치다 'to have an influence on (health)', (전쟁)의 영향을 받다 'to be influenced by (war)', 악영향 'bad effect, harmful influence', and 영향력 '(the power of) influence'.

GU9.3

~만 해도 '(even) just (talking about; taking as an example)'

제 친구들**만 해도** 한국어를 배우는 학생들이 많아지고 있어요.
Even just among my friends, the number of students who are learning Korean is increasing.

일주일 전**만 해도** 추웠는데 이제 완전히 봄이 되었어요.
Even just a week ago it was still cold, but now spring has finally arrived.

▶ This pattern consists of the particle 만 'only', 해 'do, say', and the connective suffix –도 'even if, though', literally meaning 'even if (I) talk about only ...'. A synonymous pattern is ~만 하더라도 'even if (I) talk about only ...', as in 몇 년 전까지만 해도 (or 하더라도) 우리 집은 몹시 가난했어요 'My family was extremely poor even until just a few years ago'.

~끼리
'among/by ourselves/themselves; in groups (of)'

방학에는 가족**끼리** 여행 갈 거야.
During the school break, (I'm) going to go on a trip with just my family.

친구**끼리** 무슨 비밀이 있어?
What secrets are there amongst friends?

학생들이 10명씩 **끼리끼리** 서서 이야기하고 있었다.
The students stood talking in groups of ten.

▶ The particle 끼리 means 'between', 'among', 'only between/among', and 'only with'. The word contains a nuance of exclusivity of the group that does not include people of other groups. Thus, 끼리 is attached to group nouns such as 우리, 학생, 가족, 아이들, etc. This particle attaches to group nouns. The word can be used in repetition as 끼리끼리 to emphasize the exclusiveness. 끼리끼리 is an adverb, meaning 'in groups'.

GU9.5

그건 그렇고
'by the way; now; on a different note; so that's that'

그건 그렇고 그 다음은 뭔가요?

So that's that, then what's next?

아 **그건 그렇고**, 너 없을 때 네 어머니가 전화하셨어.

By the way, your mother called while you were out.

▶ This pattern is a contraction of 그것은 그렇고, literally meaning 'that is so and'. Its derived meanings include 'by the way', 'now', 'well', and 'on a different note'. It is used to change the topic from one to another.

GU9.6

~더러 'to'

엄마가 남동생**더러** 빨리 가라고 하셨어.

Mom told my little brother to leave quickly.

누가 너**더러** 이런 일을 하라고 했어?

Who told you to do this sort of thing?

▶ The colloquial "goal" particle 더러 means 'to (a person)' and is most frequently used with a quotative clause and a verb of saying (e.g., 하다 'say'), as in 용수는 나더러 바보라고 했다 'Yongsu told me that I was a fool', 용수는 나더러 가라고 했

다 'Yongsu told me to go', 용수는 나더러 가(느)냐고 물었다 'Yongsu asked me if I was going', 용수는 나더러 가자고 했다 'suggested (to me) we go'. 더러 is also used with a causative construction, as in 엄마는 나더러 집에서 쉬게 하셨다 'Mom made me rest at home'. In simple sentences, 더러 is rarely used. Instead, particles like 에게, 한테, and 보고 are used, as in 친구에게/친구한테/친구보고 말했다 '(I) said to a friend', but not 친구더러 말했다.

▶ 더러 (as well as 보고) is used only on people of a similar or lower status than the speaker. In terms of the honorific level of the different "goal" particles, 께 is the highest, followed by 에게/한테, and then 보고/더러, in that order.

GU9.7

~시켜 주다 'to allow/do/arrange something for someone/something'

한국어를 배우고 싶어 하는 친구를 선생님에게 연결**시켜 주**었어요.
I've put a friend who wants to learn Korean in contact with a teacher.

내가 서울 구경**시켜 줄**게.
I'll show you around Seoul.

우리 개는 매일 산책을 **시켜 줘**야 해요.
Our dog should be walked every day.

▶ The expression 시켜 주다 is composed of the verb stem 시키– 'make/have (a person) do' + the infinitive suffix –어 and the auxiliary verb 주다 'for'. 시키다 is a causative form of the 하다 verb. 시켜 주다 is used to express that someone does/arranges/allows/causes a favorable action for someone else. Further examples include: 한국을 해방시켜 주었다 '(They) allowed Korea to be liberated'; 기분 전환을 시켜 주기 위해 영화를 보러 같이 갔어요 'I took them to a movie to help them feel better'.

GU9.8

~다(가) 보니(까) 'while doing … (one realizes that)'

책을 읽**다(가) 보니(까)** 벌써 밤이 늦었다.

I was reading a book and I realized it was already the middle of the night.

숙제가 어렵**다(가) 보니(까)** 끝내는 데 시간이 오래 걸렸다.

Since the homework was difficult it took a while to finish.

▶ This pattern consists of the change of action/state suffix –다(가) 'and then, while' and the verb stem 보 'see, look' + the causal/temporal connective suffix –니(까) 'as, when', literally meaning 'when I see/look while doing/being …'. The extended meaning of this pattern is 'while as a result of doing/being …' or 'as a result of doing/being …', as in 날마다 놀다 보니까 바보가 되어 버렸어요 'Since I goofed off every day, I ended up a fool' and 공부를 하다 보니까 새로운 보물을 찾은 기분이었어요 'While I was studying, I felt as though I were discovering treasure'.

활동

가... 아래 빈 칸에 가장 적당한 말을 고르세요.

1. 이 거리에서는 연인들_____ 데이트를 하는 모습을 자주 볼 수 있다.

   ㄱ. 하고   ㄴ. 끼리   ㄷ. 같이   ㄹ. 더러

2. 여기는 조용하니까 두 분이 차 마시면서 편하게 이야기 _____.

   ㄱ. 나누세요   ㄴ. 말하세요   ㄷ. 대화하세요   ㄹ. 말씀하세요

3. 어제 동물원에서 동물들이 _____ 해서 길거리에 나왔어요.

   ㄱ. 자유   ㄴ. 탈출   ㄷ. 탈북   ㄹ. 적응

4. 요즘에는 K-pop을 좋아하는 미국 학생들을 _____ 볼 수 있어서
   K-pop이 정말 인기가 많다는 것을 느낄 수 있어요.

   ㄱ. 너무   ㄴ. 정말   ㄷ. 차차   ㄹ. 흔히

5. 어제는 정말 추웠는데 바람도 불고 _____ 눈도 와서 여행하기 정말
   힘들었어요.

   ㄱ. 심지어   ㄴ. 또는   ㄷ. 즉   ㄹ. 혹시

6. 가: 오늘 일이 많아서 힘들었어요.

   나: 네, 그런데 일이 잘 돼서 다행이에요. _____ 내일 스케줄은 어떻게
       되지요?

   ㄱ. 아시다시피   ㄴ. 그건 그렇고   ㄷ. 하루빨리   ㄹ. 물론

7. 저는 남자친구를 부모님께 인사를 _____.

    ㄱ. 시켜 드렸어요   ㄴ. 받았어요   ㄷ. 했어요   ㄹ. 드렸어요

나... 아래 밑줄 친 단어와 바꿔 쓸 수 있는 말을 고르세요.

1. 평양에서도 젊은이들이 데이트하는 것을 <u>흔히</u> 볼 수 있어요.

    ㄱ. 아주   ㄴ. 제일   ㄷ. 자주   ㄹ. 급속하게

2. 토마토는 건강에 좋은 음식으로 <u>여겨집니다</u>.

    ㄱ. 궁금합니다   ㄴ. 익숙합니다   ㄷ. 바랍니다   ㄹ. 생각됩니다

3. 가: 그동안 바빠서 연락도 못 했네요. 요즘 어떻게 지내셨어요?

    나: 저도 시험 때문에 정신 없었어요. <u>그런데</u> 부모님은 요즘 건강하세요?

    ㄱ. 그건 그렇고   ㄴ. 하지만   ㄷ. 아시다시피   ㄹ. 하루빨리

4. 운동을 열심히 해서 건강이 <u>차차</u> 좋아지고 있습니다.

    ㄱ. 급속하게   ㄴ. 몰래   ㄷ. 하루빨리   ㄹ. 점점

5. 엄마가 나<u>더러</u> 청소를 하라고 하셨다.

    ㄱ. 만 해도   ㄴ. 한테   ㄷ. 끼리   ㄹ. 도

6. 눈이 오고 바람<u>마저</u> 불어서 밖에 나갈 수가 없었다.

    ㄱ. 도   ㄴ. 만 해도   ㄷ. 더러   ㄹ. 처럼

다... 주어진 표현을 사용해서 문장을 완성해 보세요.

1. ~만 해도

ㄱ: 서울은 요즘 날씨가 어때요?

ㄴ: _____ 너무 추웠는데 이제 완전히 따뜻해졌어요.

2. ~의 영향으로

ㄱ: _____ 한국어를 배우는 학생들이 많아지고 있어요.

ㄴ: 저는 _____ 매일 열심히 공부합니다.

3. ~다시피

ㄱ: 여러분들도 잘 _____ 요즘 환경 문제가 심각합니다.

ㄴ: 너도 _____ 한국에는 산이 많아.

4. ~다(가) 보니까

ㄱ: _____ 돈이 하나도 없어졌어요.

ㄴ: _____ 한국어를 잘하게 됐어요.

라... 다음 문장을 완성해 보세요.

1. 인터넷의 영향으로 _____.

2. 한류의 영향으로 _____.

3. 요즘 매일 놀다 보니까 _____.

4. 열심히 한국어를 공부하다 보니까 _____.

5. 20년 전만 해도 _____.

6. 요즘은 취직하기 힘들어서 제 친구들만 해도 _____.

읽기

남한과 북한

1945년 8월 15일, 제2차 세계 대전이 끝나게 되면서 한반도는 일제 강점기**에서 벗어나게**[GU9.9] 되었다. 미국 군과 소련 군은 한반도의 안정을 위해 38선 북쪽은 소련 군이, 남쪽은 미국 군이 통치하기로 합의했다. 원래는 빠른 시간 **이내에**[GU9.10] 한반도에 하나의 정부를 세우는 것이 목표였지만 미국과 소련 사이에 냉전이 시작되면서 한반도는 남과 북으로 분단되었다. 그리하여 3년 후 1948년에 남쪽에서는 대한민국(Republic of Korea) 정부가 수립되었고 북쪽에서는 조선민주주의인민공화국(Democratic People's Republic of Korea) 정부가 수립되었다. 한국에서는 조선민주주의인민공화국을 보통 북한이라고 부르고, 한반도 문제에 대해서 이야기할 때 한국을 남한이라고 부르기도 한다. 북한에서는 한국을 남조선이라고 부르고 북한을 조선이나 공화국이라고 부른다.

1950년에는 남한과 북한 사이에 전쟁이 발발했다. 이 전쟁은 한국 전쟁이라고도 하고 6월 25일에 일어났기 때문에 6·25 전쟁이라고도 한다. 북한의 남침으로 시작된 한국 전쟁은 3년 동안 계속되었고 미국을 비롯한 UN 연합군과 소련, 중국 등이 참가하는 국제전으로

제2차 세계 대전 World War II 벗어나다 to get out of 군 military 소련 the Soviet Union
안정 stability 38선(삼팔선) 38th parallel 통치하다 to rule, govern 합의하다 to agree
정부 government 수립하다 to establish 냉전 the Cold War 그리하여 therefore
발발하다 to break out 일어나다 to occur, break out ~(으)ㄹ 비롯한 including ...
연합군 the Allied Forces 국제전 international war

발전되었다. 이 전쟁으로 수많은 사람들이 사망하거나 다쳤고 한반
도의 대부분의 산업 시설들이 파괴되었다. 그리고 참전한 외국의 군
인들도 큰 **피해를 입었다.**^{GU9.11} 또한 전쟁 때문에 많은 가족들이 남한
과 북한으로 헤어져서 서로 만나지 못하는 이산가족이 되었다.

　　1953년에 판문점에서 휴전 협정이 이루어져서 전쟁은 멈췄지만
아직 전쟁이 완전히 끝난 것은 아니며 지금도 남한군과 북한군이 대
치하고 있다. 남한과 북한의 경계선을 군사분계선이라고 하는데 38
선과는 조금 다르다. 군사분계선에서부터 남북으로 2km 범위에는
비무장지대가 설치되어 있다. 이런 분단 상태로 인해 남한과 북한에
는 병역 의무 제도가 있다. 남한의 경우 건강한 대한민국 남성은 법
적으로 2년 정도 군복무를 해야 한다. 북한의 경우 남녀 모두 군복무
를 마쳐야 하며 군복무 기간이 남한에 비해 훨씬 더 긴 것으로 알려
져 있다.

　　많은 사람들이 한반도의 통일을 기원하고 있지만 이를 위해서는
해결해야 할 문제들이 많이 있다. 그중의 하나는 남한과 북한의 경제
력과 사람들의 사고방식이 너무 달라져서 갑자기 통일이 되면 큰 혼
란이 생길 **수도 있다는**^{GU9.12} 점이다. 하지만 남북한이 통일을 하기 위
해 서로 노력을 한다면 머지않아 통일을 이룰 수 있을 것이다.

사망하다 to die 산업 시설 industrial facilities 파괴되다 to be destroyed 참전하다 to
enter a war 피해를 입다 to be damaged 이산가족 separated families 휴전 협정 armistice
agreement 대치하다 to confront 경계선 line of demarcation 군사분계선 Military
Demarcation Line 비무장지대 Demilitarized Zone (DMZ) 병역 의무 compulsory duty of
military service 제도 system 군복무 military service 기원하다 to pray, wish
해결하다 to resolve 경제력 economic power 사고방식 way of thinking 통일 unification
혼란 confusion, chaos 머지않아 in a short time, soon

이해 문제

가... 본문과 내용이 맞으면 ○, 틀리면 X에 표시하세요.

1. 제2차 세계 대전이 끝나기 바로 전에는 일본이 한반도를   ○   X
   지배하고 있었다.

2. 한반도가 남한과 북한으로 나누어진 것은 한국 전쟁 때문이다.   ○   X

3. "대한민국", "한국", "남한", "남조선"은 모두 같은 말이다.   ○   X

4. 소련과 중국은 UN 연합군의 회원이었다.   ○   X

5. 한국 전쟁은 1953년에 끝났다.   ○   X

나... 본문을 읽고 다음 질문에 대답해 보세요.

1. 한반도가 남북으로 나누어지게 된 배경은 무엇입니까?

2. 북한의 공식 명칭은 무엇입니까?

3. 한국 전쟁은 어떻게 시작되었습니까?

4. 이산가족이 무엇인지 설명해 봅시다.

5. 남북한이 갑자기 통일되었을 때에는 어떤 문제가 생길 수 있을까요?

문법과 용법

GU9.9

~에서 벗어나다 'to get out of'

1945년 한반도는 일제 강점기**에서 벗어났다**.

The Korean Peninsula exited the Japanese Colonial Period in 1945.

나는 도시**에서 벗어나(서)** 바닷가에 가고 싶다.

I want to get out of the city and go to the beach.

▶ 벗어나다 'to get out of, free oneself, escape' is a compound verb consisting of 벗다 'take off' and 나다 'come out'. It is preceded by the particle 에서 'from', 를, or (으)로부터, which are usually interchangeable, although speakers may prefer to use one over another:

감시에서/감시를/감시로부터 벗어나다   to escape surveillance

가난에서/가난을/가난으로부터 벗어나다   to break away from poverty

기대를/기대에서/기대로부터 벗어나다   to be different from expectations

예상을/예상에서/예상으로부터 벗어나다   to be unanticipated

스트레스로부터/스트레스에서/스트레스를 벗어나다   to be relieved of stress

GU9.10

이내에/이내로 'within'

한 달 **이내에** 연락 드리겠습니다.

I will contact you within a month.

숙제로 한국 전쟁에 대해서 다섯 장 **이내로** 쓰세요.

As homework, please write about the Korean War in under five pages.

▶ The Sino–Korean bound noun 이내 means 'within, not more than', as in 우리 집에서 학교까지는 걸어서 20분 **이내**예요 'Our school is less than a 20 minute walk from our house'. The expression 이내에/이내로 is used to express a given limit or range of time, distance, or quantity.

GU9.11

(피해)를 입다 'to be harmed'

우리 아버지는 사업을 하시면서 많은 손해**를 입고** 그만두셨어요.

My father gave up the business at a great loss.

홍수로 인해 철도가 곳곳에서 큰 피해**를 입었어요.**

The railroad was seriously damaged from the flood.

▶ The basic meaning of 입다 is 'to put on, wear'. One of its extended meanings is 'to suffer, sustain, incur (an adverse situation)', as in 상처를 입다 'to get hurt',

부상을 입다 'to get injured', and 손해를 입다 'to suffer a loss'. Another extended meaning is 'to receive (a favor)', as in 은혜를 입다 'to be blessed or favored'.

~(으)ㄹ 수도 있다; ~(으)ㄹ지도 모르다 'might'

오늘 비가 **올 수도 있**으니까 우산을 가지고 나가라.

Take your umbrella with you since it might rain today.

범인은 우리 중에 한 사람**일지도 몰라**요.

The culprit may be among us.

▶ The bound noun 수 means 'case, way, means, ability, possibility'. The expression ~(으)ㄹ 수 있다, in which ~(으)ㄹ 'will/may' is a prospective modifier suffix and 있다 is an existential adjective, literally means 'there is a way/possibility that someone/something will/may'. Its extended meaning is 'can'. On the other hand, the pattern ~(으)ㄹ 수도 있다 literally means 'there is also/even a possibility that someone/something will/may ...', its derived meaning being 'might' This means there is also a possibility for the opposite.

▶ A similar expression is ~(으)ㄹ지도 모르다 where the bound noun 지 'whether, if' and the verb 모르다 'to not know' occur. It literally means '(We/I) don't know even whether something will happen or not'. Its derived meaning is 'might'. The two expressions ~(으)ㄹ 수도 있다 and ~(으)ㄹ지도 모르다 are usually interchangeable.

활동

가... 다음 뜻에 맞는 단어를 찾아서 써 넣으세요.

> 국제전, 이산가족, 사고방식, 통일, 통치, 합의, 휴전

1. 전쟁을 멈추는 것   _____

2. 여러 나라가 참가하는 전쟁   _____

3. 헤어져서 서로 만나지 못하는 가족   _____

4. 생각하는 방법이나 태도   _____

5. 나누어진 것을 하나로 합치는 것   _____

6. 나라나 지역을 다스리는 것   _____

7. 의견이 같아지는 것   _____

나... 다음 빈 칸에 가장 알맞은 말을 고르세요.

1. 운동을 하다가 다쳐서 다리에 상처를 _____.

  ㄱ. 벗어났다   ㄴ. 입었다   ㄷ. 비롯했다   ㄹ. 받았다

2. 선생님께 _____ 은혜를 어떻게 갚아야 할지 모르겠어요.

  ㄱ. 벗어난   ㄴ. 보는   ㄷ. 드린   ㄹ. 입은

3. 이 나라는 예전에는 가난했지만 국민들이 열심히 일해서 이제는 가난으로부터 완전히 _____.

    ㄱ. 입었다   ㄴ. 계속됐다   ㄷ. 벗어났다   ㄹ. 들어갔다

4. 스티브는 사업을 하다가 처음에는 많은 손해를 _____ 그 후에 성공했습니다.

    ㄱ. 입었지만   ㄴ. 벗어났지만   ㄷ. 여겼지만   ㄹ. 들었지만

5. 저는 답답한 도시 생활에서 _____ 여행을 가고 싶어요.

    ㄱ. 벗어나서   ㄴ. 이내에   ㄷ. 돌아가서   ㄹ. 입어서

다... 아래 주어진 표현을 사용해서 문장을 완성하세요. 문맥에 맞게 형태를 고쳐 쓰세요.

> 벗어나다, ~(으)ㄹ지도 모른다, ~(으)ㄹ 수도 있다, 이내에/이내로, 입다

1. 한국 전쟁 이후에 많은 사람들이 가난에서 _____ 위해서 열심히 일했습니다.

2. 이 숙제는 1주일 _____ 제출해 주세요.

3. 그동안 비가 안 와서 걱정했는데 하늘을 보니 오늘은 비가 _____.

4. 그동안 선생님께 많은 은혜를 _____. 졸업해도 잊지 않겠습니다.

5. 지금 너무 늦어서 제니가 _____ 내일 전화하는 게 좋겠어.

라... 다음은 북한에서 쓰는 말들입니다. 무슨 뜻일지 생각해 보고 한국 표준말로
써 봅시다.

북한 문화어	남한 표준어
1. 손기척	
2. 닭알	
3. 곽밥	
4. 몸까기	
5. 자동계단	
6. 머리비누	
7. 과일단물	
8. 이닦이 약	
9. 동무	
10. 원주필	
11. 위생실	
12. 손전화	

〈정답〉 1. 노크 2. 달걀 3. 도시락 4. 다이어트 5. 에스컬레이터 6. 샴푸 7. 주스 8. 치약
9. 친구 10. 볼펜 11. 화장실 12. 휴대 전화

북한의 수도 평양

평양은 북한의 수도이자 최대 도시이다. 북한의 정치, 문화, 교육의 중심지이고 인구는 300만 명 정도이다. 과거 고구려의 수도였고 고려 시대, 조선 시대에도 군사적으로 중요한 도시였기 때문에 역사 유적도 많이 남아 있다. 평양의 중심에는 대동강이 흐르고 대동강을 중심으로 옛날부터 농업이 발달했다. 여름에는 비가 많이 오지만 겨울에는 아주 건조하고 추운 날씨가 계속된다.

평양에는 북한의 주요 기관들이 모여 있고 평양 시민들은 대부분 북한의 핵심 계층에 속하는 사람들이다. 평양 시내에서는 고층 빌딩도 볼 수 있고 차도 많이 다니고 스마트 폰을 사용하는 시민들도 쉽게 볼 수 있어 다른 나라의 대도시들과 비슷한 모습이다. 하지만 평양 이외의 북한의 다른 도시들은 많이 낙후되어 있다고 한다. 평양은 북한의 상류층이 사는 도시이고 통행증을 받은 사람만 들어갈 수 있는 특별한 곳인 만큼 평양 모습만 보고 북한 전체가 그렇다고 생각할 수는 없는 것이다.

한국 국민은 평양에 가는 것이 제한되어 있지만 많은 외국인들은 평양으로 여행 가는 것이 가능하다. 하지만 아무 곳이나 여행할 수는

군사 military 역사 유적 remains of history 흐르다 to flow 농업 farming 주요 major, main
기관 organization, institution, agency 핵심 계층 the core social class of North Korea
고층 빌딩 skyscraper 낙후되다 to lag behind 상류층 the upper class 통행증 pass (card)
불가능하다 to be impossible

없고 북한에서 허락하는 곳들만 가이드와 함께 다닐 수 있다. 평양에서 관광객들에게 유명한 곳들로는 세계에서 가장 큰 개선문인 평양 개선문, 평양을 가로지르는 대동강, 고구려를 건국한 동명왕의 무덤인 동명왕릉, 평양 냉면을 비롯한 북한의 음식을 맛볼 수 있는 식당인 옥류관 등이 있다. 앞으로 북한이 세계인들에게 개방된다면 평양이 관광할 만한 도시로 관심을 끌 것으로 여겨진다.

개선문 triumphal arch 가로지르다 to cross 건국하다 to found a country 무덤 grave, tomb
개방되다 to be open to

북한의 유명한 관광 명소

백두산

한반도에서 제일 높은 산으로 높이가 2,744m이다. 백두산 정상에는 "천지"라는 호수가 있다.

금강산

옛날부터 한반도에서 가장 아름다운 산으로 알려져 있고 역사적으로 중국이나 일본에까지 아름다운 산으로 유명했다고 한다.

총석정

금강산 북쪽의 바닷가에 있는 육각형, 팔각형의 돌기둥들과 절벽이다. 화산 작용으로 생긴 지형으로 예전부터 아름답기로 유명한 곳이다.

동명왕릉

고구려를 건국한 동명왕의 무덤이다. 고구려 무덤 중 규모가 가장 큰데, 둘레는 34×34m, 높이는 11m이다.

정상 top, summit 알려지다 to become known 육각형 hexagon 팔각형 octagon
기둥 pillar 절벽 cliff 화산 작용 volcanic action 지형 geographical features 규모 scale, size
둘레 perimeter

■■ 번역문 ■■

CONVERSATION: The Younger Generation of North Korea

On a TV Talk Show

Host: Today, we have brought guests who have escaped from North Korea and live in South Korea to talk about the younger generation of North Korea.

(Ŭn-hŭi) Kim: Hi. I am 22 years old and I am Ŭn-hŭi Kim who defected from North Korea two years ago.

(Yŏng-ch'ŏl) Yi: Hi. I have been in South Korea for ten years. I am 46 years old and my name is Yŏng-ch'ŏl Yi.

Host: It's nice to meet you. As you know, lately North Korea is changing rapidly due to the influence of China and the Korean Wave. In particular, they say that the younger generation is active and daring. I am curious about how young North Koreans date. Do couples walk around, holding hands and such, in North Korea?

Yi: Yes, actually even as late as the 1990s, we didn't see couples walking around holding hands much during the day, but now things have changed greatly. So, they say lovers are dating freely.

Kim: Yes, there are many couples who are walking hand in hand or arm locked in the date's arm on the street these days. In Pyongyang, it is common to see lovers even drinking beer and bowling together.

Host: Oh, people date freely in North Korea, too. And I heard that they watch a lot of Korean dramas in North Korea these days. Is that really true?

Kim: Yes, everyone secretly watches not only K-drama, but they all secretly watch Korean movies and listen to K-pop too. Korean popular culture videos are brought directly to North Korea as DVDs or flash drives through China, you see. Even I secretly watched Korean drama every day like that, being anxious that I might get caught.

Host: Oh, what happens if they are caught watching something like that?

Kim: In the case of a student, if they are caught, they can be expelled from their schools.

Host: Many students must be watching.

Yi: Because of Korean dramas and music, they say that *hallyu* is in fashion among young people of North Korea. They follow hairstyles and fashions of South Korean celebrities. They even follow the Seoul accent a lot. This is because they think those who speak in Seoul dialect are more sophisticated, so they practice Seoul speech and such.

Host: Oh, I see. That's interesting. By the way, you all came to South Korea, after having had a hard time escaping North Korea. While living in South Korea, are there any difficulties?

Yi: At first, it was very hard. When I first came to South Korea, I tried to get a part-time job. But saying that my accent is strange, no one gave me any job. So, I was really hurt. Since there was no place that would even give me a part-time job, making a living felt difficult. But as I worked hard over the years, I came up with ways, you know.

Kim: I, too, had a hard time correcting the way I spoke. As you know in South Korea, people use a lot of English words, so I didn't understand them at first, making things difficult. In North Korea, elevators are called *sŭngganggi*, you know. At first, I didn't understand what the *ellibeitŏ* (elevator) meant, and I didn't know what *skŭrin doŏ* (screen doors), *naepk'in* (napkins), *polp'en* (ballpoint pens), or *sŭt'eip'ŭlŏ* (staplers), etc., were. Now I have adjusted, and I am doing well because many good people helped me.

Host: I saw on the news that many North Korean defectors said it was not easy adjusting to the South Korean society. I hope that the people of South and North Koreas can come and go freely as soon as possible.

READING: South Korea and North Korea

On August 15th, 1945, the Korean Peninsula was freed from Japanese occupation with the ending of World War II. For the stability of the Korean Peninsula, the U.S.

and Soviet armies agreed that the Soviet army would govern north of the 38th parallel and the United States, the south. Originally, the goal was to establish a single government on the Korean Peninsula in a timely manner, but the Cold War began between the United States and the Soviet Union, so the Korean Peninsula became divided into two Koreas. Three years later, the Republic of Korea was established in 1948 in the South, and the Democratic People's Republic of Korea in the North. South Korea commonly calls the Democratic People's Republic of Korea (DPRK) "Pukhan (North Korea),"and refers to itself as "Namhan (South Korea)" when discussing issues about the Korean Peninsula. North Korea calls South Korea "Nam-Chosŏn (South Chosŏn)," and North Korea "Chosŏn" or "Konghwaguk (Republic)."

In 1950, a war broke out between North and South Korea. This war is also called the Korean War or the War of 6·25 because it began on June 25th. The Korean War, which began as an invasion from North Korea, continued for three years. The United States, along with others like the UN Allied Forces, the Soviet Union, China, etc., also participated, thereby turning it into an international war. As a result of this war, many people were killed or injured, and most industrial facilities on the peninsula were destroyed. Additionally, the foreign soldiers who fought in the war suffered severe losses. Moreover, many families were broken up between the South and North, turning them into separated families who cannot even see each other.

In 1953, a truce agreement was reached at Panmunjeom, which halted the war, but the South Korean and North Korean armies are still confronting each other. The boundary line between South Korea and North Korea is called the Military Demarcation Line, which is a little different from the 38th Parallel. Within a 2-kilometer range to the south and north of the Military Demarcation Line, the DMZ was established between the two Koreas. Due to this state of division, both South and North Korea have mandatory military service systems. In the case of South Korea, healthy male citizens of the Republic of Korea are required by law to perform one and a half years to two years of military service. In the case of North Korea, both men and women must complete military service, the time period for which is known to be much longer in comparison to South Korea.

Many people are wishing for the reunification of the two Koreas, but there are many issues to be solved before reunification can take place. One of them would be that the economic strength and mentalities of the two Koreas have become so different, a sudden reunification could cause major confusion. But if South and North Korea both make the effort towards reuniting, they may be able to achieve unification in the near future.

FURTHER READING: Pyongyang, the Capital of North Korea

Pyongyang is both the capital of North Korea and its largest city. It is the center of North Korean politics, culture, and education and the population is about 3 million. It was the capital of Koguryŏ in the past and because it was a militarily important city even during the Koryŏ and Chosŏn Dynasties, a lot of historical relics still remain. In the center of Pyongyang flows the Taedong River, around which farming had developed since ancient times. Although a lot of rain falls during summer, it is quite dry in autumn as cold weather continues.

All of the main institutions are gathered in Pyongyang, with the majority of its citizens belonging to the core social class of North Korea. In downtown Pyongyang one can easily see tall buildings, cars driving around, and citizens using smartphones, so it has an appearance that is similar to large cities in other countries. However, the other cities in North Korea have lagged behind in their development. As Pyongyang is a city where the North Korean upper class live and is a special place where only people with passes can enter, one cannot merely look at Pyongyang and think that all of North Korea looks the same.

Although South Korean citizens' visits to Pyongyang have been limited, it is possible for many foreigners to travel to Pyongyang. However, they cannot travel to just anywhere and can go only to the places approved by North Korea accompanied by a guide. Places that are well known to tourists include the Pyongyang Triumphal Arch, which is the largest of its kind in the world, the Taedong River that cuts across the city, the Royal Tomb of King Tongmyŏng, which is a tomb dedicated to King Tongmyŏng who founded the Koguryŏ Dynasty, and *Okryu-gwan*, which is a restaurant where people can taste Pyongyang cold noodles amongst other North Korean foods. It is believed that if North Korea were to be open to the rest of the world, Pyongyang would draw attention as a city that is worth going to see.

CULTURE: Famous Tourist Spots in North Korea

Paektu Mountain

As the tallest mountain on the Korean Peninsula, it is 2,744 meters high. At the top of Paektu Mountain there is a lake called "Ch'ŏnji."

The Kŭmgang Mountains

It has become known as the most beautiful mountain on the Korean Peninsula since long ago and historically has been famous for its beauty even as far as China and Japan.

Ch'ongsŏkchŏng

These are hexagon- or octagon-shaped stone pillars and cliffs located at the seashore north of the Kŭmgang Mountains. As geographical features formed through volcanic activity, they have been famous for their beauty since ancient times.

Tomb of King Tongmyŏng

This is the tomb of King Tongmyŏng who founded the Koguryŏ Dynasty. It is the largest amongst the Koguryŏ tombs, with a perimeter of 34 by 34 meters and a height of 11 meters.

▦ 단어 ▦

38선(삼팔선)	38th parallel	다들	everyone
가로지르다	to cross	당	political party
개방되다	to be open to	대담하다	to be bold, daring
개선문	triumphal arch	대중문화	popular culture
건국하다	to found a country	대치하다	to confront
걸리다	to be caught	둘레	perimeter
경계선	line of demarcation	들키다	to get caught
경제력	economic power	–마저	even, as well
고층 빌딩	skyscraper	막막하다	to feel lost and gloomy
고치다	to fix	말투	one's way of speaking
국제전	international war	머지않아	in a short time, soon
군복무	military service	모습	appearance
군사분계선	Military Demarcation Line	몰래	secretly
군사	military	무덤	grave, tomb
군	military	발발하다	to break out
궁금하다	to be curious	벗어나다	to get out of
규모	scale, size	변화하다	to change
그리하여	therefore	병역 의무	compulsory duty of military service
급속하게	rapidly		
기관	organization, institution, agency	분단	division
		불가능하다	to be impossible
기둥	pillar	비무장지대	Demilitarized Zone (DMZ)
기원하다	to pray, wish	사고방식	way of thinking
끼리	among or by ourselves or themselves	사망하다	to die
		사회자	emcee
낙후되다	to lag behind	산업 시설	industrial facilities
남북 관계	South Korea–North Korea relations	상류층	the upper class
		성형 수술	plastic surgery
냉전	the Cold War	세대	generation
농업	farming	세련되다	to be sophisticated

소련	the Soviet Union	즐겨 먹다	to enjoy eating (frequently)
수립하다	to establish	지형	geographical features
시켜 주다	to let or allow someone/ something	차이	difference
		차차	gradually
심지어	even, what is more	참전하다	to enter a war
안정	stability	청바지	jeans
알려지다	to become known	탈북하다	to escape from North Korea
여겨지다	to be considered, regarded	탈출하다	to escape
역사 유적	remains of history	통일	unification
연합군	the Allied Forces	통치하다	to rule, govern
영상	video	통행증	pass (card)
왕래하다	to come and go	퇴학당하다	to be expelled from a school
육각형	hexagon	파괴되다	to be destroyed
~(으)ㄹ 비롯한	including ...	팔각형	octagon
이산가족	separated families	팔짱을 끼다	to link arms
이야기를 나누다	to talk (with)	패션	fashion
익숙하다	to be familiar	피해를 입다	to be damaged
일어나다	to occur, break out	하루빨리	as soon as possible
자유롭게	freely	한국 전쟁	the Korean War
적극적이다	to be active	한반도	Korean Peninsula
적응하다	to adjust	한자	Chinese character
절벽	cliff	합의하다	to agree
정부	government	해결하다	to resolve
정상	top, summit	핵심 계층	the core social class of North Korea
정해 주다	to decide (something for someone)		
		혼란	confusion, chaos
제2차 세계 대전	World War II	화산 작용	volcanic action
제도	system	휴전 협정	armistice agreement
제한되다	to be limited	흐르다	to flow
조마조마하다	to be anxious	흔히	commonly, often
주요	major, main		

한국의 주거 문화

Lesson 10 Housing in Korea

학습 목표

내용
- 한국의 주거 형태와 관련된 표현을 익힌다.
- 집을 찾거나 이사할 때 유용한 표현을 배운다.

문화
- 한국의 단독 주택 및 아파트 등 주거 형태를 살펴본다.
- 한국의 거주 상황을 이해한다.

주거 residence　형태 format　유용하다 to be useful　단독 주택 single-unit house

■ 생각해 봅시다

가 ▸▸ 다음 질문에 대해 이야기해 봅시다.

   1. 여러분이 살고 있는 집에 대해서 이야기해 보세요.

   2. 지금 살고 있는 집의 장단점은 무엇입니까?

   3. 여러분은 어떤 주거 형태를 선호합니까?

   4. 집을 구하거나 이사할 때 필요한 표현들은 어떤 것이 있습니까?

나 ▸▸ 다음 질문에 대해 자신의 경험을 이야기해 보세요.

   1. 여러분은 보통 어떻게 집을 구합니까?

   2. 집을 찾을 때 여러분이 중요하게 생각하는 것은 무엇입니까?

   3. 집을 계약할 때 주의해야 할 점은 무엇이 있습니까?

   4. 여러분이 알고 있는 한국의 주거 형태는 어떤 것이 있습니까?

선호하다 to prefer 구하다 to obtain 계약하다 to contract 주의하다 to be careful

집 구하기

학생 식당에서 지윤, 민준, 지호가 함께 점심을 먹고 있다.

지호: 지윤아, 너 어디 사니?

지윤: 학교 기숙사. 지호, 너는?

지호: 난 지금 고모 집에서 다니고 있는데 고모가 너무 엄격해서 불편해. 집에 늦게 들어가면 눈치 보이고, 친구를 데려오는 것도 쉽지 않고… 그래서 기숙사로 옮길까 해. 기숙사 어떠니?

지윤: 뭐 나쁘지는 않아. 기숙사는 학교에서 관리해 주니까 편하기는 한데 룸메이트랑 잘 안 맞으면 불편하지. 지난 번에 룸메이트랑 싸웠는데 다음 날 분위기가 너무 어색하더라고. 그래서 **참다못해**GU10.1 결국 내가 먼저 말을 걸고 화해했지.

민준: 그건 그래. 룸메이트랑 안 맞으면 정말 불편해. 난 방 세 개 있는 아파트에서 룸메이트랑 사는데 다행히도 우리는 성격이 잘 맞는 편이야.

지호: 집주인은 어때?

민준: 계약할 때 한 번 봤는데 까다롭지 않았어. 보통 불편한 게 있으면 부동산을 통해서 얘기를 하니까 볼 기회는 거의 없어.

지윤: 맞아. 집주인 **잘못**GU10.2 만나도 고생하더라구.

엄격하다 to be strict 눈치 보이다 to care about what others think 옮기다 to move
관리하다 to supervise 싸우다 to fight 분위기 atmosphere 어색하다 to be awkward
참다못해 beyond one's endurance 말을 걸다 to initiate a conversation 화해 reconciliation
집주인 landlord 까다롭다 to be particular 부동산 real estate (agent)

민준: 지금 우리 룸메이트 한 명이 이번에 군대 가거든. 그래서 마
       침 룸메이트를 구하고 있는데 관심 있으면 말해.

지호: 한 달에 얼마야?

민준: 120만 원인데 세 명이 나눠서 내.

지호: 전기세, 수도세… 뭐 인터넷은?

민준: 그런 건 다 포함돼 있어.

지윤: 비싼 거 아니야? 그 돈이면 월세를 **사느니 차라리**^{GU10.3} 전세가
       낫지 않나?

민준: 전세는 목돈이 필요한데 내가 돈이 어디 있냐? 집값이 자꾸
       올라 정말 **죽을 지경이다.**^{GU10.4}

지윤: 민준아, 너네 아파트 몇 평인데?

민준: 33평이야. 굉장히 넓고 깨끗해. 욕실도 2개고. 가장 좋은 것
       은 지하철역이랑 마트가 바로 앞에 있어.

지호: 부모님들은 내가 기숙사에 **들어갔으면 하시는데**^{GU10.5} …

민준: 그런데, 기숙사도 **싸지 않을걸.**^{GU10.6}

지윤: 그래! 기숙사도 **비싸다니까.**^{GU10.7} 집 구하는 게 쉬운 일이 아닌
       데 잘 됐으면 좋겠다. 나는 주로 학교 주변에서 생활하니까
       기숙사가 제일 좋은데 지호는 민준이네 아파트도 괜찮지 않
       을까?

민준: 그래. **일단**^{GU10.8} 와서 봐. 서울아파트 105동 1204호야.

지호: 그럴까? 다음 주에 시간 되니?

민준: 난 좋아. 룸메이트한테 물어보고 문자 보낼게.

군대 military 나누다 to divide 수도세 water bills 전기세 electricity bill 포함되다 to be
included 월세 monthly rent 차라리 rather 전세 long-term lease with large sum deposit
as a rental 목돈 lump sum of money 지경 situation 평 units to measure space in Korea,
about 35.5 square feet 욕실 bathroom 주변 surrounding 생활하다 to live 일단 first of all
동 counter for building 호 counter for unit 문자 text message

이해 문제

가... 다음 내용이 대화 내용과 맞으면 ○, 틀리면 X에 표시하세요.

1. 지윤이는 룸메이트하고 싸운 적이 있다. ○ X

2. 지호는 고모 때문에 새로운 룸메이트를 구하고 있다. ○ X

3. 전세는 목돈이 필요하다. ○ X

4. 전체적으로 집값이 많이 올라가고 있다. ○ X

5. 민준이는 한 달에 월세로 40만 원 정도 내고 있다. ○ X

6. 민준이는 군대에 가야 한다. ○ X

나... 대화를 읽고 다음 질문에 대답해 보세요.

1. 지윤, 지호, 민준이는 지금 어디에서 살고 있습니까?

2. 지호가 지금 살고 있는 곳에서 불편한 점은 무엇입니까?

3. 민준이는 왜 룸메이트를 찾고 있습니까?

4. 민준이가 사는 곳은 어떻습니까?

5. 지윤이가 룸메이트와 살아서 불편한 점은 무엇입니까?

문법과 용법

~다 못해 'unable to'

친구를 기다리**다 못해** 혼자 영화관으로 들어갔어요.

Unable to wait for my friend any longer, I just went into the theater by myself.

힘든 과제를 견디**다 못해** 학교를 그만두었어요.

Unable to bear the difficult assignments, I quit school.

더위를 참**다못해** 저는 택시를 타고 집에 가 버렸어요.

Unable to stand the heat, I just ended up taking a taxi home.

▶ The pattern ~다 못해 is a contraction of ~다가 못해서, in which the suffix –다가 means 'and then, while doing', the verb 못해 'cannot do', and the connective suffix –서 'and so'. It literally means 'while doing something, it is unable to continue it, and so'. Its derived meaning is '(being) unable to do …', as in 우리가 계속 싸우니까 선생님은 보다 못해 화를 내셨다 'Since we kept fighting, the teacher, unable to stand by and watch any longer, got mad at us', and 너무 많이 먹어 배가 부르다 못해 터질 것 같아 'I ate too much and now my stomach is unbearably full and feels like it's going to burst'. 참다못해 is idiomatized and does not need a space between 참다 and 못해.

GU10.2

잘못 ~　'mistakenly, wrong(ly), erroneously'

음식을 **잘못** 먹어 배탈이 났다.

I got a stomachache from eating some bad food.

친구가 전화번호를 **잘못** 알려 줘서 며칠 동안 연락을 할 수 없었다.

I was unable to contact my friend for a few days because
he gave me the wrong phone number.

이 단어는 발음을 **잘못** 하면 사람들한테 오해받을 수 있다.

This word may lead to a communication error if you pronounce it incorrectly.

▶ 잘못 is both a noun and an adverb. As a noun, it means 'an error, a fault, a mistake', as in 그것은 내 잘못이다 'It is my fault'. As an adverb, it modifies a verb, as in 잘못 계산하다 'to calculate erroneously', 생각을 잘못하다 'to think in an incorrect way', and 잘못 알아듣다 'to misunderstand someone's words'. The present pattern illustrates the cases that it is used as an adverb.

▶ The compound 잘못하다 functions as a verb, meaning 'to make a mistake/error, do improperly, as in 발음을 잘못하다 'to pronounce incorrectly', 판단을 잘못하다 'to err in one's judgement', and 나는 직업의 선택을 잘못했다 'I chose the wrong job'.

▶ 잘못하다 can be compared to 잘 못하다 'cannot do well', in which the adverb 잘 'well' modifies the verb 못하다 'cannot do' and there is a slight pause after 잘 in pronunciation. There is a slight difference in meaning between the two expressions, as observed in 민지는 영어를 잘못한다 'Minji speaks English the wrong way' and 민지는 영어를 잘 못한다 'Minji does not speak English well'.

GU10.3

~느니 (차라리) 'would rather … than'

동생이랑 같이 여행을 가**느니 차라리** 혼자 집에서 자는 게 낫겠어요.

I would rather sleep at home than go on a trip with my brother.

내가 생물학을 전공하**느니** 학교를 안 다니겠다.

I would rather quit school than major in biology.

너랑 결혼하**느니 차라리** 죽을래.

I would rather die than marry you.

그 식당에서 밥을 먹**느니 차라리** 집에서 라면 먹는 게 낫겠네.

I would rather eat instant ramen at home than eat at that restaurant.

▶ The connective suffix –느니 '(rather) than', which is attached only to action verbs, indicates that the contents of the second clause are better than or preferable to those of the first clause. –느니 may be followed by the comparative particle 보다 'than' with no change in meaning, as in –느니보다. The second clause can be preceded by the adverb 차라리 'rather, preferably' for emphasis, as in 버스를 타느니보다 차라리 걷는 것이 낫겠다 'I would rather walk than ride the bus'. The preferred action denoted by the second clause often ends in the conjectural suffix –겠다'.

GU10.4

~(으)ㄹ 지경이다
'to be on the verge of; to be in a tight position'

요즘 숙제가 많아서 죽을 **지경**이다.
I might die I have so much homework.

두 사람이 이혼할 **지경**이에요.
They're on the verge of divorce.

이번 주에 시험이 매일 있어서 정말 미칠 **지경**이야.
I feel like I'm going crazy with exams every day this whole week.

며칠 동안 잠을 못 자고 일했더니 쓰러질 **지경**이에요.
I am at the brink of collapse since I haven't slept for several days
to continue working.

▶ 지경 basically means 'a boundary, border'. Its extended–often exaggerated–meanings are 'a situation, a condition, circumstances'. These extended meanings serve in the pattern ~(으)ㄹ 지경이다. The situation or circumstances referred to in this pattern are typically those that cause trouble or discomfort, and in general have adverse repercussions. This expression is often preceded by a verb of hardship, such as 포기하다 'to give up', 쓰러지다 'to collapse', 죽다 'to die', 울다 'to cry', 쫓겨나다 'to be kicked out', or 넘어지다 'to fall down'.

GU10.5

~었으면/았으면 하다
'one wishes that; one should be grateful if'

우리 엄마는 내가 이번 학기에 장학금을 받**았으면 하**셔.

My mother hopes I receive a scholarship this semester.

난 네가 잘못했다는 걸 알**았으면 해**.

I want you to know that you were wrong.

그렇게 거짓말 안 **했으면 해**.

I wish you would not lie like that.

나 대신 네가 김 교수님한테 말해 **줬으면 해**.

I would be grateful if you would tell Professor Kim for me.

부모님은 내가 행복**했으면 하**셔.

My parents want me to be happy.

▶ This pattern consists of a past conditional clause followed by the general verb 하다 'do', literally meaning 'it would do if … happened'. Its derived meaning is 'I/someone wish(es) that …'. When the subject is the speaker, it additionally means 'I would be grateful if …' and is somewhat similar in meaning to ~었으면/았으면 좋겠다 'I wish/hope …', as in 저는 마이클이 올해 꼭 졸업했으면 해요/좋겠어요 'I hope Michael will graduate by any means this year'.

GU10.6

~(으)ㄹ걸(요) 'I guess, I think'

가: 민호는 언제 중국에 가니?

When does Minho go to China?

나: 아마 모레 떠날걸↗.

I think he is going to leave the day after tomorrow.

가: 오늘 미아 졸업식은 몇 시에 있어요?

What time is Mia's graduation ceremony today?

나: 지금쯤 벌써 시작했을걸요↗.

I think it should have already started.

▶ This pattern has its origins in the combination of the prospective suffix –(으) ㄹ and the bound noun것(>거) 'fact, that' followed by the object particle –을(> ㄹ). With the prospective suffix and rising intonation, the pattern has obtained the function of a sentence ending with the meaning of the speaker's inference, guess, or conjecture. When it is used without the polite ending 요, it is in the familiar speech level. The pattern can occur not only with verbs, but also with adjectives and copulas, as in 이번 시험은 어려울걸↗ 'I guess this time the exam will be difficult' and 민수는 아직 고등학생일걸요↗ 'I think Minsu is still a high school student'. Although the expressions end with rising intonation, they are statements indicating the speaker's conjecture and are not yes/no questions. Note further that, as observed in 지금쯤 벌써 시작했을걸요↗, the pattern can occur after a past construction.

Another usage of this pattern is to express the speaker's regret in the sense of 'should have'. In this case, falling intonation is used, as in 그 영화를 보러 갈 걸↘ 'I should have gone to see that movie' and 나는 공부를 더 열심히 할걸↘

'I should have studied harder'. Note that although such expressions always connote a past state of affairs, the past tense marker –었/았 is not used. As it is uttered only in soliloquy, the polite ending is not used.

GU10.7

~다니까(요) 'I told you that …'

가: 어젯밤에 어디 있었어?

　　Where were you last night?

나: 도서관에 있었**다니까**! 몇 번 얘기했는데.

　　I told you I was at library! I've told you several times.

가: 이것 좀 먹어 봐.

　　Why don't you take a bite of this?

나: 나 이거 싫**다니까**요.

　　I told you I don't like that.

▶ The pattern consists of a sentence ending (statement –다/라, question –(느)냐, proposal –자, command –(으)라) and the connective suffix –니까 (contracted from –고 하니까) 'since/as/because I say that …', literally meaning 'as I say/ask/ suggest/tell that …'. This pattern functions as a sentence ending to repeat, clarify, or reiterate something previously said, as in 나는 사과가 좋다니까(요) 'I told you that I like apples', 학교에 안 가냐니까(요) 'I asked you whether you were going to school or not', 빨리 가자니까(요) 'I told you we have to hurry', and 빨리 가라니까(요) 'I told you to hurry up'. This pattern usually shows the speaker's frustration or anger that the interlocutor is not listening to him/her.

일단 'for the time being; first of all; once'

일단 밥을 먹고 나서 얘기합시다.
For now, let's just eat first and then talk about it.

일단은 우리집에서 만나자. 그러고 나서 계획을 세우는 게 어때?
For the time being, let's just meet at my house. Then we can make the plan once there, how does that sound?

마이클은 **일단** 술을 마시기 시작하면 너무 많이 마신다.
Once Michael starts drinking, he drinks too much.

▶ The Sino–Korean adverb 일단 (*lit.* 'one–morning'; pronounced as 일딴) means 'once, for the moment'. It can be paraphrased as (a) 우선 먼저 'first of all' (e.g., 일단 거기에 가 보지요 'First off, why don't we go over there and see.'); (b) 우선 잠깐 'for the moment' (e.g., 일단 기다리고 봅시다 'For the moment let's wait and see.'), and 만일 한번 'if once' (e.g., 일단 계획을 하면 반드시 지켜라 'Once you make a plan, please follow through on it.'). Notice that, as an adverb, 일단 takes a sentence–initial or predicate–initial position. The topicalized form 일단은 is always used as a sentential adverb, taking the entire sentence as its scope, in the sense of 'first of all' or 'for the moment'. It usually comes at the beginning of a sentence.

활동

가... 주어진 설명에 적절한 단어를 다음에서 찾으세요.

> 부동산, 수도세 , 욕실, 월세, 집주인

1. 땅이나 건물처럼 움직이거나 옮길 수 없는 재산 _____

2. 집이나 방을 매달 빌려 쓸 때 내는 돈 _____

3. 수돗물을 사용한 만큼의 요금 _____

4. 목욕할 수 있도록 시설을 갖춘 공간 _____

5. 집을 대표하는 사람 또는 집을 소유하고 있는 사람 _____

나... 빈 칸에 가장 어울리는 표현을 고르세요.

1. 제가 아직 운전이 서투르니까 운전 중에는 저한테 _____ 마세요.

　ㄱ. 따라가지　　ㄴ. 말을 걸지　　ㄷ. 옮기지　　ㄹ. 나누지

2. 제 친구는 알레르기 때문에 음식을 고를 때 아주 _____.

　ㄱ. 까다로워요　　ㄴ. 깨끗해요　　ㄷ. 나눠요　　ㄹ. 낫지 않아요.

3. 외국에서 _____ 때, 급한 일이 생기면 영사관에 연락하세요.

　ㄱ. 화해할　　ㄴ. 포함할　　ㄷ. 엄격할　　ㄹ. 생활할

4. 초등학교 친구를 오랜만에 만났더니 _____.

　ㄱ. 주의했어요　　ㄴ. 유용했어요　　ㄷ. 어색했어요　　ㄹ. 선호했어요

다... 주어진 표현을 사용하여 다음 대화를 완성해 보세요.

1. ~다 못해

ㄱ: 마이클하고 너 싸웠어?

ㄴ: 응. 항상 약속 시간에 늦으니까 이번에 내가 _____ 화를 냈어.

2. 잘못 ~

ㄱ: 어디 가니?

ㄴ: 신발 가게. 어제 신발을 샀는데 점원이 _____.
영수증을 보니까 3만 원인 신발 가격이 5만 원으로 되어 있더라구.

3. ~(으)ㄹ걸╱

ㄱ: 민준이 어디 갔니?

ㄴ: _____.

4. ~느니 (차라리) ~겠다

ㄱ: 여름방학 때 뭐 할 거니?

ㄴ: 동생하고 여행 가려고?

ㄱ: 동생하고? 나는 동생하고 _____.

5. ~(으)면 하다

ㄱ: 졸업하면 뭐 할 거야?

ㄴ: 난 대학원에 가고 싶은데 우리 부모님은 내가 _____.

6. ~(으)ㄹ 지경이다

ㄱ: 너 어디 아파? 왜 그래?

ㄴ: 요즘 _____.

7. **일단**

ㄱ: 다음 달 캠프 가는 거 어떻게 할까?

ㄴ: _____.

8. **~다니까**

ㄱ: 어제 왜 파티에 안 왔어?

ㄴ: _____.

라... 다음 주제에 대해서 반 친구와 이야기해 보세요.

1. 집 구할 때 가장 힘든 점은 무엇입니까?

2. 여러분이 생각하는 이상적인 룸메이트는 어떤 사람입니까?

3. 여러분이 집주인이라면 어떤 세입자(tenant)가 마음에 들지 않을까요?

마... 여러분은 다음 상황에서 어떻게 할지 반 친구와 역할극을 해 보세요.

1. 집주인이 미리 나에게 얘기하지 않고 내 방을 다른 손님에게 보여 주러 왔다.

2. 집주인이 계약을 두 주 남기고 방을 비워 달라고 부탁했다.

3. 집주인이 다음 달부터 월세를 20만 원 올리려고 한다.

4. 룸메이트가 나에게 미리 말하지 않고 집에서 파티를 하고 있다.

5. 룸메이트 가족이 놀러 와서 일주일 동안 같이 지내야 한다.

6. 룸메이트가 청소를 하지 않는다.

바... 다음 광고를 보고 틀린 내용을 고르세요.

1. 현재 이 방은 아무도 살지 않는다.

2. 전기료, 가스비 등은 안 낸다.

3. 방에 세탁기, 냉장고, 가스레인지가 설치되어 있지 않다.

4. 적어도 1년은 계약해야 한다.

5. 지하철 서울대입구역까지 멀다.

6. 부동산 소개비는 내지 않아도 된다.

사... 다음 광고를 비교해 보고 여러분은 어느 방을 선호하는지 이야기해 보세요.

1.

성공 고시텔

- 개인 화장실, 샤워 시설, TV, 옷장, 책상, 인터넷, 에어컨 포함
- 공용 부엌, 휴게실, 세탁실 등 각종 편의시설
- 2층 여성 전용, 3층 남성 전용
- 내 집 같은 분위기, 조용하고 쾌적한 환경
- 2호선 신촌역에서 버스로 10분
- 월 50만

2.

> ### <u>전세 있어요</u>
>
> - 전세 1억 2000만
> - 30평, 넓은 거실, 방 3개, 욕실 2개
> - 지하철 OO역 도보 10분 거리
> - XX 쇼핑센터, OO마트 근처
> - 문의: 가나다 부동산
> - 전화번호: 02-1234-5678

3.

> ### <u>아주 넓은 홍대역 근처 원룸 있습니다.</u>
>
> - 홍대역 1번 출구 도보로 5분 거리
> - 공용 주차장 무료 사용
> - 맛집, 카페 등 상가가 밀집되어 있어 편리하고 안전
> - 에어컨, 인터넷 완비
> - 세탁실 공용
> - 보증금 1000만원 /월세 40만원

아... 여러분이 지금 살고 있는 집의 세입자를 구하는 광고를 만들어 보세요.

읽기

한국의 현대 주거 문화

한 신문사에서 30-40대 직장인을 대상으로 "로또 1등에 당첨되면 무엇을 할 것인가"라는 주제로 설문 조사를 했는데, 3분의 2에 가까운 응답자가 "집을 사겠다"고 답했다. 그러나 안타깝**게도**^{GU10.9} 대학을 졸업하고 나서 30년 이상 저축해도 서울에서는 집을 사기 힘들 정도로 '내 집 마련'은 서민들의 꿈이 되어 버렸다. 부모 세대 때만 해도 '내 집 마련'은 인생의 중요한 목표 중 하나였고, 집을 소유하는 것에 대하여 큰 의미를 두고 있었다. '내 집 마련'은 가족의 안정을 뜻했고 일이 십 년 열심히 일한 수입을 모아 저축하면 내 집 마련이 가능했다. 그러나 젊은 세대는 현실적으로 '내 집 마련'이 쉽지 않기 때문에 그 열망이 부모 세대**만 못하다.**^{GU10.10}

로또 lotto 당첨되다 to win (a prize) 안타깝다 to be pitiful 저축하다 to save money
마련 owning; preparation 수입 income 현실적 to be realistic 열망 desire

'내 집 마련'을 하기 전까지는 임대료를 주고 집을 빌리는데 월세와 전세가 가장 일반적인 임대 유형이다. 월세는 매달 집세를 내고 집을 빌리는 것인데 보통 1년이나 2년 단위로 계약한다. 월세로 들어갈 때 적게는 한 달 월세의 몇 배 많게는 몇 십 배에 해당하는^{GU10.11} 금액을 보증금으로 내야 한다. 이 보증금은 계약이 만료되면 돌려받을 수 있다. 전세의 경우는 한국에만 있는 임대 유형으로 상당히 큰 액수의 목돈을 내고 일정 기간을 계약해서 집을 빌리는 제도이다. 전세는 매달 임대료를 내지 않고 살 수 있고, 계약 기간이 끝나면 전세금을 전액 돌려받을 수 있다는 장점이 있다.

한국인이 제일 많이 살고 있는 주거 형태는 아파트이다. '아파트'는 영어의 apartment에서 온 외래어인데 5층 이상의 공동 주택을 말한다. 미국의 apartment는 월세를 내고 생활하는 주거 공간이지만 한국의 아파트는 미국의 condominium에 가까운 형태로 아파트의 각 세대는 개인 소유이다. 많은 사람들이 아파트에 살고 싶어 하기 때문에 점점 더 높은 아파트 단지가 여기 저기 생겨났다. 한국은 '아파트 공화국'이라고 불릴 정도로 아파트가 밀집되어 단지로 구성되어 있다. 2000년대부터는 20층이 넘는 아파트가 보편화되었고 주상복합 형태의 50층 이상의 초고층 아파트가 등장하기도 했다.

임대료 rental fee 빌리다 to borrow 임대 rented; leased 유형 type 집세 house rent
단위 units –배 -fold 해당하다 correspond; applicable to 금액 amount of money
보증금 deposit 만료 expiration 일정 fixed, set 전액 total amount 외래어 loan word
공동 common; public 공간 space 단지 complex 공화국 republic 밀집되다 to be
concentrated 구성 composition 보편화 generalization 등장하다 to appear

요즘은 원룸이나 고시원, 오피스텔 등 새로운 주거 형태가 젊은 사람들에게 인기를 끌고 있다. 원룸은 미국의 스튜디오에 해당하는데 방 안에 욕실과 부엌이 다 갖추어져 있다. 고시원은 고시텔이라고도 한다. 원룸보다는 작은 규모로 화장실이나 욕실을 같이 써야 하는 경우도 있다. 고시원은 공무원 시험을 장기간 준비하고 있는 사람이나 한 달이 안 되는 단기간 동안 머무는 사람들이 많이 찾는다. 오피스텔은 주거와 업무를 겸할 수 있는 형태이다. 주로 문화 시설이나 편의 시설이 좋은 곳에 위치하고 아파트 임대료보다는 저렴하여 젊은 사람들에게 인기가 있다.

원룸 studio 고시원 small studios mostly for government test takers 공무원 public servant 장기간 long term 단기간 short term 업무 business 겸하다 to combine 시설 facilities 편의 convenience 저렴하다 to be cheap

이해 문제

가... 다음 내용이 맞으면 ○, 틀리면 X에 표시하세요.

1. 30년 정도 저축해도 서울에서 집을 사기가 힘들다.   ○   X

2. 전세는 매달 임대료만 내면 보증금을 나중에 돌려받을 수 있다.   ○   X

3. 보증금은 보통 월세에 해당하는 정도의 금액이다.   ○   X

4. 원룸, 오피스텔, 고시원은 보통 월세로 임대한다.   ○   X

5. 고시원은 화장실이나 욕실을 공동으로 사용하기도 한다.   ○   X

6. 한국인이 가장 많이 살고 있는 주거 형태는 오피스텔이다.   ○   X

7. 부모 세대에 비해 젊은 세대는 '내 집 마련'이 쉬워졌다.   ○   X

나... 본문을 읽고 다음 질문에 대답해 보세요.

1. '내 집 마련'에 대한 인식이 세대 간에 어떻게 다릅니까?

2. 한국의 임대 유형에는 어떤 것이 있습니까?

3. 한국의 주거 형태를 본문에서 모두 찾아보세요.

4. 전세와 월세의 차이는 무엇입니까?

5. 미국의 아파트와 한국의 아파트의 다른 점은 무엇입니까?

문법과 용법

> **GU10.9**
>
> ~계도　'indeed, enough'

친구가 고맙**게도** 돈을 빌려 주었어요.

My friend was kind enough to lend me some money.

공교롭**게도** 그날은 비가 몹시 내렸다.

Unexpectedly, that day was quite rainy.

올 겨울은 유난스럽**게도** 추워요.

It is unusually cold this winter.

이상하**게도** 그 집에는 아무도 살고 있지 않았다.

Strangely enough, nobody was living in that house.

▶ Adjectives can be made into adverbs by attaching the adverbializer suffix –게, as in 이상하다 'to be strange' + –게 '–ly' → 이상하게 'strangely'. All these derived adverbs can further be followed by the particle –도 'also, even, indeed' for emphasis, as in 이상하게도 'strangely enough, very strangely'. Similar examples include 슬프게도 'sadly indeed', 안타깝게도 'regretfully indeed', 그렇게도 'so much', and 불행하게도 'unfortunately'.

~만 못하다   'to be not as good as'

제 영어는 중국어**만 못해**요.

My English is not as good as my Chinese.

부모님 건강이 예전**만 못해**서 슬퍼요.

I am sad because my parents' health is not as good as it used to be.

이 식당 음식은 제가 만든 요리**만 못해**요.

The food at this restaurant is not as good as my own cooking.

▶ This pattern, in which 만 means 'as much as' and 못하다 means 'to be inferior', is used to say that something (A) does not reach the level or degree of the other thing (B) that is being compared. It can be translated as 'is worse than', 'not as good as' or 'inferior to'. It can be paraphrased as –만큼 좋지 않다, as in 제 영어는 중국어만 못해요 = 제 영어는 중국어만큼 좋지 않아요. The particle 만 is similar in meaning to the particle 만큼 'as much as', but their uses are not the same. For example, 제 영어는 중국어만큼 유창해요 'My English is as fluent as my Chinese' is acceptable but 제 영어는 중국어만 유창해요 is not.

> **GU10.11**

~에 해당하다 'to correspond to; to be applicable to'

영어의 **R에 해당하**는 한국어 발음은 뭐예요?

What is the Korean sound that corresponds to English 'R'?

물고기의 지느러미는 사람의 팔**에 해당한**다.

The fin of a fish corresponds to the arm of a person.

한국의 원룸은 미국의 스튜디오**에 해당한**다.

The Korean 'one-room' is equivalent to an American studio.

▶ The compound verb 해당하다 'to correspond (to), be applicable (to), come under' is composed of the Sino–Korean noun 해당 'appropriateness, conformity, corresponding' and the native Korean verb 하다. It requires the goal particle 에 to occur before it, as in 그 범죄에 해당하는 벌 'the appropriate punishment to fit the crime'. 해당 combines with other Sino–Korean nouns to form compound nouns, as in 해당 학과 'the appropriate (university) department' and 해당 자료 'pertinent/relevant data'.

활동

가... 빈 칸에 가장 어울리는 표현을 고르세요.

　　1. 버스, 라디오, 컴퓨터, 바나나 등은 ＿＿＿＿＿에 속한다.

　　　　ㄱ. 외국어　　　　ㄴ. 한글　　　　ㄷ. 한자　　　　ㄹ. 외래어

　　2. 우리 집 주변에 아파트가 많이 생겨서 ＿＿＿＿＿ 시설이 잘 되어 있다.

　　　　ㄱ. 편의　　　　ㄴ. 보편화　　　　ㄷ. 마련　　　　ㄹ. 안정

　　3. 학생들의 요구로 오늘 행사 마지막에 유명한 가수가 ＿＿＿＿＿.

　　　　ㄱ. 당첨됐다　　ㄴ. 저렴했다　　ㄷ. 해당했다　　ㄹ. 등장했다

　　4. 우리 동네는 다양한 종류의 음식점들이 ＿＿＿＿＿ 해 있어서 아주 편리하다.

　　　　ㄱ. 인기　　　　ㄴ. 구성　　　　ㄷ. 열정　　　　ㄹ. 밀집

　　5. 제 아파트 계약이 다음 달에 ＿＿＿＿＿ 돼서 빨리 다른 집을 찾아야 돼요.

　　　　ㄱ. 만료　　　　ㄴ. 업무　　　　ㄷ. 유형　　　　ㄹ. 공동

　　6. 이번 행사는 졸업식과 스승의 날을 ＿＿＿＿＿ 진행할 예정입니다.

　　　　ㄱ. 저축해서　　ㄴ. 겸해서　　ㄷ. 마련해서　　ㄹ. 빌려서

나... 다음 예문과 같이 밑줄 친 표현을 사용하여 문장을 완성하세요.

　　1. 이 영화는 같은 제목의 소설만 <u>못해요</u>.

　　　　ㄱ: 학교 식당은 ＿＿＿＿＿＿＿＿＿＿＿＿＿＿.

ㄴ: 우리 학교 기숙사는 _____.

ㄷ: 제 한국어 실력은 _____.

2. 안타깝게도 우리 팀이 축구 결승전에서 졌습니다.

ㄱ: _____ 제가 이사할 때 친구들이 도와줬어요.

ㄴ: _____ 제가 조깅하러 나갈 때마다 비가 와요.

ㄷ: _____ 제니는 아직까지 취직을 못 했어요.

3. '스킨십'에 해당하는 영어 표현은 뭐가 있을까요?

ㄱ. 한국의 수학능력시험은 미국의 _____.

ㄴ. 미국의 추수감사절은 한국의 _____.

ㄷ. 1킬로그램을 파운드로 하면 _____.

다... 다음 주제에 대해서 이야기해 보세요.

1. 미국에서 집을 찾으려면 보통 어떤 과정을 거치는지 설명해 보세요.

2. 단독 주택과 아파트의 장단점을 비교하여 토론해 보세요.

3. 여러분이 살고 싶은 이상적인 집은 어떤 형태입니까?

4. 여러분이 로또 1등에 당첨되면 무엇을 하겠습니까?

5. 여러분 인생 목표에 "내 집 마련"도 포함됩니까?

추 가 읽 기

아파트 광고

한국 사람들이 가장 선호하는 주거 형태가 아파트인 만큼 한국의 건설사들은 아파트를 판매하기 위해 브랜드 마케팅에 많은 노력을 기울였다. 그 노력의 하나가 유명 연예인들을 광고 모델로 쓴 것이다. 톱모델들의 이미지는 아파트의 고급 이미지를 강조해 주고, 아파트는 나의 삶의 수준을 평가하는 상품이 되어 버렸다.

　　'당신이 사는 곳이 당신이 누구인지 말해 줍니다.'
　　'세상은 당신이 사는 곳을 동경합니다.'

이러한 광고 카피 속 아파트는 궁전이나 호텔을 연상시키고 여기에 살고 있는 사람들은 모두 행복해 보인다. 그러나 이것은 현실 생활과는 거리가 멀다는 비판을 받기도 했다.

반면에, 톱모델의 효과나 고급 이미지에서 벗어나서 아파트 자체의 가치나 실용성을 강조하거나 다양한 감성적 요소로 소비자에게 어필하는 광고도 있다. 다음의 광고 카피들은 아버지의 따뜻한 이미

건설사 construction firm 품질 quality 평가하다 to evaluate 상품 product
동경하다 to yearn 연상시키다 to remind 벗어나다 to deviate 실용성 practicality
감성적 to be emotional

지와 가족의 소중함을 알려 주거나 자연과 가깝고 아이들에게 좋은 환경이라는 메시지를 전달하고 있다.

> '바쁜 사람들도, 굳센 사람들도, 바람과 같던 사람들도,
> 집에 돌아오면 아버지가 된다.'
> '연예인 이름보다 꽃 이름을 더 많이 아는 아이로 키우고
> 싶습니다.'

이러한 광고 카피에는 소비자들의 많은 호응과 칭찬이 이어졌다. 이렇듯 현대의 아파트는 우리가 사는 주거 공간 이상의 의미를 가지고 있다.

굳세다 to be strong and firm 연예인 celebrity 호응 positive response

이사와 관련된 풍수 인테리어

한국의 풍수 인테리어를 참고하여 집 분위기를 바꿔 봅시다.

1. 침실은 아침에 햇살이 드는 방이 좋고 꽃을 두면 애정운이 상승한다.
2. 거실은 집의 중심이므로 반드시 밝아야 한다.
3. 소파는 앉은 사람에게 현관이 안 보이는 곳에 두어야 한다.
4. 지갑을 주방에 두면 금전적 손실이 있다.
5. 작은 실내 분수나 어항이 있으면 재물운이 좋다.
6. 현관이 깨끗하면 항상 좋은 소식이 들어온다.

풍수 feng shui, geomancy 햇살 sunlight 들다 to enter 애정운 being lucky in love
상승 increase 거실 living room 지갑 wallet 주방 kitchen 금전적 monetary 손실 loss
실내 interior 분수 fountain 어항 fish tank 재물운 being fortunate in property 소식 news

▪▪ 번역문 ▪▪

CONVERSATION: Finding a House

At the student cafeteria, Chiyun, Minjun, and Chiho are eating lunch together.

Chiho:　Chiyun, where do you live?

Chiyun:　School dorms. What about you, Chiho?

Chiho:　I am staying at my aunt's house now, but it's awkward because she's really strict. If I come home late, I feel like she disapproves and it's not easy to have friends over ... so, I'm thinking of moving to the dorms. How are the dorms?

Chiyun:　I mean they're not bad. It's convenient because the school maintains the dorms but if you don't get along with your roommate, then it's going to be uncomfortable. Last time I fought with my roommate, the next day the atmosphere was really awkward. I couldn't stand it, so I ended up speaking up first and we settled it.

Minjun:　That's true. If you don't get along with your roommate, it's super awkward. I'm living in a 3-bedroom apartment with roommates and luckily our personalities match pretty well.

Chiho:　How's your landlord?

Minjun:　I saw them once when I signed my contract and they weren't difficult. Usually, if there's something wrong, I talk to them through the realty office. So, I really don't have a chance to see them.

Chiyun:　Exactly. If you have a bad landlord, it gets really hard.

Minjun:　One of our roommates is about to go into the military. So we happen to be looking for another roommate. If you're interested, let me know.

Chiho:　How much is it per month?

Minjun:　It's 1, 2 million won but the three of us divide it up and pay.

Chiho:　What about the electricity bill, the water bill ... and internet?

Minjun:　Those are all included.

Chiyun: Isn't that expensive? If it's that much, instead of paying month to month, wouldn't it be better to do *chŏnse*?

Minjun: *Chŏnse* requires a lump sum up-front—do you think I have that kind of money? I am literally on the verge of death with house prices that keep rising.

Chiyun: Minjun, how many *p'yŏng* is your apartment?

Minjun: It is 33 *p'yŏng*. It's really spacious and clean. There are 2 bathrooms and the best thing is the subway station and a convenience store is right out front.

Chiho: My parents want me to go into the dorms, though ...

Minjun: But, the dorms aren't going to be inexpensive either.

Chiyun: Right! That's what I said, the dorms are expensive. Finding a house isn't easy but I hope it turns out well. Since I usually live near the school, the dorm is the best but Minjun's apartment would also be good for Chiho, right?

Minjun: Right. First come and see (it). It is Seoul Apartment, Buidling 105 Unit 1204.

Chiho: Shall we? Do you have time next week?

Minjun: That's good for me. I'll ask my roommates and text you.

READING: Modern Housing Culture of Korea

A newspaper agency conducted a survey of office workers in their 30s and 40s with the theme of "What would you do if you won 1st place in the lottery?" Two out of 3 respondents said, "I would buy a house." Unfortunately, however, 'home ownership' has become a dream for Korea's citizens, as it is difficult to buy a house in Seoul even if one saves money for over 30 years after graduating college. During even just one's parents' generation, 'home ownership' was one of life's important goals, as people attached significance to the idea of owning a house. 'Home ownership' meant stability for the family, and it was possible if someone saved up their hard-earned income for decades. However, since 'home ownership' is not realistically easy for the younger generation, their desire for it is not as strong as their parents' generation.

Before attaining 'home ownership' people rent a house, with monthly rentals and *chŏnse* or lease deposits as the most common type of house rentals. Monthly rental involves paying rent every month, usually with 1- or 2-year contracts. When someone moves in, they must pay a sum of at least several months' worth of rent to as much as ten months' worth of rent in the form of a security deposit. One can get this security deposit back when the contract expires. In the case of *chŏnse*, it is a type of house renting that is unique to Korea. It is a system in which people pay significantly large sums of money to borrow a house for a fixed period of time under contract. *Chŏnse* has the advantage of not having to pay rent every month, while being able to get back the entire deposit amount once the contracted period finishes.

The type of housing in which the highest number of Koreans live is the *ap'at'ŭ*. *Ap'at'ŭ* is a loan word that comes from the English 'apartment', and refers to common housing with five stories or more. The American apartment is a housing space for which monthly rent is paid, but the Korean apartment is closer to the American condominium, where the units are privately owned by each household. Since many people want to live in such apartments, more and more high-rise apartment complexes have emerged all over the place. To the extent that Korea has been called an 'Apartment Republic', apartments are concentrated and organized into complexes. From the 2000s, 20-plus-story apartment buildings became widespread and even residential-commercial high rises over 50 stories tall started to appear.

Nowadays new types of housing including one-rooms, *koshiwŏn*, and *op'isŭt'el* are attracting popularity amongst young people. One-rooms correspond to American studios, where rooms are equipped with a bathroom and kitchen. *Koshiwŏn* are also called *koshit'el*. They are smaller in size than one-rooms, and in many cases people have to share lavatories or bathrooms. People undergoing long-term preparations for public servant examinations or those staying for short periods of time under a month often go to *koshiwŏn*. *Op'isŭt'el* can be used for both housing and business. They are usually located in places with good cultural facilities or amenities and are cheaper than apartment rentals, making them popular among young people.

FURTHER READING: Apartment Advertisements

As apartments are the type of housing most preferred by Koreans, Korean construction firms have put in much effort towards brand marketing in order to sell apartments. One of those efforts has been using famous celebrities as advertisement models. The images of top models emphasize a luxurious image of apartments, as they have become a product for evaluating one's standard of living.

'The place that you live in tells who you are.'
'The world yearns for the place you live in.'

The apartments in these types of advertisement copies remind one of palaces or hotels, and the people living there all look happy. However, such advertisements have received criticism that it is far from real life.

On the other hand, there are also advertisements that deviate from the effect of top models or luxurious images by appealing to consumers through their emphasis on various emotional factors such as an apartment's intrinsic value or its practicality. The next advertisement copy tells about the warm images of a father or the preciousness of a family, or they convey a message of being close to nature as a good environment for the children.

'Busy people, strong people, people who were like the wind, all become fathers when they come home.'
'I want to raise children who know the names of more flowers than the names of celebrities.'

This kind of advertisement copy has elicited many positive responses and compliments from consumers. In this manner, modern apartments have taken on a meaning that is more than just a living space.

CULTURE: *Feng Shui* Interior Design as It Relates to Moving

Let's try and change the ambience of your house in reference to Korean *feng shui* interior design.

1. For the bedroom, a room that lets in sunlight in the morning is good, and if it has flowers, luck in love will increase.

2. The living room is the center of the house, so it must be bright.

3. One must put the sofa in a place where the entrance is not visible to those sitting on it.

4. If one leaves their wallet in the kitchen, there will be monetary losses.

5. If there is a small indoor fountain or fish bowl, one will have financial fortune.

6. If the entrance is clean, good news will always come in.

∷ 단어 ∷

감성적	to be emotional	등장하다	to appear
거실	living room	로또	lotto
건설사	construction firm	마련	owning; preparation
겸하다	to combine	만료	expiration
계약하다	to contract	말을 걸다	to initiate a conversation
고시원	small studios mostly for government test takers	매료시키다	to attract
공간	space	목돈	lump sum of money
공동	common; public	문자	text message
공무원	public servant	밀집	to be concentrated
공화국	republic	–배	-fold
관리하다	to supervise	벗어나다	to deviate
구성	composition	보증금	deposit
구하다	to obtain	보편화	generalization
군대	military	부각되다	to stand out
굳세다	to be strong and firm	부동산	real estate (agent)
금액	amount of money	분수	fountain
금전적	monetary	분위기	atmosphere
까다롭다	to be particular	빌리다	to borrow
나누다	to divide	상승	increase
눈치 보이다	to care about what others think	상품	product
단기간	short term	생활하다	to live
단독 주택	single-unit house	선호하다	to prefer
단위	units	성장하다	to grow
단지	complex	소식	news
당첨되다	to win (a prize)	손실	loss
동	counter for building	수도세	water bills
동경하다	to yearn	수입	income
들다	to enter	시설	facilities
		실내	interior
		실용성	practicality

싸우다	to fight	전세	long-term lease with large sum deposit as a rental
안타깝다	to be pitiful		
애정운	being lucky in love	전액	total amount
어색하다	to be awkward	주거	residence
어항	fish tank	주방	kitchen
엄격하다	to be strict	주변	surrounding
업무	business	주의하다	to be careful
연상시키다	to remind	지갑	wallet
연예인	celebrity	지경	situation
열망	desire	집세	house rent
예전	the old days	집주인	landlord
옮기다	to move	차라리	rather
외래어	loan word	참다못해	beyond one's endurance
욕실	bathroom	편의	convenience
원룸	studio	평	units to measure space in Korea, about 35.5 square feet
월세	monthly rent		
유용하다	to be useful	평가하다	to evaluate
유형	type	포함되다	to be included
일단	first of all	품질	quality
일정	fixed, set	풍수	feng shui, geomancy
임대	rented; leased	해당하다	correspond; applicable to
임대료	rental fee	햇살	sunlight
장기간	long term	현실적	to be realistic
재물운	being fortunate in property	형태	format
저렴하다	to be cheap	호	counter for unit
저축하다	to save money	호응	positive response
전기세	electricity bill	화해	reconciliation

한국의 풍습과 미신

Lesson 11 Customs and Superstitions of Korea

■ 학습 목표

내용
- 행운과 불운에 관련된 표현들을 익힌다.
- 금지 사항이나 주의할 점에 대해서 이야기하는 연습을 해 본다.

문화
- 한국의 풍습과 미신에 대해서 알아본다.
- 다른 문화의 풍습이나 미신과 비교해 본다.

풍습 custom 미신 superstition 행운 good luck 불운 bad luck 금지 사항 prohibited matters

■ 생각해 봅시다

가 ▸ 다음은 한국에서 주의해야 하거나 하면 좋은 행동들입니다. 다음을 읽고
여러분 나라의 풍습이나 미신에 대해 이야기해 봅시다.

1. 밥 그릇을 들고 밥을 먹으면 안 된다.

2. 새로 이사를 하면 이웃들에게 떡을 선물한다.

3. 윗사람에게 물건을 드릴 때는 두 손을 사용한다.

4. 다른 사람들과 술을 마실 때 보통 자기 술잔에 자기가 따르지 않는다.

5. 남의 결혼식에 갈 때 흰색 옷을 입는 것은 실례이다.

6. 빨간색으로 이름을 쓰면 안 된다.

7. 밤에 손톱이나 발톱을 깎지 않는다.

8. 여자친구나 남자친구에게 신발을 선물하지 않는다.

9. 식사할 때 밥에 젓가락을 꽂으면 안 된다.

10. 시험을 보기 전에 미역국을 먹지 않는다.

나 ▸ 여러분은 징크스가 있습니까? 있으면 이야기해 보세요.

그릇 bowl 행동 behavior 이웃 neighbor 술잔 glass for alcohol
손톱/발톱을 깎다 to clip one's fingernail/toenail 꽂다 to stick into 징크스 jinx

세계의 미신

한국어 수업에서 한국과 여러 나라의 미신에 대해서 이야기한다.

선생님: 혹시 여러분들이 한국에 살면서 알게 된 한국 미신이 있나요?

노아: 제가 지난번에 밤에 휘파람을 불었더니 제 친구가 뱀 나온다고 휘파람을 **불지 말라고 했어요**.^{GU11.1}

제니: 말도 안 돼요. 요즘 뱀이 어디 있어요? 특히 도시에…

선생님: 뱀은 없지만 옛날부터 밤에 휘파람을 불면 뱀이나 귀신이 나온다는 말이 있어요.

제니: 밤에 휘파람을 불면 시끄러우니까 그런 말을 **만들어 낸**^{GU11.2} 것 아닐까요?

선생님: 아마도 그렇겠지요.

노아: 저는 지난번에 아는 한국 분이 저더러 다리를 떨면 복이 달아난다고 하셨어요.

선생님: 맞아요. 그리고 특히 어른들 앞에서 다리를 떠는 것은 예의에도 어긋나는 일이에요. 여러분 나라에는 어떤 미신들이 있어요?

제니: 미국이나 영국에서는 집 안에서 우산을 펴면 안 좋은 일이 생긴다는 말이 있어요.

휘파람을 불다 to whistle 뱀 snake 귀신 ghost 아마(도) maybe 다리를 떨다 to shake one's leg 복 luck 달아나다 to run away 예의에 어긋나다 to go against etiquette 펴다 to unfold, spread

노아:　그리고 검은 고양이를 보면 운이 안 좋다고 해요. 그런데, 저는 검은
　　　　고양이가 두 마리나 있는데 고양이를 키우고 나서 더 좋은 일만 생기
　　　　는걸요.^{GU11.3}

제니:　그렇지 않아도 저도 그 얘기 **하려던 참**^{GU11.4}이었어요. 사실 저도 검은
　　　　고양이를 키우는데 외롭지 않고 좋기만 한데요.

노아:　그리고 사다리 아래로 지나가면 불행한 일이 생길 수 있다는 말이 있
　　　　어요.

선생님:　사다리 아래로 지나가면 당연히 위험할 것 같은데요.

노아:　그렇죠. 위험하니까 그런 말이 생긴 **거겠지요**.^{GU11.5} 그 외에도 나쁜 일
　　　　이 일어나는 것을 방지하려면 나무로 만든 책상이나 식탁 같은 것들
　　　　을 노크하는 것처럼 두드리면 돼요.

제니:　그리고 많은 서양 사람들이 거울을 깨면 7년 동안 재수가 없다고 생각
　　　　해요.

선생님:　정말요? 얼마 전에 거울을 하나 깨뜨렸는데… **어쩐지** 요즘 나쁜 일이
　　　　자꾸 일어나**더라니**…^{GU11.6}

제니:　하하. 선생님은 한국 사람이니까 괜찮으실 거예요.

선생님:　그럼 행운을 주는 것들로는 뭐가 있죠?

노아:　네 잎 클로버, 숫자 7, 또 미국에서는 토끼 발을 가지고 다니면 운이
　　　　좋다고 해요.

선생님:　진짜 토끼 발이요?

노아:　옛날에는 진짜도 있었다는데 요즘은 토끼 발 모양으로 만든 액세서리
　　　　가 있어요.

선생님:　문화마다 참 여러 가지 재미있는 미신들이 있네요!

키우다 to raise 사다리 ladder 불행하다 to be unlucky 당연히 naturally 그 외에도 in
addition 방지하다 to prevent 노크하다 to knock 두드리다 to tap 재수(가) 없다 to be
unlucky 어쩐지 no wonder; somehow 네 잎 클로버 four-leaf clover 토끼 rabbit
운이 좋다 to be lucky

이해 문제

가... 대화의 내용과 맞으면 ○, 틀리면 X에 표시하세요.

1. 한국에는 뱀이 많이 있다.	○	X
2. 한국에서 다리를 떠는 것은 예의 바르지 않은 행동이다.	○	X
3. 영국과 미국에서는 집 안에서 우산을 펴는 것을 안 좋게 생각한다.	○	X
4. 서양에서는 검은 고양이가 불운을 뜻한다.	○	X
5. 서양에서는 토끼 발이 행운을 가져다준다고 생각한다.	○	X

나... 대화를 읽고 다음 질문에 대답해 보세요.

1. 나라마다 불운에 관련된 미신을 정리해 봅시다.

2. 나라마다 행운에 관련된 미신을 정리해 봅시다.

3. 여러분들의 나라에는 어떤 미신들이 있는지 이야기해 봅시다.

문법과 용법

GU11.1

~지 말라고 하다 'to tell someone not to …'

엄마가 늦게 다니**지 말라고 했**어요.

Mom told us not to stay out late.

환경에 좋지 않은 플라스틱을 사용하**지 말라고 했**어요.

(They) told us not to use plastic materials as they are not good
for the environment.

▶ The pattern ~지 말라고 하다 is used to report what someone orders someone else
not to do. It consists of the negative nominalizer suffix –지, the negative verb
stem 말 'stop, not do', imperative sentence ending –라, the quotative particle 고
'that', and the main verb 하다 'to say, told', literally meaning 'A tells B that B
should stop doing'. Only action verb constructions can come before –지 말다, as
in 가지 마세요 'Don't go'; therefore 슬프지 마세요 is not a correct sentence, but
that meaning can be conveyed using –어/아하다, as in 슬퍼하지 마세요 'Don't be
sad'.

GU11.2

~어/아 내다 'to do something eventually'

제 친구는 병을 **이겨 내고** 건강해졌어요.

My friend eventually recovered from his illness and is now healthy.

소방관은 모든 사람을 **구해 냈**어요.

The fireman saved everyone in the end.

이렇게 많은 일들을 어떻게 **해냈**어요?

How did you manage to do so many things?

한국이 축구, 야구에서 금메달을 **따냈**어요!

Korea managed to win gold medals in both soccer and baseball!

▶ As a main verb, ~내다 means 'to produce, put forth'. When used as an auxiliary verb as in ~어/아 내다, it highlights the relentless effort given to successfully achieve a goal or endpoint that involved difficulty. Thus, the meaning is 'to do something eventually, manage to …, do something to the very end despite the difficulty'. Thus, many of the daily action verbs such as 먹다, 잠들다, 놀다, 갖다, 놓다 are not used with ~어/아 내다 since the degree of effort for those is relatively low.

GU11.3

~는걸요/(으)ㄴ걸요   'indeed, despite anticipations or reservations to the contrary'

가: 이사하려면 힘들겠어요. 제가 도와 드릴게요.

It must be hard to move (houses). Let me help you.

나: 괜찮아요. 짐도 별로 없**는걸요**.

That's okay. I don't have a lot of things anyway.

가: 왜 길에 사람들이 별로 없지요?

Why aren't there many people on the street?

나: 오늘 날씨가 이렇게 바람이 불고 추**운걸요**. 누가 이런 날 나오고 싶겠어요.

Well today's weather is this windy and cold. Who would want to come out on this kind of day?

가: 민지가 술을 마셔도 돼요?

Can Minji drink alcohol?

나: 21살**인걸요**. 괜찮아요.

She's 21 years old. It's fine.

▶ This ending is used when one explains one's thoughts or argument, or gives a reason for it. It conveys that the action or state expressed occurs or is the way it is despite and/or contrary to whatever expectations one might normally have.

GU11.4

~(으)려는/(으)려던 참
'at the point of (doing), just when'

내가 지금 나가**려는 참**이었어.

I was just about to leave home.

저녁을 막 먹**으려던 참**에 뜻하지 않은 손님이 찾아왔어요.

Just when we were going to have dinner, an unexpected guest came to visit.

▶ The time word 참 'break, recess, rest period, moment' is a bound noun that must be preceded by the pre-noun 한 'one, big, large' as in 한참 'for a while', or by a clause ending in the intention-indicating suffix –(으)려는 or –(으)려던. The two suffixes –(으)려는 and –(으)려던 are contractions, respectively, of the intention-indicating clauses –(으)려고 하는 and –(으)려고 하던 with –고 하 deletion. The two constructions are used interchangeably, with a slight difference in connotation. The intention is simultaneous with the moment of the time (참) when –(으)려는 is used, but is slightly antecedent to it when –(으)려던 is used.

GU11.5

~는/(으)ㄴ 거겠지(요)   'it may be that, I guess that'

유명인을 광고에 쓰는 것은 광고 효과를 극대화하기 위해서 그러**는 거겠지**요.

I suppose the use of celebrities in commercials is to maximize the advert's effect.

가: 민지가 어디를 저렇게 빨리 가는 걸까요?

Where do you think Minji is heading in such a rush?

나: 학교에 가**는 거겠지**요.

 I guess she must be on her way to school.

▶ The pattern ~는/(으)ㄴ 거겠지(요) 'I guess that ...' is a contraction of ~는/(으)ㄴ 것이겠지(요), where ~는 (non–past of verbs)/(으)ㄴ (past of verbs and non–past of adjectives/copulas) are modifier suffixes, the bound noun 것 means 'a fact, (the fact) that', 이 is the copula stem 'be', –겠 is a conjecture–indicating suffix meaning 'may', and –지(요) is a sentence ending meaning 'I assure you, I suppose'. The compound ending –겠지 is rendered as 'I guess'. The clauses that end in the modifier suffix –는/(으)ㄴ modify 것/거, as in 미아는 학교에 간 거겠지 'I guess Mia went to school'.

GU11.6

어쩐지 ~더라니(까) 'no wonder'

오늘은 **어쩐지** 운수가 좋**더라니**.

I had good luck today, no wonder.

컴퓨터가 고장 났는지 안 켜져요. **어쩐지** 지난 주부터 엄청 느리**더라니**.

The computer isn't turning on, maybe it's broken. It's been so slow since last week, no wonder.

가: 비가 많이 오고 있어요.

 It is raining a lot.

나: **어쩐지** 아침부터 많이 흐리**더라니까**요.

 No wonder it was so cloudy this morning.

▶ The sentential adverb 어쩐지 means 'somehow, without knowing why', as in 어쩐지 울고 싶은 기분이다 'For some reason I feel like crying'. The sentence ending ~더라 means 'I observed, experienced that …'. The final suffix –니(까) 'because, that's why' indicates the speaker's belated realization of the causal relation between the 어쩐지 clause and the previous expression. Together with 어쩐지 and –니까 the phrase is rendered as 'no wonder'.

활동

가... 아래 빈 칸에 어울리는 단어를 고르세요.

1. 옆집 아저씨가 매일 밤 휘파람을 _____ 너무 시끄러워요.

   ㄱ. 불어서   ㄴ. 불러서   ㄷ. 놀아서   ㄹ. 연주해서

2. 갑자기 비가 오기 시작해서 급하게 우산을 꺼내서 _____.

   ㄱ. 열었다   ㄴ. 닫았다   ㄷ. 켰다   ㄹ. 폈다

3. 우리 부모님은 개를 두 마리 _____ .

   ㄱ. 키우세요   ㄴ. 자라세요   ㄷ. 크세요   ㄹ. 재배하세요

4. 경찰들이 교통사고 _____을/를 위해서 노력하고 있어요.

   ㄱ. 방지   ㄴ. 풍습   ㄷ. 대조   ㄹ. 대상

5. 밤에 갑자기 남의 집에 가는 것은 예의에 _____ 행동이에요.

   ㄱ. 맞는   ㄴ. 바른   ㄷ. 지키는   ㄹ. 어긋나는

나... 주어진 표현을 사용하여 다음 대화를 완성해 보세요.

1. ~지 말라고 하다

   ㄱ: 오늘 회식에 안 가세요?

   ㄴ: 의사가 저한테 술을 _____. 그래서 일찍 집에 가려고요.

2. ~어/아 내다

   ㄱ: 이 수학 문제는 너무 어려웠지만 1시간 만에 결국 _____.

   ㄴ: 정말 잘 했어요!

3. ~(으)려던/려는 참이다

ㄱ: 지난번에 빌려 간 돈 언제 갚으실 거예요?

ㄴ: 그렇지 않아도 오늘 _____. 늦게 드려서 미안해요.

4. ~ 거겠지요.

ㄱ: 여자친구한테서 1주일 동안 연락이 없어요.

ㄴ: 아마 수업이 많아서 _____. 좀 더 기다려 보세요.

5. 어쩐지 ~더라니

ㄱ: 저 두 사람 사귄 지 한 달 됐대요.

ㄴ: 어쩐지 둘이 매일 _____.

6. ~는/~(으)ㄴ걸요

ㄱ: K-pop이 정말 인기가 많은가요?

ㄴ: 그럼요. 요즘 학생들이 _____.

다... 한국에는 재미있는 미신들이 많이 있습니다. 왜 다음과 같은 미신이 생겼는지 그 이유를 한국 사람들과 함께 이야기해 봅시다.

1. 문지방을 밟으면 안 된다.

2. 방문을 닫고 선풍기를 켜고 자면 죽는다.

3. 돼지꿈을 꾸면 돈이 생긴다.

4. 숫자 4는 죽음을 의미한다.

5. 대학 입학 시험을 보는 사람에게는 찹쌀떡이나 엿을 선물한다.

> 문지방 threshold 선풍기 electric fan 꿈을 꾸다 to dream 찹쌀떡 sticky rice cake
> 엿 Korean-style sticky taffy

읽기

선물할 때 주의할 점들

감사를 표현하거나 축하하기 위해 선물을 주고받는 것은 인간관계에 좋은 영향을 **끼친다**.[GU11.7] 하지만 문화에 따라 의미가 다른 물건들이 있기 때문에 다른 문화의 사람들에게 선물할 때에는 조심해서 물건을 골라야 한다.

한국에서는 연인에게 신발이나 손수건을 선물하면 헤어진다는 말이 있다. 신발은 떠난다는 뜻이 있고 손수건은 눈물을 뜻하기 때문이다. 그리고 친구에게 칼을 선물하면 친구 관계를 끊고 싶다는 뜻으로 오해할 수 있다. 날카로운 칼이 위험할 수 있는 것은 **말할 것도 없다**.[GU11.8] 그래서 한국 사람에게는 **기왕이면**[GU11.9] 신발, 손수건, 칼은 선물로 주지 않는 것이 좋다.

꽃도 좋은 선물이지만 꽃에 담긴 의미는 문화마다 다를 수 있다. 예를 들어 한국에서는 흰색 국화가 장례식에 사용하는 꽃이므로 일반적인 선물로는 **금물이다**.[GU11.10] 그리고 한국 사람들은 어버이날이나 스승의 날에 부모님, 선생님들에게 감사의 마음을 전하기 위해 카네이션을 드리는데 서양에서는 카네이션이나 백합은 장례식에 사용하는 꽃이기 때문에 선물할 때 주의해야 한다. 또,

---

영향 effect 끼치다 to cause 고르다 to choose 손수건 handkerchief 눈물 tears 칼 knife,
blade 오해하다 to misunderstand 날카롭다 to be sharp 위험하다 to be dangerous
기왕이면 if that is the case anyway 국화 chrysanthemum 장례식 funeral 일반적인 usual,
general 금물 taboo 어버이날 Parents' Day 스승 teacher, mentor

서양에서는 빨간 장미는 보통 연인에게 주는 꽃이기 때문에 빨간 장미를 선물할 때는 오해가 없도록 주의해야 한다.

중국에서는 시계를 선물한다는 말이 장례를 치른다는 말과 발음이 같**다고 해서**^{GU11.11} 중국 사람들은 시계를 선물하지 않는다. 그리고 우산이나 과일 중의 배도 이별을 의미하는 말과 발음이 비슷하기 때문에 보통 선물하지 않는다. 또한 중국 말로 부채가 헤어진다는 말과 발음이 비슷하기 때문에 친구 사이에 해서는 안 되는 선물로 알려져 있다.

상대방의 종교에 따라서 주의해야 하는 선물들도 있다. 무슬림들은 술과 돼지고기를 먹으면 안 되기 때문에 이들에게 술이나 돼지고기를 선물하면 곤란하다. 또 힌두교도들은 소를 신성한 동물로 생각하기 때문에 소가죽을 이용한 지갑이나 가방 같은 제품들을 선물**했다가는**^{GU11.12} 큰 실례가 될 것이다.

선물을 받을 때 예절로는 미국에서는 선물을 받고 그 자리에서 열어 보고 감사의 마음을 전하는 것을 예의로 생각하지만 한국에서는 감사히 선물을 받고 내용물은 나중에 확인하는 것이 더 적절하다고 여겨진다. 이처럼 선물에 관련된 관습이 문화마다 다르므로 외국인에게 선물을 준비할 때에는 미리 잘 알아보는 것이 바람직하다.

장례를 치르다 to hold a funeral 발음 pronunciation 이별 farewell 부채 fan 상대방 the other party 종교 religion 주의하다 to be careful 무슬림 Muslim 곤란하다 to be awkward 힌두교도 Hindu 신성하다 to be sacred 소가죽 cowhide 내용물 content items 확인하다 to check 여겨지다 to be considered 관습 custom

이해 문제

가... 대화의 내용과 맞으면 ○, 틀리면 X에 표시하세요.

1. 한국에서 신발이나 손수건은 이별을 뜻한다.   ○   X

2. 한국에서 흰색 국화는 죽음과 관련이 있다.   ○   X

3. 한국 사람들은 카네이션을 부모님께 선물한다.   ○   X

4. 중국에서 시계는 좋아하는 선물이다.   ○   X

5. 무슬림에게는 술을 선물하면 안 된다.   ○   X

6. 힌두교도들은 돼지고기를 안 먹는다.   ○   X

7. 한국 사람들은 보통 선물을 받자마자 뜯어본다.   ○   X

나... 대화를 읽고 다음 질문에 대답해 보세요.

1. 한국에서 카네이션은 어떤 경우에 쓰입니까?

2. 서양에서 선물할 때 조심해야 하는 꽃들은 어떤 꽃들이 있습니까?
   왜 조심해야 할까요?

3. 중국에서 이별을 뜻하는 물건들은 어떤 것들이 있습니까?

4. 종교에 따라 주의해야 하는 선물들은 어떤 것들이 있습니까?

5. 한국에서 선물을 받을 때 어떤 점을 주의해야 합니까?

문법과 용법

끼치다 'to cause, exert'

불편을 **끼쳐** 드려 죄송합니다.
Sorry to inconvenience you.

부모님께 걱정을 **끼쳐** 드려서는 안 된다.
You should not make your parents anxious.

오랜 가뭄은 한국 경제에 나쁜 영향을 **끼쳤**다.
The long drought negatively influenced the Korean economy.

▶ The transitive verb 끼치다 means 'to cause X to Y'. X is expressed by abstract nouns often with negative effects such as 불편 'inconvenience', 폐 'trouble', 걱정 'worry, concern', 손해 'damage', 걱정 'worry', 수고 'trouble', and 해 'harm', while Y is expressed by a wide variety of concrete or abstract nouns including human beings. The goal particles equivalent to 'to' are 께, 에게, 한테, and 에 depending on the status of Y.

> **GU11.8**
>
> 말할 것도 없다   'It is a matter of course that; There is no need to say'
>
> 말할 것도 없이   'needless to say'

그 사람이 정직하다는 것은 **말할 것도 없**어요.

It is obvious that that person is honest.

한국인의 온돌 사용이 촉각 문화 때문임은 **말할 것도 없**다.

Needless to say, Koreans' use of ondol is a direct result of their culture surrounding the sense of touch.

말할 것도 없이 한국에서 제일 큰 도시는 서울입니다.

Needless to say, the largest city in Korea is Seoul.

▶ The pattern 말할 것도 없다 literally means 'there is even nothing that we should say'. The derived meaning is 'there is no need to say that …' or 'it is a matter of course that …'. The expression 두말할 것도 없다 is often used in the same sense, where 두말 means 'two words'. In order to trigger the use of this pattern, a clause must precede the pattern.

▶ The adverbial form (두)말할 것도 없이 is an idiomatic expression to mean 'needless to say', as in (두)말할 것도 없이 미국은 세계의 최강국이다 'Needless to say, the United States is the strongest nation in the world'.

GU11.9

기왕이면/이왕이면 'if that is the case anyway'

기왕이면 나하고 같이 갑시다.

If you're going anyway, why don't you just go with me?

외국어 수업을 들어야 되면 **이왕이면** 한국어 수업을 들으세요.

If you have to take a foreign language class anyway, you might as well take Korean.

▶ The Sino–Korean nouns 기왕 and 이왕 mean 'the past, bygones'. While as an adverb, it means 'already, now that'. When it is followed by 이면 'if it is', the whole construction means 'while (since, if) one is already at it; all in all; if it has already happened, things being what they are anyway'.

GU11.10

~은/는 금물이다 'be prohibited'

운전 중에 방심**은 금물이다**.

Not paying attention while driving is prohibited.

지나친 욕심**은 금물이다**.

Excessive greed is taboo.

환자에게 술과 담배**는 금물이다**.

Alcohol and smoking are prohibited for patients.

▶ The Sino–Korean noun 금물 means 'a tabooed, prohibited, or forbidden item, something to be carefully avoided'. It takes the copula 이다 to function as a predicate to indicate that a certain action (a subject referent) is a taboo or is prohibited, as 과식은 금물이에요 'Overeating must be avoided' and 환자가 담배 피우는 것은 금물이에요 'Patients are prohibited from smoking'.

GU11.11

~다고/라고 해서 'be called (entitled; known as)... and (so/then)'

3월 14일은 화이트 데이**라고 해서**, 남자들이 여자들한테 사탕을 선물해요.
March 14th is called White Day and on this holiday men gift candy to women.

제주도는 공기가 맑고 기후가 따뜻하**다고 해서** 많은 관광객이 몰려든다.
Cheju Island is known to have fresh air and warm weather,
so many tourists flock to visit.

▶ This pattern consists of the indirect quotation pattern 다고 or 라고 (the latter after the copula 이다), the verb 해 'say; call' and the suffix –서 'and so, and then', literally meaning 'it is said that ...', 'and so/then ...'. Frequently, the causal ('and so') or temporal sequence ('and then') meaning of –서 becomes weakened and only its connective meaning 'and' remains, as in the first sentence above. The second sentence has a cause–effect meaning.

GU11.12

~다가는 'do … and then; if … (with negative consequence)'

천천히 드세요. 그렇게 급하게 먹**다가는** 체하겠어요.

Eat slowly. You will get an upset stomach if you eat that fast.

이러**다가는** 큰일 나요.

If you just leave things like that, you will find yourself in a pickle.

쉬지 않고 일만 하**다가는** 병나요.

All work and no play will lead you to get sick.

▶ This pattern consists of the suffix –다가 'while, and then', followed by the topic particle 는. Its basic meaning is 'to do and then', as in 가다가는 서고 서다가는 간다 'It goes and stops, and stops and goes'. The construction's derived function is to provide a condition for a certain negative consequence. While its conditional equivalent, ~(으)면, is used neutrally, ~다가는 is limited to cases with negative consequences. For example, 비가 오면 집에 있겠다 is a natural expression, but 비가 오다가는 집에 있겠다 is ungrammatical. Similarly, 주말 밤에 예약하지 않고 들렀다가는 원하는 영화를 볼 수 없다 'If you don't make a reservation on a weekend night, you will not be able to watch the movie you wanted to' is fine, but 주말 밤에 예약하지 않고 들렀다가는 원하는 영화를 볼 수 있다 is ungrammatical.

활동

가... 다음 빈 칸에 가장 어울리는 단어를 고르세요.

1. 땅이 미끄러우니까 넘어지지 않도록 _____.

ㄱ. 주의하세요   ㄴ. 알아보세요   ㄷ. 두드리세요   ㄹ. 사용하세요

2. 어머니, 제가 전화를 안 받아서 걱정하셨지요? 걱정을 _____ 드려서 죄송합니다.

ㄱ. 전해   ㄴ. 실례해   ㄷ. 끼쳐   ㄹ. 치러

3. 초대받았을 때에는 작은 선물을 준비해서 가는 것이 _____.

ㄱ. 적절합니다   ㄴ. 부족합니다   ㄷ. 금물입니다   ㄹ. 실례입니다

4. 저는 친구한테 칭찬을 하려고 했는데 친구가 제 말을 _____ 화를 냈어요.

ㄱ. 이해해서   ㄴ. 알아서   ㄷ. 오해해서   ㄹ. 따라서

5. 산에서 담배를 피우면 불이 날 수 있습니다. 그렇기 때문에 산에서 담배를 피우는
것은 _____.

ㄱ. 금물입니다   ㄴ. 바람직합니다   ㄷ. 적절합니다   ㄹ. 실례입니다

6. 이번 행사는 졸업식과 스승의 날을 _____ 진행할 예정입니다.

ㄱ. 저축해서   ㄴ. 겸해서   ㄷ. 마련해서   ㄹ. 빌려서

나... 다음에서 알맞은 단어를 골라 대화를 완성하세요.

> 금물이다, 기왕이면/이왕이면, 적절하다, 말할 것도 없다, 끼치다

1. ㄱ. 제가 서태지의 음악을 들어 봤는데 아주 좋았어요.

   ㄴ. 맞아요. 서태지의 음악은 K-pop에 큰 영향을 _____.

2. ㄱ. 제가 새로운 외국어를 배우면 직업을 찾는 데 도움이 될까요?

   ㄴ. 물론이지요. 취업에서 외국어가 중요하다는 것은 _____.

3. ㄱ. 요즘 일이 너무 재미없어요.

   ㄴ. 어차피 해야 되는 일이니까 _____ 즐겁게 하려고 노력하세요.

4. ㄱ. 이번 경기에서는 한국 팀이 꼭 이길 거예요.

   ㄴ. 상대편도 요즘 꽤 잘하기 때문에 방심은 _____.

5. ㄱ. 한국에서 장례식에 갈 때에는 어떤 옷을 입어야 해요?

   ㄴ. 화려하지 않고 단정하게 검은색 옷을 입는 것이 _____.

다... 주어진 문형으로 다음 문장을 완성해 보세요.

1. ~다고/(이)라고 해서

ㄱ. 이 식당이 비빔밥으로 _____ 와 봤어요. 듣던 대로 정말 맛있네요.

ㄴ. 음력 8월 15일은 _____ 한국에서 중요한 명절이에요.

2. ~다가는

ㄱ. 조심하세요. 이렇게 위험하게 ＿＿＿＿＿＿＿＿＿＿＿＿ 사고가 날 거예요.

ㄴ. 매일 공부도 안하고 ＿＿＿＿＿＿＿＿＿＿＿ 좋은 성적을 못 받을 거예요.

ㄷ. 이렇게 추운 날 ＿＿＿＿＿＿＿＿＿＿＿ 감기에 걸릴 거예요.

라... 다음의 경우에 여러분 나라에서는 보통 어떤 선물을 하는지 이야기해 봅시다.

1. 생일:

2. 결혼:

3. 집들이:

4. 입학/졸업:

5. 명절:

마... 여러분 나라에서 특별한 선물을 하는 경우는 어떤 경우들이 있습니까?

바... 여러분 나라에서 선물할 때 주의해야 할 점을 알아보고 함께 이야기해 봅시다.

한국에서 특별한 의미가 있는 동물

한국에서는 옛날부터 새가 하늘과 인간의 세계를 이어 주는 동물이라고 생각해서 많은 새들이 사람들의 사랑을 받아 왔다. 특히 학과 까치는 행운의 상징이었다. 학은 장수나 행운을 의미하고 까치는 좋은 소식을 알려 주는 새라고 생각되어 왔다. 그리고 기러기는 사랑과 의리를 지키는 새라고 생각되어 결혼할 때 신랑이 신부 집에 나무로 만든 기러기 한 쌍을 보내는 풍습이 있었다.

새 이외에 사랑을 받는 동물들로는 호랑이, 돼지, 양, 거북 등이 있다. 호랑이는 용맹함을 상징하는데 한국 사람들은 무서운 호랑이를 오히려 사람과 친한 이미지로 만들어 두려움을 극복했다. 그리고 돼지는 부를 상징해서 사람들이 꿈에 돼지를 보면 돈이 생긴다고 생각한다. 그리고 온순한 양은 평화를, 오래 사는 거북은 장수를 상징한다.

이어 주다 to connect 학 crane 까치 magpie 장수 longevity 소식 news 기러기 wild geese
의리 loyalty 쌍 pair of 호랑이 tiger 돼지 pig 양 sheep 거북 turtle 용맹함 brevity
두려움 fear 극복하다 to overcome 부 richness 온순하다 to be gentle, docile 평화 peace

한국인들의 사랑을 받는 동물
들 중에는 용, 봉황, 해태 같은 상
상의 동물도 있다. 용은 힘과 권위
를 상징하여 임금의 얼굴을 용안
이라고 했다. 그리고 또 용은 바다
에서 일을 하는 어민들에게 안전을 기원하는 대상인 동시에 고기를
많이 잡을 수 있도록 기원하는 대상이다. 봉황은 왕을 상징하는 동물
로 한국 대통령 휘장에도 쓰인다. 해태는 선악을 판단할 수 있는 동
물이라고 생각되어 법을 상징하고 지금은 서울시의 마스코트로도 쓰
인다. 이러한 동물들은 한국의 전설, 문학, 미술, 지역 이름에 이르기
까지 한국인의 생활 속에 밀접하게 자리잡고 있다.

용 dragon 봉황 phoenix 해태 *haetae* (a unicorn lion) 상상 imagination 권위 authority
어민 fisherman 안전 safety 기원하다 to pray, wish 대상 object 동시에 at the same time
휘장 insignia 선악 good and evil 판단하다 to judge 법 law 전설 legend 땅 land
밀접하다 to be closely related 자리잡다 to settle

혈액형과 성격

대부분의 한국 사람들은 자신의 혈액형을 알고 있고 많은 사람들이 혈액형과 성격이 관계가 있다고 생각한다. 과학적 근거는 없지만 재미로 서로 혈액형을 물어보고 상대방의 성격을 추측해 보기도 한다. 아래 혈액형별 성격을 읽어 보고 여러분의 성격과 맞는지 살펴보자.

혈액형	성격
A형	소심하고 꼼꼼하고 성실하게 자기가 해야 할 일을 열심히 한다. 약속을 잘 지킨다. 가끔 너무 신중해서 우유부단할 때도 있다.
B형	사교적이라 친구를 잘 사귀고 아이디어가 좋다. 말을 잘 한다. 쉽게 사랑에 빠진다. 가끔 변덕스러울 때도 있다.
O형	활발하고 적극적이다. 리더십이 있다. 여러 사람들과 잘 지낸다. 돈을 잘 계획해서 쓴다. 가끔 너무 털털하다.
AB형	합리적이고 계획을 잘 세운다. 일을 혼자 하는 것을 좋아한다. 인간관계가 좋다. 성격이 까다로운 사람들이 많다.

혈액형 blood type 대부분 most of 자신 oneself 관계 relationship 과학적 근거 scientific basis 추측하다 to guess 소심하다 to be timid 꼼꼼하다 to be meticulous, precise 성실하다 to be faithful, sincere 신중하다 to be cautious 우유부단하다 to be indecisive 사교적이다 to be sociable 변덕스럽다 to be unpredictable 활발하다 to be outgoing 적극적이다 to be active 리더십 leadership 털털하다 to be easygoing 합리적이다 to be rational 까다롭다 to be fastidious, picky

▓▓ 번역문 ▓▓

CONVERSATION: Superstitions around the World

In Korean class, they are discussing superstitions of Korea and other countries.

Teacher: Have any of you heard of any Korean superstitions while living in Korea?

Noah: I whistled at night a bit ago and my friend told me not to whistle because snakes will come out.

Jenny: That's absurd. These days, snakes are to be found nowhere, especially in cities.

Teacher: There are no snakes, but since the old days, there is a saying that whistling at night will make snakes or ghosts come out.

Jenny: Maybe people invented such a saying because whistling at night is noisy?

Teacher: Maybe so.

Jenny: The other day, a Korean person I know said that if I shake my leg, my luck will run away.

Teacher: That is right. And it's not polite to shake your leg, especially in front of elders. What superstitions are there in your country?

Noah: In the U.S. or Great Britain, there is a saying that if you open your umbrella indoors, something bad will happen.

Noah: Also, seeing a black cat, is bad luck. But, I have two black cats, and only more good things have happened since I started raising cats, you know.

Jenny: As a matter of a fact, I was about to talk about that. Actually, I too am raising a black cat, so I am not lonely, and it is nothing but nice.

Noah: And there is a saying that if you walk under a ladder, bad things can happen.

Teacher: It would surely be dangerous to walk under a ladder.

Noah: Right. I think that such a saying was made because it's dangerous. And people think if one wants to prevent bad things from happening, they should tap on a desk or a table made of wood, like knocking.

Noah: Also, many Westerners think that breaking a mirror will bring them seven years of bad luck.

Teacher: Really? I broke a mirror a while back … No wonder bad things have been happening lately.

Jenny: Haha. You'll be fine because you're a Korean.

Teacher: Then, what are some of the things that will bring good luck?

Jenny: Four-leaf clovers, number seven. And in the U.S., they say carrying around a rabbit–foot will bring good luck.

Teacher: Do you mean real rabbit feet?

Jenny: In the old days, they say there were real rabbit feet, but these days there are accessories made in the shape of rabbit feet.

Teacher: Every culture has so many interesting superstitions!

READING: Things to Be Careful of When Giving Presents

The act of giving presents to express gratitude or congratulations causes a positive effect on people's relationships. However, because there are objects with different meanings depending on the culture, one must carefully choose them when giving presents to people of other cultures.

In Korea, it is said that when one gives shoes or a handkerchief as a present to his or her significant other, they will break up. That is because shoes have the meaning of leaving while a handkerchief means tears. And if one gives a knife to his or her friend, they can misunderstand this as wanting to cut off their relationship as friends. It also goes without saying that a sharp blade could be dangerous. So if one is going to give a present to a Korean person, it is best to not give shoes, a handkerchief, or a knife as a present.

Flowers are also a good present, but the meanings contained in flowers can differ for each culture. For example, since white chrysanthemums are used for funerals in Korea, they are taboo as common presents. And on Parents' Day or Teachers' Day, Koreans give carnations in order to convey feelings of gratitude to parents or teachers. However, since carnations or lilies are used for funerals in the West, one must use caution when giving them as presents. On another note, red roses are usually given to one's significant other in the West, so one must use caution when giving red roses as presents in order to avoid any misunderstandings.

In China, saying that one will give a clock has a similar pronunciation to saying that one will hold a funeral, so Chinese people do not give clocks as presents. And because the word for umbrella or pear is similar in pronunciation to a word that means separation, they usually are not given as presents. Also, since the Chinese word for 'fan' is similar to a word that means breaking up, it is also known to be a forbidden present among friends.

There are also presents that one must be cautious of depending on the religion of the other person. Since Muslims cannot drink or eat pork, things will be awkward if one gives them alcohol or pork. And because Hindus think of cows as sacred animals, one will end up causing serious offense if he or she gives leather products that use cowhide such as wallets or bags.

As for present-receiving etiquette, people in the United States think that opening a present right then and there while conveying one's feelings of gratitude is polite, but in Korea, gratefully accepting a present and checking its contents later is considered to be more appropriate. It is in such ways that customs concerning presents differ from culture to culture, and so it is desirable to thoroughly find out about things ahead of time when giving presents to foreigners.

FURTHER READING: Animals with Special Meanings in Korea

In Korea, people from a long time ago have thought of the bird as an animal that connects the sky with the world of humans, so many birds have been beloved by them. The crane and magpie especially were symbols of good luck. Cranes meant longevity or good luck while magpies were thought of as birds that bring good news. Wild geese were thought of as birds that defended love and loyalty, so there was a custom of sending a pair of wild geese made from wood to the houses of the groom and bride getting married.

Other beloved animals besides birds included tigers, pigs, sheep, and turtles. Tigers symbolized bravery, which had occurred as a result of Korean people creating friendly images of ferocious tigers to overcome their fear of them. Pigs symbolized wealth, so people thought that they would get money if they saw a pig in their dreams. The gentle sheep symbolized peace while the long-living turtle represented longevity.

There are also imaginary animals such as dragons, phoenixes, and *haetae* (unicorn lions) amongst the animals beloved by Koreans. Dragons symbolized strength and authority, so the king's face was called *yong'an* meaning dragon's face. Dragons were also objects of prayers for safety amongst fishermen working on the seas as well as for catching plenty of fish. As animals that were symbolic of the king, phoenixes are also used for the insignias of Korean presidents. *Haetae* were thought of as animals that could judge between good and evil, so they symbolized the law and are even used as mascots for the city of Seoul now. These animals have settled into intimate places within our daily lives, including Korean legends, literature, arts, and even place names.

CULTURE: Blood Types and Personalities

Most Koreans know their own blood type and many of them think that there is a relationship between blood types and personalities. Although there is no scientific basis, people ask each other about their blood types for fun and even try to guess about the other's personality. Read about the personalities for each blood type and see if they match your own!

Blood Types	Personalities
Type A	Timid, meticulous, and diligently carries out one's duties with sincerity. Keeps promises. Occasionally too cautious, which results in being indecisive at times.
Type B	Sociable, good at making friends, has good ideas. Speaks well. Falls in love easily. Occasionally unpredictable.
Type O	Outgoing and active. Possesses leadership. Gets along well with many people. Good with money. Occasionally too easygoing.
Type AB	Rational, good at making plans. Likes to work alone. Has good relationships with people. Many have fastidious personalities.

■■ 단어 ■■

거북	turtle	당연히	naturally
고르다	to choose	대부분	most of
곤란하다	to be awkward	대상	object
과학적 근거	scientific basis	동시에	at the same time
관계	relationship	돼지	pig
관습	custom	두드리다	to tap
국화	chrysanthemum	두려움	fear
권위	authority	땅	land
귀신	ghost	리더십	leadership
그 외에도	in addition	무슬림	Muslim
그릇	bowl	문지방	threshold
극복하다	to overcome	미신	superstition
금물	taboo	밀접하다	to be closely related
금지 사항	prohibited matters	발음	pronunciation
기러기	wild geese	방지하다	to prevent
기왕이면	if that is the case anyway	뱀	snake
기원하다	to pray, wish	법	law
까다롭다	to be particular;	변덕스럽다	to be unpredictable
	to be fastidious, picky	복	luck
까치	magpie	봉황	phoenix
꼼꼼하다	to be meticulous, precise	부	richness
꽂다	to stick into	부채	fan
꿈을 꾸다	to dream	불운	bad luck
끼치다	to cause	불행하다	to be unlucky
날카롭다	to be sharp	사교적이다	to be sociable
내용물	content items	사다리	ladder
네 잎 클로버	four-leaf clover	상대방	the other party
노크하다	to knock	상상	imagination
눈물	tears	선악	good and evil
다리를 떨다	to shake one's leg	선풍기	electric fan
달아나다	to run away	성실하다	to be faithful, sincere

소가죽	cowhide	자신	oneself
소식	news	장례를 치르다	to hold a funeral
소심하다	to be timid	장례식	funeral
손수건	handkerchief	장수	longevity
손톱/발톱을 깎다	to clip one's fingernail/toenail	재수(가) 없다	to be unlucky
술잔	glass for alcohol	적극적이다	to be active
스승	teacher, mentor	전설	legend
신성하다	to be sacred	종교	religion
신중하다	to be cautious	주의하다	to be careful
쌍	pair of	징크스	jinx
아마(도)	maybe	찹쌀떡	sticky rice cake
안전	safety	추측하다	to guess
양	sheep	칼	knife, blade
어민	fisherman	키우다	to raise
어버이날	Parents' Day	털털하다	to be easygoing
어쩐지	no wonder; somehow	토끼	rabbit
여겨지다	to be considered	판단하다	to judge
엿	Korean-style sticky taffy	펴다	to unfold, spread
영향	effect	평화	peace
예의에 어긋나다	to go against etiquette	풍습	custom
오해하다	to misunderstand	학	crane
온순하다	to be gentle, docile	합리적이다	to be rational
용	dragon	해태	*haetae* (a unicorn lion)
용맹함	brevity	행동	behavior
우유부단하다	to be indecisive	행운	good luck
운이 좋다	to be lucky	혈액형	blood type
위험하다	to be dangerous	호랑이	tiger
의리	loyalty	확인하다	to check
이별	farewell	활발하다	to be outgoing
이어 주다	to connect	휘장	insignia
이웃	neighbor	휘파람을 불다	to whistle
일반적인	usual, general	힌두교도	Hindu
자리잡다	to settle		

한국의 설화와 속담

Lesson 12 Korean Folktales and Proverbs

학습 목표

내용
- 이야기를 전달할 때 쓰이는 유용한 표현들을 익힌다.
- 속담을 활용하는 문형을 연습한다.

문화
- 한국의 설화와 속담을 통해 한국의 전통 문화와 사상을 이해한다.
- 다른 문화 속의 설화 및 속담과 비교해 본다.

설화 folktales, fairy tales 전달하다 to deliver 활용하다 to utilize; apply 사상 thought, idea

■ 생각해 봅시다

가 ▸ 다음 한국의 옛날 이야기를 알고 있습니까? 이와 비슷한 내용의
이야기가 여러분 나라에도 있습니까?

1. 콩쥐 팥쥐
2. 해님 달님
3. 선녀와 나무꾼
4. 흥부와 놀부

나 ▸ 여러분이 들었던 무서운 이야기가 있습니까? 다음 등장인물에 대해서
들어 본 적이 있습니까?

> 도깨비, 저승사자, 구미호, 삼신 할매, 처녀 귀신

다 ▸ 여러분 나라에서 자주 쓰는 속담이나 격언이 있으면 몇 가지 소개해
봅시다.

라 ▸ 다음 한국 속담의 뜻을 생각해 보세요. 여러분 나라에도 비슷한 뜻의
속담이 있습니까?

1. 낮말은 새가 듣고, 밤말은 쥐가 듣는다.
2. 세 살 버릇 여든까지 간다.
3. 콩 심은 데 콩 나고 팥 심은 데 팥 난다.
4. 남의 떡이 더 커 보인다.

> 선녀 fairy 나무꾼 lumberjack 등장인물 character (in book, story) 격언 maxim 새 bird
> 쥐 mice 버릇 habit

은혜 갚은 꿩

한국 문화 체험 활동을 다녀와서

선생님: 여러분, 주말 동안 잘 쉬었어요? 지난 주 템플스테이를 하면서 많이 배웠을 텐데 질문 없어요?

토니: 저요, 선생님! 그때 구전… 뭐를 스님이 설명해 주셨잖아요?

선생님: 아, 구전설화요? 입에서 입으로 전해지는 이야기죠.

토니: 네, 꿩 이야기였는데 이해를 잘 못 했어요. 죄송하지만, 선생님이 다시 한 번 이야기해 주시**면 안 되나요?**^{GU12.1}

선생님: 네, 그러지요. 우리가 갔던 곳은 강원도 치악산(雉岳山)이에요. 원래는 적악산이었는데 이 전설 때문에 꿩이라는 뜻을 가진 한자 '치(雉)'를 써서 치악산이 된 거예요. 그럼 다시 들어 보세요. 옛날 강원도 **어느**^{GU12.2} 마을에 활을 잘 쏘는 젊은이가 있었는데, 과거 시험을 보기 위해 서울로 떠났어요. 이 젊은이가 며칠을 계속 걷다가 어느 날 적악산 속으로 들어갔어요. 그때, **바로**^{GU12.3} 눈 앞에서 큰 뱀이 꿩을 잡아먹으려는 **게 아니겠어요.**^{GU12.4}

은혜 kindness 갚다 to repay 꿩 pheasant 체험 experience 템플스테이 experiencing temple life ("temple stay") 구전 oral tradition handed down verbally 스님 monk 전해지다 to go down 원래 originally 전설 legend 어느 one 마을 village 활 bow 쏘다 to shoot 젊은이 young person 뱀 snake

그래서 젊은이는 얼른 활을 쏘아서 꿩을 구해 주었어요. 그리고 날이 어두워져 쉴 곳을 찾다가 어느 어여쁜 여자 집에서 하룻밤을 묵게 됐지요. 이 젊은이는 너무 피곤해서 금방 잠이 들었어요. 근데 갑자기 숨을 쉬기 힘들어서 눈을 떠 보니까, 아까 그 여자가 엄청 큰 뱀으로 변해서 이 젊은이 몸을 감고 있었어요. 그리고 이 뱀은 "나는 아까 너의 화살에 맞아 죽은 뱀의 아내다! 아침 해가 뜨기 전에 네가 종을 울려 내 남편을 위로해 주면 살려 주겠다"고 말했어요.

그렇지만 젊은이는 이 뱀에게 잡혀 있어서 움직일 수도 없고, 어두운 밤 산속에 종이 어디에 있는지 알 수도 없었어요. 그래서 포기하고 죽을 때만 기다리고 있었지요. 그런데 이때 어디선가 종소리가 울렸는데 뱀은 종소리가 나**기 무섭게**^{GU12.5} 도망쳤어요. 그리고 이 젊은이는 아침 일찍 종소리가 났던 곳으로 가 봤는데 거기에는 자기가 구해 준 꿩이 피를 **흘린 채로**^{GU12.6} 죽어 있었던 거예요. 좀 이해됐어요? 질문 있으면 해 보세요.

린다: 선생님! 꿩이 종을 **쳤단 말이에요**^{GU12.7}? 어떻게요?

선생님: 네, 맞아요.이 젊은이에게 은혜를 갚기 위해서 피투성이가 되도록 온몸으로 종을 친 거지요. 또 질문 없어요?

얼른 quickly 구하다 to rescue 어여쁘다 to be pretty 묵다 to stay, put up 숨을 쉬다 to breathe 눈을 뜨다 to open one's eyes 엄청 awfully, very 감다 to wind up, coil up 화살 arrow 아내 one's wife 위로하다 to comfort someone 종을 울리다 to ring a bell 살려 주다 to save one's life 종소리 peal or sound of bells 도망치다 to run away 피를 흘리다 to shed blood 종을 치다 to hit a bell

토니: 젊은이가 과거 시험을 보러 갔다고 하셨는데 과거 시험이 뭐예요?

선생님: 요즘으로 말하면 고급 공무원 시험 같은 거예요.

토니: 아… 그때도 시험이 있었네요.

선생님: 네. 그래요. 그런데 이 설화를 통해서 어떤 교훈을 얻을 수 있을까요?

린다: 음, 내가 도움을 받으면 다른 사람을 도와줘야 한다는 것 같은데요.

선생님: 네, 잘 얘기했어요. 이 설화는 은혜를 입으면 꼭 갚을 수 있는 사람이 되어야 한다는 교훈을 가르쳐 주고 있어요. 이렇게 설화를 통해서 교훈을 배울 수 있는데 한국의 유명한 관광지를 가 보면 이러한 전설이 있는 곳이 많으니까 한번 찾아서 읽어 보면 재미있기도 하고 유익할 거예요.

과거 old government official exam 고급 high-level; advanced 공무원 public official
교훈 lesson 도움을 받다 to receive help 은혜를 입다 to be indebted to 유익하다 to be
helpful; to be instructive

이해 문제

가... 대화 내용과 맞으면 ○, 틀리면 X에 표시하세요.

1. 학생들은 템플스테이를 할 예정이다.   ○   X

2. 강원도 치악산의 원래 이름은 적악산이었다.   ○   X

3. 젊은이는 여행을 하기 위해 서울을 가고 있었다.   ○   X

4. 여자가 뱀으로 변해서 꿩을 잡아먹으려고 했다.   ○   X

5. 젊은이는 종을 쳐서 죽은 꿩을 위로했다.   ○   X

나... 대화를 읽고 다음 질문에 답하세요.

1. 윗글이 주는 교훈은 무엇입니까?

2. 윗글에 나오는 등장인물과 소재를 모두 찾아 보세요.

3. 여러분이 지나가던 젊은이라면 다음 상황에 어떻게 하겠습니까?

ㄱ. 위험에 처한 꿩을 봤을 때

ㄴ. 날이 어두워져 하룻밤 잘 곳을 찾아야 할 때

ㄷ. 뱀이 몸을 감고 잡아먹으려고 할 때

ㄹ. 자기에게 은혜를 갚고 죽은 꿩을 발견했을 때

문법과 용법

GU12.1

~(으)면 안 돼요?   'Would you do me the favor of ...?'

우리 결혼하**면 안 돼요**?

Can't we get married?

죄송하지만, 돈 좀 빌려주시**면 안 되나요**?

I'm sorry, but could you lend me some money?

▶ The expression ~(으)면 안 돼요 literally means 'if you …, it is not okay/it is not right/it will not do'. This expression is used when telling someone what they should/must not do, as in 두 사람 결혼하면 안 돼요 'You/Those two should not get married'. The question form of this expression, ~(으)면 안 돼요?, literally means 'is it not right if I/we …?', and is appropriate to make a polite request or to ask someone for permission.

GU12.2

어느   'a certain, any, some (… or other)'

미아가 프랑스의 **어느** 고등학교에 갔다고 들었어요.

I heard that Mia went to some high school in France.

나는 그 사건을 **어느** 신문에서 읽었어.

I read about that event in some newspaper or other.

내가 민지를 마지막으로 만난 것은 5월 **어느** 날이었다.

The last time I met up with Minji was some day in May.

▶ While 이, 그, and 저 are definite demonstratives, 어느 is an indefinite demonstrative, as observed in 이 집 'this house', 그 집 'that house near you', 저 집 'that house over there', and 어느 집 'which/any/some house'. Like other question words, 어느 has both a question meaning 'which?' and a non–question meaning 'some, one, a certain, any'. Like other demonstratives, 어느 must be followed by a noun as in 어느 날 'which day?; one day, someday, any day' and 어느 마을, 'which village?; a certain village, any/every village'. In general, when used in a question sentence, 어느 has a question meaning, and when used in a statement sentence it has a non-question meaning.

GU12.3

바로 'precisely, right(ly), exactly'

내가 찾던 것이 **바로** 이거다!

This is precisely what I was looking for.

호랑이도 제 말 하면 나타난다더니 수지 이야기를 하고 있었는데
바로 그때 수지가 나타났다.

As if speaking of the devil*, Suji appeared right as (we/they) were talking about her.   *lit., 'as it is said, a tiger shows up when (we) talk about it'

수업 끝나고 **바로** 집에 가세요.

Go straight home immediately after class.

▶ The adverb 바로 is derived from the adjective 바르다 'to be upright, straight, right'. 바로 variously means 'rightly, correctly, properly, straight, precisely, just, at once, immediately, directly, with no delay', as in 바로 말하면 'to tell the truth', 바로 그때에 'just at that moment', and 지금 바로 가세요 'You had better go right now'.

GU12.4

~(으)ㄴ/는 게 아니겠어요? 'Oh! … but it's that …!'

샌디가 깨끗한 줄 알았는데 엄청 더러운 **게 아니겠어요?**

I thought Sandy was a clean person, but it turns out she's filthy!

서로 친구라고 하더니 둘이 사귀는 **게 아니겠어요?**

After calling each other just friends, they're now dating!

▶ This pattern is a fossilized rhetorical question, in that the speaker habitually uses a negative question form to express his/her emphatic positive assertion. It literally means 'Surely it be not the case that …?' It is used when narrating or reporting a past situation or event that is difficult to believe. –는 게 is a contraction of –는 것이 'to be the fact/case that …'

GU12.5

~기(가) 무섭게 'as soon as …'

교통 신호가 바뀌**기가 무섭게** 차들이 출발했어요.

The cars took off as soon as the traffic light changed.

수업이 끝나**기가 무섭게** 학생들이 급하게 체육관으로 갔어요.

The students rushed to the gym as soon as class ended.

▶ The pattern ~기가 무섭게 'as soon as' is interchangeably used with ~자마자 which also means 'as soon as'. ~기가 무섭게 is a slightly stronger expression with an emphasis on the immediacy of the action that follows ~기가 무섭게. The meaning of the adverb 무섭게 'scarily' is not to be taken literally but more as an indicator of immediacy. Only verb stems may be placed before ~기가 무섭게 and ~자마자.

GU12.6

~(으)ㄴ 채(로)
'just as it is, intact, as it stands, with no change'

텔레비전을 켜 **놓은 채로** 잠이 들었어요.

I fell asleep with the TV turned on.

안경을 **낀 채** 수영장에 들어갔어요.

I got into the swimming pool with my glasses still on.

▶ The expression ~(으)ㄴ 채(로) consists of the past modifier ending –(으)ㄴ, the bound noun 채 meaning 'intactness, no change, just as it is', and the instrument particle 로 meaning 'with'. It is used to describe a situation when the condition has not changed but instead is maintained as it is. Only verb stems may occur before this pattern, as in 그 사람은 신을 신은 채 방에 들어왔다 'He came into the room with his shoes still on'. This phrase is always used with the past tense.

> GU12.7

~단/란 말이다 '(I) mean'

비가 와도 갈 거**란 말이**에요?

Do you mean you are going even if it rains?

오늘 수업에 안 가겠**단 말이**야?

Are you saying you aren't going to class today?

수업이 취소됐**단 말이**야.

I mean the class was cancelled.

농구를 하다가 다리를 다쳐서 병원에 입원해야 된**단 말이**에요.

I'm telling you that I should be hospitalized since I injured
my leg playing basketball.

▶ The colloquial pattern ~단/란 말이다 is a contraction of the quotative construction ~다고/라고 하는 말이다 literally meaning 'it is my words that ...' or 'I am
saying that ...'. Its derived meaning is 'I mean (that) ...'. The suffix –다/라 before the quotative particle 고 is a plain–level statement ending, as in 좋단 말이
다 'I mean it's good' and 학생이란 말이다 'I mean (he) is a student'. Instead of
the statement ending, the question ending –(느)냐, the proposal ending –자, and
the command ending –(으)라 can be used, as in 먹–느냐/잔/으란 말이다 'I mean
whether (he) eats; I mean I propose to eat; I mean you should eat'.

The pattern can be used in questions to mean 'do you mean (that) ...?' with
appropriate question endings and rising intonation.

활동

가... 다음 빈 칸에 가장 어울리는 단어를 고르세요.

1. 제가 어려울 때 도와줘서 정말 고마워요. 이 _____을/를 어떻게 갚지요?

   ㄱ. 은혜   ㄴ. 교훈   ㄷ. 인사   ㄹ. 감사

2. 요즘 취직이 어려운데 _____은/는 인기가 많은 직업이다.

   ㄱ. 과거   ㄴ. 체험   ㄷ. 공무원   ㄹ. 위로

3. 유럽 여행을 계획하고 있는데 _____ 곳을 아직 정하지 못했다.

   ㄱ. 구할   ㄴ. 숨을 쉴   ㄷ. 잡아먹을   ㄹ. 묵을

4. 한국 영화를 자주 보는데 한국어 공부에 _____ 표현들이 많이 나온다.

   ㄱ. 어여쁜   ㄴ. 유익한   ㄷ. 피를 흘리는   ㄹ. 감는

5. 기차가 떠나려고 해요. _____ 타세요.

   ㄱ. 일찍   ㄴ. 한번   ㄷ. 어느   ㄹ. 얼른

나... 주어진 표현을 사용하여 대화를 완성하세요.

1. 가: 이 사건의 범인이 누구예요?

   나: 바로

   _____.

2. 가: 너는 왜 룸메이트랑 싸웠어?

   나: ~는 게 아니겠어?

   _____.

3. 가: 지난 번에 파티에 왜 안 왔어?

　　나: 어느

　　　　　_____.

4. 가: 어젯밤에 기숙사에서 무슨 일이 있었나 봐. 얘기 좀 해 줘.

　　나: ~(은)ㄴ 채(로)

　　　　　_____.

5. 가: 오늘 저녁은 집에서 요리해서 먹을까요?

　　나: ~(으)면 안 돼요?

　　　　　_____.

6. 가: 민지 씨 어디 있는지 알아요?

　　나: ~기가 무섭게

　　　　　_____.

7. 가: 시험 다 끝났어요?

　　나: ~단/란 말이에요.

　　　　아니요. _____.

다... 여러분 나라의 설화에 자주 나오는 동물이나 소재는 어떤 것이 있는지 이야기해
보세요.

라... 다음을 소재로 한 한국의 구전 설화를 찾아서 한 문단으로 정리해 보세요.

    1. 도깨비

    2. 용이나 뱀

    3. 잉어

    4. 호랑이

마... 구전 설화를 모티프로 한 한국의 드라마나 영화를 찾아보세요.

바... 여러분 나라의 설화 중 하나를 골라 소개해 보세요.

읽기

미운 놈 떡 하나 더 준다

우리 인생에서 인간관계가 중요하다는 것은 말할 필요도 없다. 그 중에서 특히 어려운 것은 내가 싫어하는 사람과의 관계도 이끌어 가야 할 때이다. 싫어하는 사람은 안 만나면 제일 좋겠지만 **그렇다고 안 만날 수도 없다.**^{GU12.8} 인간관계라는 것이 현실적으로 **피한다고 해결되는 일이 아니기 때문이다.**^{GU12.9}

"미운 놈 떡 하나 더 준다"라는 한국 속담이 있다. 이 속담은 다음과 같은 이야기에서 유래한다. 옛날에 고약한 시어머니 때문에 화병이 난 며느리가 있었다. 도저히 견딜 수 없었던 며느리는 점쟁이를 찾아가서 이 미운 시어머니를 죽일 수 있는 방법을 물었

다. 점쟁이는 시어머니가 제일 좋아하는 음식을 백일 동안 해 드리면 이름도 모르는 병에 걸려 그 시어머니가 죽을 거라고 충고해 주었다. 며느리는 아침, 점심, 저녁으로 정성껏 인절미를 만들어 드렸다.

밉다 to hate 놈 dude 인생 life 이끌다 to lead 피하다 to avoid 해결되다 to resolve
고약하다 to be nasty 시어머니 mother-in-law 화병 emotional disorder from suppressed
anger 도저히 utterly; absolutely 견디다 to endure 며느리 daughter-in-law
점쟁이 fortune teller 충고하다 to advise 정성껏 with one's utmost sincerity
인절미 Korean traditional rice cake coated with bean flour

그런 줄도 모르고[GU12.10] 시어머니는 좋아하는 인절미를 먹으며 잘 지냈다. 그래도 며느리를 여전히 무시하고 구박했다. 그러나 한 달 두 달 지나자 시어머니는 떡 해 주는 며느리가 고마워졌다. 나중에는 이 며느리의 정성에 감동하여 여기저기 돌아다니며 동네 사람들에게 며느리 칭찬을 했다. 그러는 사이 며느리도 시어머니와 관계가 좋아졌다.

이 며느리는 자기를 항상 칭찬해 주고 웃어 주는 시어머니가 죽을까 봐 걱정이 되었다. 그동안 시어머니를 미워했던 것을 후회하며 며느리는 다시 점쟁이를 찾아가서 시어머니가 죽지 않는 방법을 알려 달라고 울며 부탁했다.

점쟁이는 크게 웃으며 "그것 봐! 그때 그 미운 시어머니는 죽었잖아". 결국 며느리가 미워했던 그 시어머니는 정말로 볼 수 없게 되었고, 며느리를 칭찬해 주고 웃어 주는 마음 좋은 시어머니하고 행복하게 살았다는 이야기이다.

이 이야기는 내가 싫어하는 사람을 어떻게 대해야 하는지 지혜를 알려 준다. 인간관계에서 누군가를 싫어하면 나도 불편하다. **그런가 하면,**[GU12.11] 나의 감정도 상대방에게 전달되어 갈수록 그 관계는 어색하고 불편해질 것이다. 우리는 조상들의 생활 경험에서 나온 이런 속담을 통해서 당시의 생활 관습과 한국인의 정서 및 시대적 배경을 배울 수 있고 현재 우리의 생활에도 적용할 수 있는 것이다.

무시하다 to ignore   구박하다 to mistreat   감동하다 to be impressed   칭찬 compliment
부탁하다 to make a request   대하다 to deal with   감정 emotion   전달되다 to be delivered
어색하다 to be awkward   당시 at that time   관습 custom; convention   정서 emotion;
sentiment   시대적 time period; periodic   적용하다 to apply

이해 문제

가... 본문을 읽고 다음 내용이 맞으면 ○, 틀리면 X에 표시하세요.

1. 시어머니와 며느리는 사이가 좋지 않았다.   ○   X
2. 시어머니는 인절미를 좋아한다.   ○   X
3. 시어머니와 점쟁이는 친구다.   ○   X
4. 시어머니는 이름도 모르는 병 때문에 죽을 뻔했다.   ○   X
5. 며느리의 정성으로 시어머니의 병이 나았다.   ○   X
6. 속담을 통해 한국인의 생활 관습을 알 수 있다.   ○   X

나... '미운 놈 떡 하나 더 준다'는 언제 쓰는 속담일까요?

다... 여러분 나라에서 이 속담과 비슷한 의미로 쓰이는 속담은 무엇입니까?

라... 윗글의 속담이 주는 교훈은 무엇입니까?

마... 여러분은 다음과 같은 상황에서 어떻게 하겠습니까?

    1. 점쟁이라면 며느리에게 어떻게 하라고 말해 주겠습니까?

    2. 시어머니한테 구박받는 며느리라면 어떻게 하겠습니까?

    3. 사이가 좋지 않았던 며느리가 갑자기 순종적으로 바뀌었을 경우,
       시어머니라면 어떻게 하겠습니까?

바... 한국 속담에서 '떡'이 들어가는 속담을 찾아봅시다.

문법과 용법

> **GU12.8**

그렇다고 ~(으)/ㄹ 수도 없다
'even so, it is not right to; even so, (one) cannot'

우리 학교는 시험이 없다. **그렇다고** 공부를 안 **할 수도 없**다.

We don't have exams. Even so, we can't not study at all.

네가 많이 바쁜 건 알아. **그렇다고** 나만 회의에 참석**할 수도 없**잖아.

I know you are very busy. Even so, I just cannot attend the meeting alone, you know.

▶ 그렇다고 is a contraction of 그렇다고 해서, which literally means 'even if it is said that it is so', where 그렇다 means 'it is so', 고 'that', 해 '(they) say', and –서 'even if'. In colloquial speech, 해서 is often omitted with the meaning retained. This expression frequently occurs with a main clause with the expression ~(으)ㄹ 수도 없다, which means literally 'there is also no way to …' and colloquially 'it is also not right to …'.

GU12.9

~다고/라고 (해서) 되는 일이 아니다
'it wouldn't work even though; just because … , it wouldn't be okay'

너의 실수는 사과한**다고 되는 일이 아니다**.

It is not enough for you to just apologize for your mistake.

성공은 공부만 한**다고 해서 되는 일이 아니다**.

Studying alone is not enough to achieve success.

한국어를 가르치는 것은 한국 사람이**라고 해서 되는 일이 아니다**.

It is not enough to simply be a Korean person to be able to teach Korean.

▶ This pattern is similar to pattern GU12.8. It consists of a concessive clause followed by a negative main clause. The concessive ending –다고/라고 'even though, even if' is a contraction of –다고/라고 해서 or –다고/라고 해도, literally 'even though someone says that …'. 되다 means 'become okay, work/do'. Thus, the whole pattern literally means 'Even though …, it is not something that will do'.

> GU12.10

그런 줄도 모르고 'without knowing it was the case; being unaware of such a fact'

오늘 춥다고 했는데 난 **그런 줄도 모르고** 코트를 안 입고 나갔다.
They said it would be cold today, but I didn't know that
and left without a coat on.

존은 한국말이 유창하더라. 그런데 나는 **그런 줄도 모르고** 존에게 영어로 말했어.
You know, John speaks fluent Korean. But I hadn't realized that
and I just spoke to him in English.

▶ The bound noun 줄 means 'a fact, a way, likelihood'. It must be preceded by a verb clause led by a modifying ender (–(으)ㄴ/는/(으)ㄹ) and is followed by the main verb 알다 'to know' or 모르다 'to not know', as in –(으)ㄴ/는/을 줄 알다/모르다 'to know or not know that/whether'. The pattern 그런 줄도 모르고, where the particle 도 'even, also' is added, means 'not even knowing that such a thing has happened'.

> GU12.11

그런가 하면 'whereas; on the other hand'

제 친구들은 보통 학교 식당에서 식사를 해요. **그런가 하면** 어떤 친구들은
자주 만들어 먹어요.
My friends usually eat in the school cafeteria. On the other hand,
some of my (other) friends prefer to eat food they made themselves.

대도시를 선호하는 사람들이 있다. **그런가 하면** 시골에서 살고 싶어 하는
사람들도 많다.

There are people who prefer big cities. On the other hand, there are also
people who would like to live in the countryside.

▶ This pattern, which consists of 그런가 'that is so' and 하면 'if one thinks/takes',
   is used as a sentence–initial conjunctive adverb. Its literal meaning is 'if one
   thinks/takes it (the content of the preceding sentence) is so'. Its derived meaning is 'whereas' and 'on the other hand'. Its function is to introduce a sentence
   that contrasts in meaning with the preceding sentence.

활동

가... 다음 빈 칸에 가장 어울리는 단어를 고르세요.

1. 복잡했던 문제가 드디어 _____.

   ㄱ. 해결되었다   ㄴ. 이사갔다   ㄷ. 안정됐다   ㄹ. 피했다

2. 친구는 내 의견을 _____ 여행 계획을 세웠다.

   ㄱ. 이끌고   ㄴ. 충고하고   ㄷ. 무시하고   ㄹ. 지내고

3. 모든 어려움을 극복하고 피아니스트로 성공한 그 사람의 이야기에 많은
   사람이 _____.

   ㄱ. 전달되었다   ㄴ. 견뎠다   ㄷ. 부탁했다   ㄹ. 감동했다

4. 나라마다 _____이/가 다르기 때문에 여행을 하기 전에 알아보는 것이 좋다.

   ㄱ. 관습   ㄴ. 칭찬   ㄷ. 정성   ㄹ. 화병

5. 알레르기가 있어서 _____ 못 먹는 음식이 있으면 알려 주세요.

   ㄱ. 그중에서   ㄴ. 도저히   ㄷ. 나중에는   ㄹ. 정성껏

6. 교통이 복잡한 시간을 _____ 1시간 일찍 집에서 출발하세요.

   ㄱ. 미워하려면   ㄴ. 감동하려면   ㄷ. 피하려면   ㄹ. 전해지려면

나... 주어진 표현을 사용하여 문장을 완성하세요.

1. 그렇다고 ~(으)ㄹ 수도 없다

ㄱ: 요즘 살 빼려고 해.

_____ .

ㄴ: 매일 요리하는 게 너무 귀찮아요.

_____ .

2. ~다고 되는 일이 아니다

ㄱ: 시험 성적이 좋지 않아서 울었다. 그렇지만

_____ .

ㄴ: 4년 동안 열심히 노력해서 이번에 졸업을 하게 됐다.

그러나 _____ .

3. 그런 줄도 모르고

ㄱ: 토니가 어제 입원했대.

_____ .

ㄴ: 오늘 아침 수업이 취소됐어.

_____ .

4. 그런가 하면

ㄱ: 저는 보통 아침 일찍 일어나서 숙제를 해요.

_____ .

ㄴ: 제니는 성격이 아주 활발하다.

_____ .

다... 다음은 한국에서 자주 쓰이는 속담들입니다. 의미가 비슷한 영어 속담과 연결해 보세요.

ㄱ. 손뼉도 마주쳐야 소리가 난다.   A. Lock the stable after the horse is stolen.

ㄴ. 옷이 날개다.   B. Even a worm will turn.

ㄷ. 콩으로 메주를 쑨다고 해도 안 믿는다.   C. It takes two to tango.

ㄹ. 미꾸라지 한 마리가 개울물을 흐린다.   D. Talk of the devil and he will appear.

ㅁ. 호랑이도 제 말 하면 온다.   E. The grass is greener on the other side of the fence.

ㅂ. 지렁이도 밟으면 꿈틀한다.   F. Too many cooks spoil the broth.

ㅅ. 남의 떡이 커 보인다.   G. You've cried wolf too many times.

ㅇ. 소 잃고 외양간 고치기.   H. Fine feathers make fine birds.

ㅈ. 짚신도 제 짝이 있다.   I. One rotten apple spoils the barrel.

ㅊ. 낮말은 새가 듣고 밤말은 쥐가 듣는다.   J. Walls have ears.

ㅋ. 사공이 많으면 배가 산으로 간다.   K. Every dog has his day.

ㅌ. 쥐구멍에도 볕 들 날 있다.   L. Every Jack has his Jill.

라... 위의 속담을 사용하여 보기와 같이 문장을 만들어 보세요.

'낮말은 새가 듣고 밤말은 쥐가 듣는다'

→ '낮말은 새가 듣고 밤말은 쥐가 듣는다'**고** 말조심을 해야 돼.

→ '낮말은 새가 듣고 밤말은 쥐가 듣는다'**더니** 어제 한 얘기가
   벌써 소문이 났어.

마... 여러분 나라에서 자주 쓰는 속담이 있으면 이야기해 보세요.

추가-읽기

새옹지마(塞翁之馬)

"인생은 새옹지마다"라는 말이 있다. "새옹지마"란 "국경 지대에 사는 노인의 말"이라는 뜻이다. 이 속담은 좋은 일과 나쁜 일, 기쁜 일과 슬픈 일이 반복될 때에 쓰이며 또 누군가가 일이 잘못되어 괴로워하거나 슬퍼할 때 위로하는 말로 쓰인다. 그렇게 쓰이는 데는 다음과 같은 연유가 있기 때문이다.

옛날 중국 북쪽 국경 지대의 한 마을에 아들과 단둘이 살고 있는 노인이 있었다. 그 노인에게는 몇 마리의 말이 있었는데, 그것이 전 재산이었다. 어느 날 말 한 마리가 갑자기 국경선을 넘어서 북쪽으로 도망갔다. 노인이 말을 따라갔으나 놓치고 말았다. 마을 사람들은 "좋은 말을 잃어서 가슴이 아프시겠습니다" 하고 노인을 위로했지만 노인은 웃으며 "할 수 없는 일이지요. 나쁜 일이 있으면 좋은 일도 생기겠지요"라고 말했다.

그러고 나서 얼마 지나자 도망쳤던 말이 노인의 집으로 돌아왔다. 그런데 혼자 온 것이 아니라 아주 훌륭한 말 한 필을 데리고 함께

새옹지마 the irony of fate 국경 지대 national border area 노인 elderly person 반복되다 to be repeated 괴로워하다 to be in agony 북쪽 northern side 마을 village 단둘이 just the two persons (adv.) 전 재산 one's entire assets 국경선 national border line 넘다 to cross over 도망가다 to escape 따라가다 to follow 놓치고 말다 to end up losing 잃다 to lose 가슴(이) 아프다 to be heartbroken 지나다 to pass 돌아오다 to return 훌륭하다 to be magnificent 필 a counter for horses and large animals meaning 'head'

돌아온 것이었다. 이번에는 마을 사람들이 부러워하면서 말했다.

"정말 잘 된 일입니다. 큰 횡재를 하셨군요."

그러자 노인은 이번에도 웃으며 말했다.

"글쎄요, 좋은 일인지 모르겠습니다. 좋은 일이 있으면 나쁜 일도 있는 법이니까요."

그리고 또 몇 달이 지났다. 그 노인의 아들이 새로 온 말을 타다가 그만 말에서 떨어지고 말았다. 다행히 목숨은 건졌으나 다리를 다쳐서 장애인이 되고 말았다. 이번에 마을 사람들은 "정말 슬프시겠습니다" 하며 노인을 위로했다. 그러자 노인은 그저 무표정한 얼굴로 이렇게 말했다.

"할 수 없지요. 나쁜 일이 있으면 또 좋은 일이 있고 그런 것이니까요."

해가 바뀌고 어느 날 전쟁이 일어났다. 그래서 마을의 젊은이들은 모두 군인으로 전쟁에 가야 했다. 그러나 노인의 아들은 다리를 다쳤기 때문에 전쟁에 나가지 않아도 되었다. 그 전쟁에서 많은 사람들이 목숨을 잃었지만 노인의 아들은 무사히 지낼 수 있었다.

부러워하다 to be envious 횡재 unexpected fortune 법 law 목숨을 건지다 to escape death
장애인 handicapped person 무표정하다 to be expressionless 전쟁 war 군인 soldier
목숨을 잃다 to lose one's life 무사하다 to be safe

문화

수수께끼

수수께끼는 정답이 있는 문제가 아니고 말장난을 이용하여 재치있게 대답해야 하는 문제이다. 다음 수수께끼의 답을 찾아보세요.

1. 내 것만 볼 수 있고 남의 것은 절대로 볼 수 없는 것은?

2. 더우면 키가 커지고 추우면 키가 작아지는 것은?

3. 더울 때는 옷을 많이 입고 추울 때는 옷을 벗는 것은?

4. 살을 빼면 커지는 것은?

5. 세상에서 제일 큰 코는?

6. 아무리 빨리 뛰어도 따라오는 것은?

7. 일을 많이 하면 키가 작아지는 것은?

8. 적에게 등을 보여야 이기는 것은?

9. 추울 때는 뚱뚱하다가 따뜻하면 날씬해지는 사람은?

10. 별 중에 가장 슬픈 별은?

11. 내 것인데 남이 더 많이 쓰는 것은?

12. 온 세상을 다 덮을 수 있는 것은?

13. 돈 낭비를 제일 많이 하는 동물은?

14. 물고기의 반대말은?

15. 사람들이 제일 좋아하는 물은?

11. 이름 12. 끄개풀 13. 사자 14. 불고기 15. 선물

〈정답〉1. 꿈 2. 온도계 3. 나무 4. 옷 5. 멕시코 6. 그림자 7. 연필 8. 줄다리기 9. 눈사람 10. 이별

■■ 번역문 ■■

CONVERSATION: The Pheasant Who Paid Back (an Archer's) Kindness

After a Korean culture experience activity

Teacher: Everyone, did you all rest well over the weekend? Last week, while doing the temple stay, you must have learned a lot. Does anyone have any questions?

Tony: I do, teacher! When we were there, the monk was explaining something about "*kujŏn ...*" something, you know?

Teacher: Ah, you are talking about "*kujŏn sŏrhwa,*" a story that has been passed down from mouth to mouth.

Tony: Yes, it was a story about a pheasant, and I wasn't able to understand it too well. Sorry, but would it be alright if you told the story again?

Teacher: Yes, of course. The place that we went was Ch'iak-san in Gangwon-do. Originally it was Chŏgak-san but because of this legend it became Ch'iak-san since the Chinese character *chi* means pheasant. Alright now, listen again. A long time ago, in a village in Gangwon-do, there was a youth who shot the bow well who left for Seoul to take a state examination. After a few days of walking continuously, one day this youth entered inside Jeogak-san. When he did, right in front of his eyes, what do you know but there was a huge snake that was trying to feed on a pheasant.

So the youth quickly shot his bow and saved the pheasant. And then when the day became dark he looked for a place to rest, and stayed the night at a beautiful woman's house. Because the youth was so tired, he fell asleep right away. But then all of a sudden it became hard to breathe, and he opened his eyes to the woman who had turned into a huge snake and was coiled around his body. And the snake said "I am the wife of the snake that you shot and killed with an arrow earlier! I will save you only if before the sun rises, you ring the bell and console my husband."

But because the youth was trapped by the snake he couldn't move, and in the darkness of the night of the mountain he didn't even know where the bell was. So the youth gave up and waited for his time to die. But then the sound of a bell rang out and soon as it did, the snake fled. And so, the youth left early in the morning to the place that the bell had rung. There was the pheasant that he had saved, bleeding to death, just as it was before. Do you understand a little more now? If you have any questions please ask.

Linda: Teacher! Does that mean that the pheasant had hit the bell? How?

Teacher: Yes, correct. To pay back the youth's kindness, (the pheasant) hit itself against the bell and became bloody. Are there any other questions?

Tony: You said that the youth was going to take a state examination, what is a state examination?

Teacher: Today we call it a civil servant exam.

Tony: Ah ... there were tests even back then.

Teacher: Yes, of course. Then, through this tale, what kind of lessons can we gain?

Linda: Hmm, like if I receive help, then I need to help other people.

Teacher: Yes, well said. This folktale teaches the lesson that if you receive kindness, then you must become one to return that kindness. We can learn lessons through folktales, and when you go to Korea's famous tourist destinations there are many places with legends like these. So if you try to find and read them, then it will be both fun and helpful.

READING: Give One More Rice Cake to the One You Hate

It goes without saying that interpersonal relationships are important in our lives. What is especially difficult among these is having to also lead relationships with people one dislikes.

Although it would be best to not meet people one dislikes, that is not a plausible way to go about things. This is because realistically, interpersonal relationships are not resolved by avoiding them. There is a Korean proverb that says, "Give one more rice cake to the one you hate." This proverb originates from the following story.

Long ago, there was a daughter-in-law who became ill due to her suppressed anger at her mother-in-law. Absolutely unable to endure things anymore, the daughter-in-law went to see a fortune teller and asked if there was a way to kill her hateful mother-in-law. The fortune teller advised her that if she gave the mother-in-law her favorite food for 100 days, she would die from a nameless disease.

The daughter-in-law earnestly made rice cakes (for her mother-in-law) for breakfast, lunch, and dinner. Without knowing anything, the mother-in-law ate her favorite rice cakes and lived happily. Even so, she continued to disregard and mistreat her daughter-in-law.

However, after a month or two, the mother-in-law became grateful to her daughter-in-law for making the rice cakes. She later went around the neighborhood, all the while praising her daughter-in-law, moved by her devotion. Meanwhile, the daughter-in-law's relationship with her mother-in-law also changed for the better. She then became worried that the mother-in-law who always complemented her and gave her a smile would die.

The daughter-in-law regretted hating her mother-in-law and went back to the fortune teller to ask for a way to prevent her from dying. The fortune teller laughed out loud and said, "See! That hateful mother-in-law from those days has died." This is a story that in the end, the mother-in-law that the daughter-in-law once hated was nowhere to be found and the daughter-in-law lived happily with a mother-in-law who praised her, smiled at her, and had a good heart.

This story imparts wisdom on how to deal with people one dislikes. In interpersonal relationships, hating someone is discomforting for oneself. On the other hand, one's emotions will also be delivered to the other person, which causes the relationship to become progressively awkward and uncomfortable. Through such proverbs that have emerged from the experiences of our ancestors, we are able to learn about the customs of that time, as well as the sentiments of the Korean people in addition to that time period's backdrop. We can also apply them to our lives today.

FURTHER READING: *Saeong-jima*, the Irony of Fate

There is a saying "Life is a *Saeong-jima*." *Saeong-jima* means the horse of an elderly person living on the border. This proverb is used when good and bad or happy and sad events are repeated, or to console a person troubled or saddened by something that has gone wrong. This usage arises from the following story (*lit.*, such a use is due to its having the following origination).

Long ago, in a village on the norther border (area) of China, an elderly man lived alone with his son. The elderly man owned a few horses, which were his entire assets. One day, one of the horses the elderly man was raising threw a temper tantrum. The horse suddenly crossed the borderline and ran away to the north. The elderly man hastily chased after the horse but could not catch the swift horse. When he trudged back to the village, everyone (*lit.*, every single person, without fail) consoled him, saying "You must be sad at having lost a good horse." But the elderly man laughed heartily and said, "It can't be helped. All sorts of things are bound to happen in life. I suppose when something bad happens, then something good is bound to happen, too."

A while after this episode, the runaway horse returned to the elderly man's home. But instead of returning alone, it brought a magnificent horse along with it. This time, all the neighbors envied him and said,

"What luck! (*lit.*, This is a good event.) You've gained a windfall."

Again, the old man laughed heartily, saying "Well, I'm not sure that a horse returning with its friend is such a good thing. As a rule, when a good thing happens, then a bad thing is bound to happen, too."

Many months had passed. Then, while riding the new horse, the elderly man's son fell off the horse. Fortunately, his life was spared, but he injured his leg and became physically handicapped. The village people, again clicking their tongues, pitied them and said, "You must be very sad." At this, the old man, a blank expression on his face, replied, "It can't be helped. Well, when something bad happens, then something good happens, too."

One day the following year, a war started. So all the young men of the village were drafted as soldiers to go out to the battlefields. But the elderly man's son did not have to go to war because of his handicap. Although many people lost their lives in the war, the elderly man's son was able to stay safe.

CULTURE: Riddles

Riddles are not questions with a correct answer, but rather ones that must be answered with wit and the use of wordplay. Try and find answers for the following riddles.

1. Something for which I can only see mine and not anyone else's.
2. Something that becomes tall when it's hot and becomes short when it's cold.
3. Something that wears a lot of clothes when it's hot, and takes off clothes when it's cold.
4. Something that grows when you lose weight.
5. The biggest nose in the world is?
6. Something that follows you no matter how fast you run.
7. Something for which it gets shorter as it works a lot.
8. Something for which you must show your back to your enemy in order to win.
9. A person who is chubby when it's cold but becomes slim when it's warm.
10. The saddest star.
11. Something that's mine but other people use it the most.
12. Something that can cover the entire world.
13. The animal that wastes the most money.
14. The antonym of a 'fish'.
15. People's favorite water.

▌▌ 단어 ▌▌

가슴(이) 아프다	to be heartbroken	대하다	to deal with
감다	to wind up, coil up	도망가다	to escape
감동하다	to be impressed	도망치다	to run away
감정	emotion	도움을 받다	to receive help
갚다	to repay	도저히	utterly; absolutely
격언	maxim	돌아오다	to return
견디다	to endure	등장인물	character (in book, story)
고급	high-level; advanced	따라가다	to follow
고약하다	to be nasty	마을	village
공무원	public official	며느리	daughter-in-law
과거	old government official exam	목숨을 건지다	to escape death
관습	custom; convention	목숨을 잃다	to lose one's life
괴로워하다	to be in agony	무사하다	to be safe
교훈	lesson	무시하다	to ignore
구박하다	to mistreat	무표정하다	to be expressionless
구전	oral tradition handed down verbally	묵다	to stay, put up
		밉다	to hate
구하다	to rescue	반복되다	to be repeated
국경 지대	national border area	뱀	snake
국경선	national border line	버릇	habit
군인	soldier	법	law
꿩	pheasant	부러워하다	to be envious
나무꾼	lumberjack	부탁하다	to make a request
넘다	to cross over	북쪽	northern side
노인	elderly person	사상	thought, idea
놈	dude	살려 주다	to save one's life
놓치고 말다	to end up losing	새	bird
눈을 뜨다	to open one's eyes	새옹지마	the irony of fate
단둘이	just the two persons (adv.)	선녀	fairy
당시	at that time	설화	folktales, fairy tales

숨을 쉬다	to breathe	전해지다	to go down
스님	monk	젊은이	young person
시대적	time period; periodic	점쟁이	fortune teller
시어머니	mother-in-law	정서	emotion; sentiment
쏘다	to shoot	정성껏	with one's utmost sincerity
아내	one's wife	종소리	peal or sound of bells
어느	one	종을 울리다	to ring a bell
어색하다	to be awkward	종을 치다	to hit a bell
어여쁘다	to be pretty	쥐	mice
얼른	quickly	지나다	to pass
엄청	awfully, very	체험	experience
원래	originally	충고하다	to advise
위로하다	to comfort someone	칭찬	compliment
유익하다	to be helpful; to be instructive	템플스테이	experiencing temple life ("temple stay")
은혜	kindness		
은혜를 입다	to be indebted to	피를 흘리다	to shed blood
이끌다	to lead	피하다	to avoid
인생	life	필	a counter for horses and large animals meaning 'head'
인절미	Korean traditional rice cake coated with bean flour		
잃다	to lose	해결되다	to resolve
장애인	handicapped person	화병	emotional disorder from suppressed anger
적용하다	to apply		
전 재산	one's entire assets	화살	arrow
전달되다	to be delivered	활	bow
전달하다	to deliver	활용하다	to utilize; apply
전설	legend	횡재	unexpected fortune
전쟁	war	훌륭하다	to be magnificent

13과

한국의 공동체 문화

Lesson 13 Korean Culture of Community

■ 학습 목표

내용 • 공동체 문화가 언어에서 나타나는 현상을 살펴본다.
• 다양한 접속사를 사용해 근거와 연결하는 표현을 연습해 본다.

문화 • 공동체 의식이 한국인의 일상생활에서 어떻게 나타나는지 살펴본다.
• 한국 대학의 주요 행사에 나타나는 공동체 문화에 대해 알아본다.

공동체 community 접속사 conjunction 근거 basis 연결하다 to connect
의식 consciousness 일상생활 daily life 행사 event

■ 생각해 봅시다

가 ▸▸ 다음에 대해 이야기해 봅시다.

1. 여러분 학교 행사는 어떤 것들이 있습니까?

2. 여러분이 참여하고 있는 대학 행사나 활동이 있으면 말해 보세요.

3. 대학 생활의 첫날을 기억나는 대로 설명해 보세요.

4. 여러분 학교에는 입학식이 있습니까? 졸업식은 있습니까?

5. 대학에서 새로운 친구는 주로 어떻게 만나게 됩니까?

6. 동아리는 어떤 종류가 있습니까?

7. 여러분 학교나 지역에서 운동 경기에 가 본 적이 있습니까?
   경험을 설명해 보세요.

나 ▸▸ 다음 어휘에 대해 여러분이 알고 있는 바를 이야기해 보세요.

1. 입학식

2. 오리엔테이션(오티/OT)

3. 엠티(MT)

4. 대동제, 축제

5. (야학) 봉사 활동

6. 사은회

7. 졸업 여행

참여하다 to participate 입학식 entrance ceremony of school 동아리 club 경기 game, match

대화

대학 행사와 활동

대학 입학식장에서 신입생인 유학생 미아와 미아의 고등학교 선배 노아가 만난다.

노아: 미아야!

미아: (손을 흔들며) 선배, 여기요!

노아: 휴우, 안 늦어**서 다행이다.**GU13.1 비가 오**는 바람에**GU13.2 길이 너무 막혔는데… 자 여기, 꽃다발 받아. 입학 축하해!

미아: 선배, 오늘 제 입학식에 와 줘서 정말 고마워요. **그렇잖아도**GU13.3 저는 한국에 가족이 없어서 선배가 와 주지 않았더라면 외로운 입학식이 **될 뻔했어요.**GU13.4

노아: 그럴 거 같았어. 그리고 미국에는 보통 입학식이라는 게 아예 없잖아.

미아: 맞아요. 그래서 입학식을 영어로 뭐라고 해야 할지조차 모르겠어요.

노아: 그렇지. 그런데 한국에서는 입학식 같은 행사에 가족과 친구들이 많이 와서 다 함께 축하해 주거든.

입학식장 entrance to ceremony hall 다행 luck, fortune 막히다 to be jammed
꽃다발 bouquet 아예 to begin with 조차 even

미아: 그런 거 같아요. 근데 선배, 오늘 들어 보니까 학교 행사가 무
        지 많던데요.

노아: 응. 개강은 3월 초지만 신입생들이 그 전에 대학 생활을 준비
        하고 적응할 수 있도록 입학식과 오리엔테이션을 일찍 하고,
        그 후에도 여러 행사들이 이어지지.

미아: 네. 오리엔테이션을 줄여서 OT라고도 하고 아니면 새내기
        배움터라고도 하던데요…

노아: 맞아. 그리고 우리 단과대학은 3월 첫 주말에 엠티(MT)를 가
        더라.

미아: 엠티라면…

노아: 응. 영어의 멤버쉽 트레이닝을 줄여서 엠티라고 하는데 우리
        대학은 1박 2일로 경기도로 가.

미아: 엠티는 가는 게 좋아요? 저는 아는 친구도 없는데요…

노아: 응, 가서 동기들과 인사도 하고, 선배들로부터 대학 생활에
        필요한 정보들도 얻고 하니까 가면 좋지. 장기 자랑도 하고,
        친밀감과 소속감을 느낄 수 있는 게임도 해.

미아: 근데 혹시 엠티에 가면 밤 늦게까지 술을 많이 마시지 않아
        요? 저는 술을 잘 못 마시는 데다가 잠도 일찍 자는 편이라서
        요…

노아: 예전에는 술을 많이 마셨는데 요즘은 강요하지 않으니까 너
        무 걱정하지 않아도 돼. 밤새 이야기하는 친구들도 있지만 힘
        들고 졸리면 먼저 방에 들어가서 자도 괜찮아.

미아: 그럼 가 봐야겠네요.

무지 really, very 개강 beginning of semester in college 적응 adaptation
새내기 배움터 college orientation 단과대학 college or school of a university 줄이다 to
shorten 동기 classmate 장기 자랑 talent show 소속감 sense of belonging 예전 former
days 밤새 all night long

노아: 그건 그렇고 동아리는 생각해 봤어?

미아: 네, 동아리에 꼭 가입하고 싶어요. 그런데 동아리들이 어찌나 **많은지**^{GU13.5} 고르기가 힘들 거 같네요.

노아: 그렇지. 오늘 오전 입학식 끝나고 오리엔테이션 때 학생회관에서 동아리 소개가 있을 거야.

미아: 그런데 선배, 5월에는 대동제가 있다던데 그게 뭐예요?

노아: 아, 대동제는 대학 축제야. 대동제라는 말이 "다 함께 크게 어울려 화합한다"는 뜻이야.

미아: 대동제 때는 뭘 해요?

노아: 캠퍼스 곳곳에서 전시, 공연, 대회 같은 행사들을 많이 해. 좋은 추억이 될 거야. 우리 학교는 인기 있는 가수도 초청해서 공연도 하고 그래.

미아: 정말 기대되네요. 유명한 가수가 왔으면 좋겠어요.

노아: **축제도 축제지만**^{GU13.6} 봄부터 우리 단과대에서 농촌 봉사 활동도 있어. 일손이 달리는 봄에 농촌에 가서 모내기도 돕는데 서울에서는 할 수 없는 경험이야. 그리고, 여름방학에는 학생들 공부도 봐주기도 하고.

미아: 미국에서도 봉사 활동을 해 봤는데 한국에서도 꼭 해 보고 싶어요.

노아: 단과대학별, 그리고 학과별 행사도 많으니까 일정을 잘 살펴보고 중요한 행사나 모임을 놓치지 말도록 해.

미아: 네, 선배. 잘 알려 줘서 고마워요. 선배가 같은 학교에 있어서 참 든든해요.

학생회관 student center 대동제 college festival 축제 festival 화합하다 to unite in harmony 대회 contest 초청 invitation 농촌 봉사 활동 volunteer service in farming communities 일손 worker, hand 딸리다 to run short 모내기 rice planting
단과대 (=단과대학) college or school of a university 봐주다 to help 든든하다 to feel secure

이해 문제

가... 다음 내용이 대화 내용과 맞으면 ○, 틀리면 X에 표시하세요.

    1. 노아는 미아의 입학식에 늦었다.   ○   X

    2. 한국에서는 입학식에 가족들이 가서 축하해 준다.   ○   X

    3. 새내기 배움터는 신입생들이 공부하는 교실이다.   ○   X

    4. 노아네 대학 학생들은 엠티를 3박 4일로 제주도로 간다.   ○   X

    5. 대동제 때는 인기 가수 초청 공연도 볼 수 있다.   ○   X

나... 대화를 듣고 다음 질문에 대답해 보세요.

    1. 미아에게 외로운 입학식이 될 뻔한 이유는 무엇입니까?

    2. 엠티에 가면 좋은 이유는 무엇입니까?

    3. 엠티에 가면 술을 많이 마셔야 됩니까?

    4. 대동제를 설명해 보세요.

    5. 노아네 단과대에서 봄에 하는 행사는 무엇이 있습니까?

문법과 용법

GU13.1

~어(서)/아(서) 다행이다 'it is fortunate/lucky that'

차 사고가 났지만 아무도 다치지 않**아서** 불행 중 **다행이다**.

In the midst of such misfortune, thank goodness no one was hurt in the car accident.

지갑을 잃어버렸는데 경찰서에서 찾았다고 연락이 **와 다행이다**.

It is very fortunate that the police contacted (me) saying that they found the wallet (I) had lost.

▶ The pattern consists of the causal connective ending ~아(서)/어(서) 'because, as', followed by the main adjective 다행이다 'to be fortunate/lucky'. The expression is used when a situation feels seemingly lucky because it turned out to be better than expected in comparison to what could have happened. Thus, people frequently use this expression in a situation where they want to show that they are thankful that the worst–case scenario did not happen.

▶ The noun 다행 comprises the characters 다(多) 'many' and 행(幸) 'luck' and means 'fortune, luck'. The adjectival forms are 다행스럽다 and 다행하다 'to be lucky, fortunate' (e.g., 다행스러운 결과 and 다행한 일). The adverbial form is 다행히 'luckily, fortunately' as in 다행히 안 다쳤다 'luckily, (someone) was not injured'.

> GU13.2

~는/(으)ㄴ 바람에
'because of, as a result of (an unexpected cause)'

인터넷 연결이 안 되**는 바람에** 제가 숙제를 못 했어요.

Since I couldn't connect to the internet, I couldn't do my homework.

눈이 많이 오**는 바람에** 비행기가 취소됐어요.

The flight was cancelled due to heavy snowfall.

▶ The expression ~는/(으)ㄴ 바람에 (*lit.* 'by the wind of …') means 'because, because of, as a result of, owing to'. The expression is used mostly when the unexpected cause expressed in the first clause has negatively affected the resulting situation given in the second (main) clause, as in 날씨가 추운 바람에 감기에 걸렸어요 'Because the weather was cold, I caught a cold'. This pattern is not usually used with a favorable cause and effect. Thus, for example, 우리 아버지는 선생님인 바람에 많은 사람으로부터 존경받으세요 is unacceptable. A synonymous pattern ~기 때문에 is more appropriate, as in 우리 아버지는 선생님이기 때문에 많은 사람으로부터 존경받으세요.

While the verb of the main consequential clause may be either in the past tense or in the non-past (e.g., 못 잤어요, 못 자요), the verb before ~는/(으)ㄴ 바람에 is usually in the present tense (e.g., 안 되는 바람에 and not 안 됐는 바람에, 안 된 바람에). In rare cases, however, the past tense ending –(으)ㄴ is acceptable, as in 어젯밤 눈이 많이 온 바람에 오늘 아침 길이 몹시 미끄럽다 'Due to the heavy snow last night, the roads are very slippery this morning'.

A final note is that the pattern cannot be used in imperative or propositive sentences. Thus, 눈이 오는 바람에 학교에 가지 마라/말자 'Because of the snowfall, don't/let's not go to school' is not grammatical.

GU13.3

그렇잖아도   'as a matter of fact, in fact'

가: 우리가 늦어서 친구가 기다리고 있을 텐데 친구에게 전화 안 해?

Our friend must be waiting for us since we are late;

aren't you going to give him a call?

나: **그렇지 않아도** 제가 지금 친구에게 전화하려고 했었어요.

As a matter of fact, I was just about to call him.

가: 나는 지금 점심 먹으러 가려는데 너는 안 가?

I am about to leave for lunch … Aren't you coming?

나: **그렇잖아도** 지금 막 떠나려던 참이었어.

In fact, I was just about to leave.

▶ 그렇지 않아도 is a contracted form of 그러하지 않아도 whose literal meaning is 'even if it's not like that', or 'even if one doesn't do so'. Its derived meaning is 'as a matter of fact; in fact'. In speaking, 그렇지 않아도 can be further contracted to 그렇잖아도. Similar expressions include the short negation form 안 그래도 'in any case, any way'.

▶ People frequently use the expression when they were about to do something that has just been suggested. Thus what follows 그렇잖아도 refers to what has just been mentioned. Often, the expression that follows 그렇잖아도 is an action that is expected to take place.

GU13.4

~(으)ㄹ 뻔하다
'almost did or happened; barely escaped doing'

오늘 아침 9시 수업에 하마터면 늦을 **뻔했어**.

(I) was almost late for my 9 a.m. class this morning.

점심도 안 먹고 10시간 이상 일을 해서 거의 쓰러**질 뻔했**어요.

(I) almost fainted after working for over 10 hours
without even stopping to eat lunch.

아이가 하마터면 자동차에 부딪**힐 뻔했**어요.

The child was nearly hit by the car.

▶ The pattern combines the prospective modifier with the verb 뻔하다 to mean 'almost do something', 'closely escape doing something', 'be on the verge of', or an event 'almost happened but did not take place'. It most often occurs in the past, with the meaning that a situation was averted at the last minute. The escaped situations are frequently adverse, but favorable situations also occur with the pattern, as in 나는 부자가 될 뻔했어 'I almost became a rich man'. Adverbs commonly used with the expression ~(으)ㄹ 뻔하다 are 거의 'almost' and 하마터면 'nearly', which provide an emphasis to the situation.

> GU13.5

어찌나 ~는/(으)ㄴ지 'so … that; too … to'

어찌나 추운지 얼어 죽는 줄 알았어요!

It was so cold I thought I was going to freeze to death!

어찌나 무서운지 대답할 수 없었다.

I was too scared to answer his question.

어찌나/얼마나 많이 먹었**는지** 배가 터질 거 같아요.

I ate so much that I think my stomach is going to explode.

▶ The adverb 어찌나 'so (much), too' derived from the combination of the adverb 어찌 'how, somehow' and the particle 나 'as much as' and is an emphasized form of the adverb 어찌. The adverb 어찌나 is followed by an adjective or a verb conjugated with the modifier suffix –(으)ㄴ/는지. If a verb is used, a manner adverb (e.g., 빨리, 많이, 높이) usually precedes it, as in KTX가 어찌나 빨리 달리는지 나는 좀 어지러웠어 'the KTX (train) went so fast that I felt a bit dizzy'. The bound noun 지 means 'whether, if, that'. It is assumed that the pattern 어찌나 ··· ~는/(으)ㄴ지 derived from 어찌나 ··· ~는/(으)ㄴ지 몰라도 'though it is not sure how much …'. With the deletion of 몰라도, 어찌나 and ···지 jointly express the meaning 'so … that …; too … to …'.

▶ A similar pattern is 얼마나 ~는/(으)ㄴ/(으)ㄹ지, where the adverb 얼마나 'so (much), too' consists of the noun 얼마 'how much/many' and the particle 나 'as much as'. 얼마나 and ···지 jointly express the meaning 'so … that; too … to'. This pattern has broader uses than the 어찌나 pattern. While 어찌나 is mainly followed by an adjective or an adverb, 얼마나 is followed by an adjective, a verb, or an adverb. While 어찌나 can only be used for past or present situations (that were experienced or are being experienced), 얼마나 can be used for past, present, or future situations. Thus, 내일은 어찌나 추울지 걱정돼요 '(I) am worried about how cold it will be tomorrow' is ungrammatical because tomorrow's cold weather obviously has not yet been experienced or witnessed. The correct expression would be 내일은 얼마나

추울지 걱정돼요. While 어찌나 is required to be followed by a causal construction such as –는(으)ㄴ지 or –어서/아서, 얼마나 does not have such restriction.

> **GU13.6**
>
> ## N도 N(이)지만   'although N is important, (something else is more important)'

건강해지려면 **운동도 운동이지만** 술부터 끊으세요.

If (you) want to get healthier, while exercise is important,

(you) should first quit drinking.

> 가: 영화 몇 시에 시작하지?
>
>   What time does the movie begin?
>
> 나: **영화도 영화지만** 밥 먼저 먹자.
>
>   While the movie is important, we should eat first.

▶ The expression N도 N(이)지만, literally meaning 'N is N but…', emphasizes the content of the second clause over that of the first clause. Its idiomatic meaning is 'N is good/okay/acceptable, but…', as in the following dialogue.

> 가: 새를 기르면 어떻겠니?
>
>   How about raising a bird?
>
> 나: **새도 새지만** 강아지를 더 기르고 싶어.
>
>   While raising a bird is okay, I'd prefer to raise a puppy.

> 가: 어떻게 하면 취직이 잘 될까?
>
>   How can I get a good job?
>
> 나: 취직하려면 **성적도 성적이지만** 면접도 중요해. 면접도 잘 봐야지.
>
>   If (you) want to get a job, while (your) GPA is important, the job interview
>
>   is also quite important too. (You) have to do well on the job interview.

활동

가... 주어진 표현을 사용하여 문맥에 맞게 빈 칸을 채워 문장을 완성해 보세요.

> ~어/아(서) 다행이다, ~는/ㄴ 바람에, 그렇잖아도, ~(으)ㄹ 뻔하다,
> 어찌나/얼마나 ~는/(으)ㄴ/(으)ㄹ지, N도 N(이)지만

1. 회의가 늦게 _____ (끝나다) 저녁 식사 약속

   시간에 늦었어요.

2. 오늘 등산하기로 했는데 비가 _____ (안 오다).

3. _____ (피곤하다)

   집에 들어오자마자 쓰러져 잤어요.

4. ㄱ: 나 좀 도와줄 수 있어?

   ㄴ: _____ 도와주려고 했어.

5. 비가 갑자기 많이 오네요. 오늘 우산을 안 가지고 왔더라면 비를

   _____ (맞다)

6. (공부) _____ 건강이 더 중요해요.

나... 다음 질문에 자세히 답해 보세요.

1. 한국 대학과 여러분 대학의 새 학년도 개강 행사를 비교하세요.

2. 입학식이나 졸업식은 어떤 순서로 합니까?

3. 장기 자랑으로 할 수 있는 활동을 설명하고 준비해 보세요.

4. 한국의 대학 축제나 행사들을 조사해 보고 설명하세요.

5. 여러분이 알고 있거나 직접 해 본 봉사 활동을 설명해 보세요.

다... 학교마다 다양한 동아리가 있습니다. 주어진 칸에 동아리에 대한 정보를 찾아 써서 친구와 교환해 보세요.

1. 여러분 학교에 있는 동아리 종류를 알아보세요. (예: 학술, 외국어, 예술, 체육, 종교, 봉사 및 게임, 여행, 요리 등의 취미)
그 외에 또 어떤 동아리가 있습니까?

2. 여러분이 가입하고 싶은 동아리를 고르세요. 그 동아리의 목적과 활동에 대해 써 보세요.

동아리명	동아리 종류	동아리 목적 혹은 활동

라... 여러분이 고른 동아리에 가입하고 싶은 이유는 무엇입니까?

마... 학과, 단과대학 등의 교내 동아리 외에도 몇 개 대학의 대학생들이 모여 만든 연합 동아리가 있습니다. 교내 동아리와 연합 동아리의 장단점을 생각해 보세요.

칸 cell 교환 exchange 학술 academics 예술 arts 체육 sports, physical education
종교 religion 가입하다 to join 목적 aim 동아리명 club name 교내 on campus
연합 alliance

읽 기

생활에 나타나는 한국의 공동체 의식

공동체 의식이란 한 사람이 어떤 공동사회의 한 구성원이라는 생각이다. 한국에서는 공동체 의식을 **바탕으로**^{GU13.7} 한 생활 문화를 쉽게 볼 수 있다. 예를 들어 '내 부모님', '내 엄마', '내 아빠'라고 하지 않고 '우리 부모님', '우리 엄마', '우리 아빠'라고 한다. 여기에서 '우리' 대신 '내'를 사용한다면 어색하고 좀 이기적**으로 여겨진다.**^{GU13.8} 이것은 나 이전에 우리 집안에서의 부모님이시자 어머니 아버지이시기 때문이다. 심지어 남편이나 아내의 경우에도 '내 남편', '내 아내'라고 하기보다는 '우리/저희 남편', '우리/저희 아내'라고 하는 것이 보통이다. 내가 다니는 학교도 '우리 학교'라고 한다.

학교 생활에 있어서도 입학식, 신입생 오리엔테이션, 엠티, 축제, 동아리, 봉사 활동, 운동회, 체육 대회, 수학여행, 졸업 여행, 사은회, 졸업식 등에 공동체 의식이 녹아 있다. 이런 공동체 의식은 어렸을 때 형성된다고 볼 수 있는데 다른 나라에서는 입학식을 하지 않는 경우도 많다. 또, 수학여행의 경우 초중고는 물론, 심지어 유치원에서도 간다.

구성원 member 바탕 base 어색하다 to be awkward 이기적 selfish 여기다 to consider
이전 previous 운동회 sports day 수학여행 school or class trip
사은회 teacher-appreciation banquet 녹아 있다 to be steeped (*lit.* melted) in
형성되다 to be formed 초중고 elementary, middle, and high schools 심지어 even
유치원 kindergarten

　　이와 같이^{GU13.9} '우리'가 중요시되는 한국 사회에서는 전통적으로 식사도 혼자보다는 가족과 함께 한다. 아마도 현대 사회처럼 먹을 음식이 넘쳐 나지 않았던 시절에는 혼자 음식을 다 먹는 것보다는 나누어 먹는 것이 중요했을 것이다. 또, 여럿이 모여 음식을 나누어 먹으면서 지켜야 하는 밥상 예절도 생겨난 것으로 보인다. 직장에서 회식이 유난히 잦은 한국의 회식 문화 역시 집단주의의 한 형태라고 할 수 있다. 회식(會食)이라는 어휘의 한자를 보면 여러 사람이 모여 함께 음식을 먹는다는 의미이다.

　　한국인들은 공간을 함께 쓰는 데에도 익숙해져 있다. 아마 예전 한옥집에서 대가족이 모여 사는 풍습 때문일 것이다. 한옥은 문과 창

중요시되다 to be considered to be important　혼자 alone　넘쳐나다 to overflow
나누다 to divide, share　밥상 dining table　유난히 especially, exceptionally
집단주의 collectivism, groupism　형태 form　어휘 vocabulary　공간 space
익숙하다 to be familiar　대가족 large family

문이 창호지로 되어 있어서 방음이 잘 되지 않**는 데다가**[GU13.10] 좁은 공간에 많은 사람들이 함께 살아야 했기 때문에 나만의 공간을 갖는 것은 쉽지 않았다. 이처럼 사적 공간이 제한돼 있다 보니 서로의 일을 잘 알고 서로의 안녕을 묻고, 남의 사적인 부분도 나의 문제처럼 함께 걱정해 주는 것이 일상이었다. 따라서 한국에서는 공공장소에서도 타인과 공간을 공유하는 것을 자연스럽게 생각해**서 그런지**[GU13.11] 가까이 다가가거나 신체가 살짝 닿거나 해도 굳이 "실례합니다, 죄송합니다"라고 하지 않는다.

이처럼 전통적으로 공동체 의식이 강조되는 한국 사회에서는 단체 생활과 협동심이 강조되어 왔다. 그런가 하면 남들과 다르거나 튀는 행동은 환영받지 않는 행동으로 여겨지기 때문에 한국 사회는 개성이 중요시되지 않는다는 비판도 있었다. 그리하여 요즘 한국 사회에서는 전통적인 공동체 의식은 조금 약화되고 개인적인 특징이 강조되는 방향으로 나아가고 있다.

창호지 traditional Korean paper 방음 soundproof 일상 daily routine 공공장소 public place or area 공유 sharing 다가가다 to go near 신체 body 닿다 to touch, reach 굳이 particularly 강조 emphasis 단체 group 협동심 cooperative attitude 튀다 to stand out 개성 individuality 비판 criticism 그리하여 therefore 약화되다 to be weakened 방향 direction

이해 문제

가... 다음 내용이 본문의 내용과 같으면 ○, 다르면 X에 표시하세요.

1. 남편에 대해 말할 때 '우리 남편'보다는   ○   X
   '내 남편'이라고 하는 게 더 맞다.

2. 한옥에서 나만의 공간을 갖는 것은 쉽지 않았다.   ○   X

3. 한국에서 사적인 공간을 함께 쓰는 것은 실례이다.   ○   X

4. 회식이라는 어휘의 한자를 보면 돌아가면서   ○   X
   순서대로 먹는다는 뜻이다.

5. 한국에서는 단체 생활과 협동심이 강조되어 왔다.   ○   X

나... 본문을 읽고 다음 질문에 대답해 보세요.

1. 한국 사회에서 예전에 음식을 나누어 먹는 것이 중요했던 이유는 무엇입니까?

2. 한국인들이 공간을 함께 쓰는 데에 익숙해져 있는 점을 어디에서 볼 수 있습니까?

3. 한국인들이 공간을 함께 쓰는 데에 익숙해져 있는 이유는 무엇이라고 합니까?

4. 공동체 의식이 중시되는 현상은 무엇이 있을까요?

5. 요즘 한국 사회에서의 공동체 의식은 어떻게 바뀌어 가고 있습니까?

문법과 용법

GU13.7

~을/를 바탕으로 'based on'

그 저자는 실제 경험을 **바탕으로** 소설을 썼어요.

The author wrote a novel based on their real-life experiences.

한글은 발음 원리와 동양 철학을 **바탕으로** 만든 과학적인 글자입니다.

Hangul is a scientific writing system created on the basis of
phonetic principles and Asian philosophy.

▶ This pattern is a shortened form of ~을/를 바탕으로 하여, where the noun 바탕
means 'foundation' or 'basis'. Preceded by the object marker 을/를 and followed
by the particle –(으)로 'as, with', the expression X를 바탕으로 means 'taking/
having X as the basis', 'on the basis of X', or 'based on X'.

GU13.8

~(으)로/고 여겨지다 'to be regarded as'

백남준의 작품은 값비싼 예술품으로 **여겨지고** 있다.

The works of Nam June Paik are regarded as valuable works of art.

과거에 텔레비전은 부자들만 가지는 것이라고 **여겨졌다.**

In the past, television was considered something only for the rich.

▶ The verb 여기다 means to 'regard, think, consider'. When the verb is compounded with the change–of–state suffix –어지다 'to become', the passive verb 여겨지다 is the result, meaning 'to be considered, regarded'. The verb 여겨지다 requires a subject and a complement, in the sense of 'X (subject) is regarded as Y (complement)'. The complement is introduced by the particle –(으)로 'as' or the quotative particle 고 'to be'. In 우리 할아버지는 진정한 애국자였다고 여겨져요 'Our grandfather is considered to have been a true patriot', 우리 할아버지 is the subject and 진정한 애국자였다 is the complement.

GU13.9

이와 같이   'like this; as such'

이와 같이 자세히 설명해 주지 않으면 1학년 학생들은 이해하지 못할 거예요.
Unless you explain it in detail like this, the first year students
will not be able to understand.

너는 천재야. **이와 같이** 어려운 시험에서 100점을 받다니!
You're a genius. You managed to score a 100 on a difficult exam like this!

그 배우는 **이와 같이** 여러 드라마에서 뛰어난 연기력을 바탕으로 많은
인기를 끌었다.

As such, this actor has drawn much popularity from his outstanding
acting skills in several dramas.

▶ The pattern 이와 같이 consists of the demonstrative pronoun 이 'this', the instrument particle 와 'with, as', the adjective stem 같 'same', and the adverbializer suffix –이 '–ly, in', meaning 'like this'. It has two functions. As a conjunctive adverb, in which 이 refers to the thing or fact that the speaker/writer mentioned in the immediately preceding expression, 이와 같이 modifies the whole subsequent sentence, as in 이와 같이 한국은 해방되었다 'Like this, Korea was liberated'. As a manner adverb, in which 이 refers either to an immediately preceding mention or to the co-occurring noun, 이와 같이 modifies the adjective that precedes the noun, as in 이와 같이 어려운 문제 'a difficult question like this,' where 이 refers to 문제 and 이와 같이 modifies 어려운.

GU13.10

~는/(으)/ㄴ 데다가 'not only… but also; additionally'

제 여동생은 학교 성적도 **좋은 데다가** 리더십도 강해요.

My younger sister not only gets good grades,

but she also has strong leadership skills.

눈도 많이 **온 데다가** 바람도 세서 정말 춥네요.

It is really cold because we not only had a heavy snowfall,

but the wind is also strong.

이 식당은 음식이 맛있**는 데다가** 가격도 싸요.

At this restaurant the food not only tastes good, but the price is also affordable.

나는 대학원생**인 데다가** 선생님이기도 하다.

I am not only a graduate student but also a teacher.

▶ The word '데' in the expression ~는/(으)/ㄴ 데다가 is a bound noun meaning 'place, spot'. And being a bound noun, 데 is always preceded by a modifier clause as in 아픈 데, which means a painful spot (on one's body). In this target expression of ~(으)/ㄴ/는 데다가, 데 is followed by the additive particle ~에다가 (often contracted to 에다, 다가, or 다) 'to; adding to this (place)'. The expression ~는(으)/ㄴ 데다가 means 'on top of …, in addition to'. The ~는(으)/ㄴ 데다가 pattern is used to express that the content in the second clause is adding up to the first clause. Thus, the meaning becomes 'in addition to …, on top of …, not only … but also'.

~어서/아서 그런지 'perhaps, maybe because'

어젯밤에 늦게 자서 **그런지** 오늘은 계속 피곤하고 졸리다.
Perhaps it's because I went to sleep late last night,
but I have been tired and sleepy all day today.

날씨가 추워**서 그런지** 공원에 사람이 별로 없네요.
Maybe because of the cold weather, the park is not very busy today.

▶ This pattern is a shortened form of ~어서/아서 그런지 몰라도 literally meaning 'I am not sure whether it is/does so because …'. Its derived meaning is 'perhaps' or 'maybe because'. This expression is used to indicate an indefinite reason explaining the situation or phenomenon at hand, which has been specified in the main clause.

활동

가... 주어진 표현을 사용하여 문장에 맞게 빈 칸을 채워 보세요.

> ~을/를 바탕으로 , ~(으)로/다고/라고 여겨지다, 이와 같이
>
> ~는/(으)ㄴ 데다가, ~어서/아서 그런지

1. 이런 디자인은 이제 유행이 _____ (지났다).

2. 저희 할머니는 운동을 _____ (열심히 하시다)
   무척 건강하세요.

3. 지금 비가 많이 _____ (오고 있다) 바람도 세요.
   그래서 오늘 대신 내일 축구 연습을 하기로 했어요.

4. 내가 본 텔레비전 프로그램은 사실 _____
   만든 다큐멘터리였어요.

5. 그 책은 50년 전에 나온 책이에요. _____
   오래된 책은 잘 가지고 있어야지요.

나... 다음 밑줄 친 곳에 어울리는 단어를 고르세요.

1. 어느 외국인이 _____ 한국어 표현으로 질문을 했다.

   ㄱ. 넘쳐난   ㄴ. 닳은   ㄷ. 방음   ㄹ. 어색한

2. 새 학년도가 시작하는 3월 2일에 신입생 _____이/가 있을 예정이다.

    ㄱ. 결혼식   ㄴ. 사은회   ㄷ. 입학식   ㄹ. 졸업식

3. 우리는 아홉 식구가 모여 사는 _____이다.

    ㄱ. 공공장소   ㄴ. 대가족   ㄷ. 추억   ㄹ. 환영

4. 직장 생활을 한 지 1년이 넘어서 이제는 직장 생활에 _____.

    ㄱ. 든든하다   ㄴ. 발달하다   ㄷ. 익숙하다   ㄹ. 환영하다

5. 병원, 학교, 지하철역과 같은 _____에서 담배를 피우면 안 된다.

    ㄱ. 공공장소   ㄴ. 방향   ㄷ. 인솔   ㄹ. 작업

다... 다음 질문에 자세히 답해 보세요.

1. 다른 나라 문화에서도 공동체 의식을 찾아볼 수 있습니까? 있다면
   예를 자세히 설명해 보세요.

2. 여러분의 문화에서 식사나 음식 습관을 통해 나타나는 공동체, 혹은 개인주의
   문화에 대해 글을 써 보세요.

3. 혼자 하면 어렵지만 힘을 모아 함께 해서 일을 해낸 경험이 있습니까?
   그 경험에 대해 이야기해 보세요.

추 가 ─ 읽 기

함께 나누는 공동체 문화, 품앗이와 김장

나보다 "우리"를 먼저 생각하는 배려와 지혜가 바로 한국의 공동체 의식이다. 한국 문화에 나타나는 공동체 의식으로는 품앗이가 있다. 품앗이란 내가 남에게 품(일)을 해 준 것만큼 다시 받아온다는 뜻으로 서로 서로 일을 돌아가며 해 주는 협동을 말한다. 즉, 한 가족의 부족한 노동력을 해결하기 위해 다른 가족들의 노동력을 빌려 쓰고 나중에 갚아 주는 것이다.

품앗이 전통의 대표적인 예로 한국 고유의 김장을 들 수 있다. 김장이란 대가족이 겨우내 먹기 위한 많은 분량의 김치를 늦가을에 한꺼번에 담그는 것이다. 김장을 담그기 위해서는 가족과 이웃 간 협력이 필수적이었다. 이렇게 담근 김치는 서로 나눠 먹기도 하는데 이런 김장 문화는 유네스코 인류무형문화유산 대표목록에 등재되면서 세계적으로 관심을 받았다. 김장을 통해 한국인들의 어울려 살면서 서로 돕는 공동체의 중요성을 볼 수 있기 때문이다.

배려 consideration 지혜 wisdom 품앗이 communal sharing of labor 돌아가다 to go around and take turns 부족하다 to be lacking 노동력 manpower 해결하다 to resolve 빌려 쓰다 to borrow (and use) 갚아 주다 to pay back 김장 kimchi making for the winter 겨우내 throughout the winter 분량 amount 한꺼번에 at once all together 담그다 to make fermented food 협력 cooperation 필수적 necessary 유네스코 인류무형문화유산 대표목록 UNESCO Intangible Cultural Heritage Representative List 등재되다 to be registered

김장뿐만 아니라 잔칫집이나 상가(喪家) 등 일손이 많이 필요한 일들은 모두 품앗이로 해결했다. 또한 노동력이 많이 필요한 농사와 관련된 모내기, 물대기, 김매기, 추수 등도 모두 품앗이로 해낼 수 있었다. 이와 같이 혼자서는 하기 어려운 작업을 많은 사람이 힘을 합쳐 이루어 내는 것을 미덕으로 여겨 온 것이다. 그러나 현대 시대에 가족 단위, 주거 형태, 식문화 등의 생활 양식이 바뀜에 따라 이러한 공동체 문화는 서서히 사라져 가고 있어 많은 사람들이 아쉬워하고 있다.

상가 household in mourning 물대기 irrigation 김매기 weeding 해내다 to accomplish
작업 work 이루어 내다 to pull something off 미덕 virtue 단위 unit 식문화 eating culture
양식 style, way 서서히 gradually 사라져 가다 to evanesce

문 화

학사 일정*

월	날짜	학사 일정
3월	3.1	3·1절 휴일
	3.2	1학기 개강, 입학식 및 오리엔테이션
	3.2–3.8	1학기 수강 신청 변경
	3.10–3.11	단과대 엠티
4월	4.19–4.26	1학기 중간시험 기간
5월	5.5	어린이날 휴일
	5.16–5.17	대동제 축제(5교시부터 휴강)
	5.22	석가탄신일 휴일
6월	6.2–6.3	농촌 모내기 봉사
	6.14	1학기 종강
	6.15–6.21	1학기 기말시험 기간

휴일 holiday 수강 신청 변경 change of course registration 중간시험 midterm examination
어린이날 Children's Day 휴강 lecture cancellation 석가탄신일 Buddha's Birthday

월	날짜	학사 일정
7월	7.9–7.15	농촌 봉사
8월	8.27–8.31	2학기 등록
9월	9.3	2학기 개강
	9.11–9.12	가을 축제
	9.24–9.26	추석 연휴
10월	10.3	개천절 휴일
	10.9	한글날 휴일
	10.22–10.26	2학기 중간시험 기간
11월	11.2	수시 면접일
12월	12.14	2학기 종강
	12.15–12.21	2학기 기말시험 기간
1월	1.30–2.1	학부 신입생 등록
2월	2.21–2.27	학과별 졸업 여행
	2.26	학위 수여식(졸업식)
	2.28	겨울 방학 종료

* 학사일정은 학사운영의 사정에 따라 변경될 수 있습니다.

수시 early college exam 면접일 interview date 학위 degree 수여식 conferment ceremony
종료 end

▪▪ 번역문 ▪▪

CONVERSATION: College Events and Activities

At the college entrance ceremony, Mia, a freshman international student, meets Noah, one of her high school's upperclassmen.

Noah: Mia!

Mia: (Waving her hand) sŏnbae (*lit.* an upperclassman), over here!

Noah: Whew, thank goodness (*lit.* it is fortunate that) I'm not late! The roads were so congested because of the rain. Okay, here you go, take this flower bouquet. Congratulations on starting college!

Mia: *Sŏnbae*, thank you so much for coming to my entrance ceremony today! In fact, since I don't have any family in Korea, if you hadn't come it would have been a lonely entrance ceremony.

Noah: (I thought) it would probably be so. And, you know in the U.S. there's usually no such thing as a school entrance ceremony.

Mia: Right. So, I don't even know what a "school entrance ceremony" would be called in English.

Noah: Exactly. But in Korea, a lot of family and friends come to events like school entrance ceremony and celebrate together.

Mia: That's how it seems. But *sŏnbae*, I found out today that there are so many school events.

Noah: Yep. The start of the semester is the beginning of March, but before then, in order to help new students prepare for and adjust to college life, they do the entrance ceremony and orientation early on. And even after those (events), there are many other events that follow.

Mia: Yes. Orientation shortened down is called "OT", or it's also called *saenae'gi paeumt'ŏ* (*lit.* new member learning center).

Noah: Right. And our college goes to MT or college retreat the first weekend in March.

Mia: MT you say ...

Noah: Yeah. MT is abbreviated English for "membership training" and our college goes to Kyeonggi-do Province for 1 night and 2 days.

Mia: Should I go to the retreat? I don't even know anyone.

Noah: Yeah, you go and meet your group peers, and it's good because you also learn important information needed for college life from upperclassmen. They also do a talent show and games that give you a feeling of closeness and belonging.

Mia: But if I go to the retreat, there's going to be people drinking a ton until way late, right? I can't drink a lot, and on top of that I'm one who tends to go to bed early ...

Noah: In the past, they drank a lot. But these days, because they don't pressure you to drink, you don't have to worry too much. There will be some friends that will stay up all night talking, but if you find it hard and feel sleepy, then it's okay to go to bed and sleep first.

Mia: Well then, I'll have to go and check it out.

Noah: So that's that, have you thought about any clubs?

Mia: Yes, I definitely want to join a club. But there are so many clubs, it seems like it will be hard to choose.

Noah: Right. This morning after the entrance ceremony, during the orientation, at the student center, there will be an explanation of the clubs.

Mia: But sŏnbae, I heard that in May there is taedongje. What is that?

Noah: Ah, "taedongje" is a college festival. Taedongje means "all coming together in grand harmony."

Mia: What do you do for taedongje?

Noah: All over campus you have many events like displays, performances, and contests. It will make for a great memory. Our school also invites popular singers and has concerts.

Mia: I'm really looking forward to it. That would be great if a famous singer came.

Noah: A festival is a festival but starting in the spring, our college has service activities at farming communities, too. Since farming communities are shorthanded in spring, we go and help plant rice seedlings, which is an experience you can't have in Seoul. And during the summer break, we also help students with their homework.

Mia: I've done service activities in the U.S., I'll definitely want to try them in Korea, too.

Noah: There are many events by college and department, so watch your schedule and make sure not to miss out on important events and meetings.

Mia: Yes, *sŏnbae*. Thank you for thoroughly explaining (these things). I feel reassured since you are in the same school (as me).

READING: Korean Sense of Community Appearing in Daily Life

Sense of community is the consideration of one person as a member of a communal society. In Korea, one can easily see a culture of living based upon a sense of community. For example, people do not say 'my parents', 'my mom', or 'my dad'. They say, 'our parents', 'our mom', or 'our dad'. If one were to use 'my' instead of 'our' in this context, it would be considered awkward and a bit self-centered. This is because they are the parents of an entire household before they are my own mother or father. Moreover, even in the cases of husbands or wives, it is common to say 'our husband' or 'our wife' rather than saying 'my husband' or 'my wife'. The school that one attends is also referred to as 'our school'.

Even in one's school life, a sense of community is steeped in various events. These include school entry ceremonies, new student orientations, membership trainings (MT) or college retreats, festivals, clubs, volunteer works, field days, athletic competitions, class trips, graduation trips, teacher-appreciation banquets, and graduation ceremonies. Such sense of community can be seen as having been formed from a young age, whereas there are many instances in which other countries do not even have school entry ceremonies. When it comes to class trips, even kindergartens have them in addition to elementary, middle, and high schools.

As such, in Korean society where the word 'our' is considered to be important, even the act of eating meals is traditionally done with families rather than alone. It was probably important to share food rather than eating it all by oneself during times when food to eat was not abundant like the modern society. It also seems that table manners that are expected to be followed emerged as people gathered to share food.

Dining get-togethers are especially frequent at one's workplace. Korea's culture of collectivism can also be described as a form of collectivism. If one looks at the Chinese characters of the word *hoeshik*, the meaning is many people gathering to eat with each other.

Koreans are also used to sharing space. This is probably because of the custom of large families living together in traditional Korean houses in the old days. The doors and windows of traditional Korean houses were made of traditional Korean paper, so in addition to being poorly soundproofed, many people had to live in a narrow space. As a result, it was difficult to attain a space that was completely one's own. Personal space was limited in such fashion. Thus, knowing much about each other's business, asking about each other's well-being, and showing concern about even the private aspects of other people's lives as if it were one's own problem was a daily routine. Therefore, it may be because people in Korea think that sharing a space with strangers in public places is so natural that even if someone approaches nearby or comes in slight bodily contact with others, people do not particularly bother to say, "Excuse me" or "I'm sorry."

It is in this manner by which living within a group, as well as a collaborative attitude, has been stressed in Korean society. And as for actions that differ or stand out from other people, they are considered unwelcome behavior, which has led to criticism that individuality is not valued in Korean society. Consequently, such a traditional sense of community has slightly weakened in Korean society these days, heading towards a direction in which individual character is emphasized.

FURTHER READING: Communal Culture of Sharing: Communal Labor Sharing and Kimchi Making

The consideration and wisdom to think of "us" before oneself is Koreans' sense of community. A sense of community that appears in Korean culture, is *p'umashi*, a communal sharing of labor. *P'umashi* has the meaning of receiving help from others in exchange for doing some of their *p'um*, or work, which involves cooperation and taking turns in helping each other with work. In other words, a family resolves its lack of manpower by borrowing the labor of another family and paying it back later.

As a typical example of the traditional communal sharing of labor, one can cite the native Korean tradition of *kimjang*, making kimchi for the winter. *Kimjang* is the act of making a large quantity of kimchi all at one time in late autumn, so that large families can eat kimchi throughout the winter. In order to make the kimchi, cooperation between the family and its neighbors is necessary. Koreans share kimchi made in such a manner, and *kimjang* received global attention when it became registered on the UNESCO Representative List of Intangible Cultural Heritage. This is because one can see through *kimjang* the importance of community in which Koreans live in harmony with one another while helping each other.

Besides *kimjang*, many other tasks requiring much manpower were resolved through communal sharing of labor, including household banquets or wakes. Farm work that required much manpower such as rice planting, irrigation, weeding, and harvesting could also be accomplished through communal sharing of labor. Thus, it was considered a virtue to join forces and pull off work that was too difficult to do alone. However, as lifestyles encompassing the family unit, forms of housing, and eating culture change in current society, this type of communal culture is gradually disappearing to the regret of many people.

CULTURE: Academic Calendar*

Month	Date	Schedule
March	March 1st	March 1st Independence Movement Day Holiday
	March 2nd	1st Term Classes Begin, Matriculation Ceremony and Orientation
	March 2nd–8th	1st Term Course Registration Changes
	March 10th–11th	Respective College's Trips
April	April 19th–26th	1st Term Midterm Examination Period

May	May 5th	Children's Day Holiday
	May 16th–17th	University Festival (Lectures cancelled from 5th period)
	May 22nd	Buddha's Birthday Holiday
June	June 2nd–3rd	Volunteer Service in Farming Community Rice Planting
	June 14th	1st Term Classes End
	June 15th–21st	1st Term Final Examination Period
July	July 9th–15th	Volunteer Service in Farming Community
August	August 27th–31st	2nd Term Registration
September	September 3rd	2nd Term Classes Begin
	September 11th–12th	Autumn Festival
	September 24th–26th	Korean Thanksgiving Holiday
October	October 3rd	National Foundation Day Holiday
	October 9th	Hangul Day Holiday
	October 22nd–26th	2nd Term Midterm Examination Period
November	November 2nd	Early College Exams Interview Day
December	December 14th	2nd Term Classes End
	December 15th–21st	2nd Term Final Examination Period
January	January 30th–February 1st	Undergraduate New Student Registration
February	February 21st–27th	Respective Majors' Graduation Trip
	February 26th	Degree Conferment (Graduation Ceremony)
	February 28th	Winter Break Ends

* The academic calendar is subject to change according to the circumstances of the university operations.

▪▪ 단어 ▪▪

가입하다	to join	단과대(=단과대학)	college or school of a university
강조	emphasis	단위	unit
갚아 주다	to pay back	단체	group
개강	beginning of semester in college	담그다	to make fermented food
개성	individuality	닿다	to touch, reach
겨우내	throughout the winter	대가족	large family
경기	game, match	대동제	college festival
공간	space	대회	contest
공공 장소	public place or area	돌아가다	to go around and take turns
공동체	community	동기	classmate
공유	sharing	동아리	club
교내	on campus	동아리명	club name
교환	exchange	든든하다	to feel secure
구성원	member	등재되다	to be registered
굳이	particularly	딸리다	to run short
그리하여	therefore	막히다	to be jammed
근거	basis	면접일	interview date
김매기	weeding	모내기	rice planting
김장	kimchi making for the winter	목적	aim
꽃다발	bouquet	무지	really, very
나누다	to divide, share	물대기	irrigation
넘쳐 나다	to overflow	미덕	virtue
노동력	manpower	바탕	base
녹아 있다	to be steeped (*lit.* melted) in	밤새	all night long
농촌 봉사 활동	volunteer service in farming communities	밥상	dining table
		방음	soundproof
다가가다	to go near	방향	direction
다행	luck, fortune	배려	consideration
		봐주다	to help

부족하다	to be lacking	유네스코	UNESCO Intangible
분량	amount	인류무형문화유산	Cultural Heritage
비판	criticism	대표목록	Representative List
빌려 쓰다	to borrow (and use)	유치원	kindergarten
사라져 가다	to evanesce	의식	consciousness
사은회	teacher-appreciation	이기적	selfish
	banquet	이루어 내다	to pull something off
상가	household in mourning	이전	previous
새내기 배움터	college orientation	익숙하다	to be familiar
서서히	gradually	일상	daily routine
석가탄신일	Buddha's Birthday	일상생활	daily life
소속감	sense of belonging	일손	worker, hand
수강 신청 변경	change of course	입학식	entrance ceremony of school
	registration	입학식장	entrance to ceremony hall
수시	early college exam	작업	work
수여식	conferment ceremony	장기 자랑	talent show
수학여행	school or class trip	적응	adaptation
식문화	eating culture	접속사	conjunction
신체	body	–조차	even
심지어	even	종교	religion
아예	to begin with	종료	end
약화되다	to be weakened	줄이다	to shorten
양식	style, way	중간시험	midterm examination
어린이날	Children's Day	중요시되다	to be considered to be
어색하다	to be awkward		important
어휘	vocabulary	지혜	wisdom
여기다	to consider	집단주의	collectivism, groupism
연결하다	to connect	참여하다	to participate
연합	alliance	창호지	traditional Korean paper
예술	arts	체육	sports, physical education
예전	former days	초중고	elementary, middle,
운동회	sports day		and high schools
유난히	especially, exceptionally	초청	invitation

축제	festival	해내다	to accomplish
칸	cell	행사	event
튀다	to stand out	협동심	cooperative attitude
품앗이	communal sharing of labor	협력	cooperation
필수적	necessary	형성되다	to be formed
학생회관	student center	형태	form
학술	academics	혼자	alone
학위	degree	화합하다	to unite in harmony
한꺼번에	at once all together	휴강	lecture cancellation
해결하다	to resolve	휴일	holiday

일제 강점기의 한국

Lesson 14 Korea during the Japanese Colonial Period

학습 목표

내용
- 일본의 한반도 식민 통치와 당시의 한국인의 생활을 이해한다.
- 인터뷰에 필요한 언어 예절을 배운다.

문화
- 태평양 전쟁과 일본의 항복 그리고 한반도의 광복을 훑어본다.
- 한국 문화의 암흑 시대를 살펴본다.

일제(= 일본 제국) Japanese Empire 일제 강점기 Japanese occupation period
식민 통치 colonial rule 당시 those days 태평양 전쟁 the Pacific War 항복 surrender
광복 restoration of independence 훑어보다 to look through 암흑 시대 dark age

■ 생각해 봅시다

가 ‣ 다음에 대해서 아는 대로 이야기해 봅시다.

    1. 제2차 세계 대전

    2. 진주만 폭격

    3. 태평양 전쟁

    4. 맥아더 장군, 아이젠하워 대통령

나 ‣ 다음 사진의 역사적 배경이 무엇인지 알아보세요.

1945년 나가사키에 투하된 원자 폭탄   1945년 포츠담 선언

진주만 Pearl Harbor 폭격 bombing 투하되다 to be air-dropped 원자 폭탄 atomic bomb
포츠담 선언 the Potsdam Declaration

일제 강점기 한국인의 생활

사회일보 장 기자가 한국대학교 손 교수를 인터뷰하고 있다.

장 기자: 안녕하세요, 교수님. 오랜만에 **뵙겠습니다.**[GU14.1]

손 교수: 정말 오랜만이네요. 요즘도 바쁘시지요?

장 기자: 네. 매일 취재하느라 바쁘게 지내고 있습니다. 그런데, 아까
전화로 잠깐 **말씀드렸듯이**[GU14.2] 저희 신문사에서 광복절 특집
기사를 준비하고 있습니다. 일제 강점기를 겪은 어르신들의
경험담을 중심으로[GU14.3] 기사를 쓰려고 합니다.

손 교수: 그때 일이 너무 오래되어 얼마나 기억하고 있을지 모르겠어요.

장 기자: 실례지만 올해 연세가 **어떻게 되시는지**[GU14.4] 여쭈어 봐도 될까
요?

손 교수: 1933년생이에요.

장 기자: 그럼 일제 시대에 초등학교를 다니셨겠네요.

손 교수: 네. 한국이 일제에서 해방되던 1945년에 나는 초등학교 6학
년이었어요.

장 기자: 그럼 2차 세계 대전을 모두 초등학교 다니실 때 경험하셨겠
어요.

사회일보 *Sahoe Ilbo* 취재하다 to collect news data 특집 special edition 기사 news (article)
겪다 to experience 어르신 esteemed elder 경험담 story of one's personal experiences
올해 this year 여쭈다 to say, ask (to a senior) 해방되다 to be liberated 제2차 세계 대전
World War II 경험하다 to experience

손 교수: 그렇죠. 초등학교 1학년 때 독일의 히틀러 군대가 폴란드를
        침공해서 제2차 세계 대전이 일어났어요.

장 기자: 한국 사람들을 힘들게 한 것은 태평양 전쟁이었겠지요?

손 교수: 맞아요. 1941년 12월 8일, 그러니까 미국 시간으로는 7일이지
        요. 일본이 하와이 진주만의 미국 함대를 공습하면서 태평양
        전쟁이 시작되었지요. 3년 9개월간의 전쟁 때문에 우리 한국
        사람들 고생은 말할 수 없었어요.

장 기자: 전쟁 당시 경험하신 일 중 가장 생각나시는 일을 하나 말씀해
        주시겠습니까?

손 교수: 그때 우리는 일본 국민이라 믿었어요. 초등학교에 들어가자
        우리는 "황국 신민 맹세"를 외워야 했어요. 그래서 우리는 미
        국, 영국을 우리 적으로 생각했고 따라서 일본의 전쟁 승리를
        위해서 온갖 희생을 다했어요.

장 기자: 일제 시대에는 학교에서 한국어를 쓰지 못하게 했다면서요?

손 교수: 학교에서 한국말을 하면 벌을 받았어요. 그때는 매일 아침 조
        회 때마다 일본 천황이 살고 있는 도쿄 쪽을 바라보고 절을
        했어요.

장 기자: 한국 사람들 이름도 바꿔야 했다지요?

손 교수: 네. 일본식 이름으로 바꾸게 했어요. 나도 물론 내 이름을 일
        본 이름으로 바꿨어요. 그뿐인가요? 한국 젊은이들이 전쟁터
        로 떠날 때마다 우리는 일본 국기를 들고 나가서 환송했어요.

독일 Germany 침공하다 to invade, attack 함대 fleet 공습하다 to make an air raid
말할 수 없다 to be beyond description 국민 citizen 황국 신민 맹세 Oath of Subjects of the
Japanese Empire 외우다 to recite 적 enemy 승리 victory 온갖 all kinds of 희생 sacrifice
다하다 to do one's best 벌을 받다 to be punished 조회 morning assembly 천황 emperor
전쟁터 battlefield 국기 national flag 환송하다 to give a hearty send-off

일본군을 위해서 많은 쌀을 바쳤고, 무기를 만들도록 집에 있는 놋그릇, 수저 등까지도 바쳤어요.

장 기자: 그러면 전쟁 때 학교 공부는요?

손 교수: 내가 5학년, 6학년 때는 수업을 거의 못 했어요.

장 기자: 왜요?

손 교수: 젊은이들이 전쟁터로 떠나서 우리들 초등학생들이 농사를 도왔어요. 봄에는 거머리에 물리면서 모를 심었어요. 가을에는 낫을 들고 벼를 벴고요. 그리고 산에 가서 소나무 뿌리를 캤어요.

장 기자: 소나무 뿌리를요? 소나무 뿌리는 왜요?

손 교수: 소나무 뿌리에서 나오는 기름을 전투기에 쓴다고 했어요.

장 기자: 어린 시절을 정말 힘들게 보내셨군요.

손 교수: 지금 생각하면 죽지 못해서 살았던 것 같아요. 먹을 것이 없어서 겨로 만든 빵을 먹고 살았고 소나무 껍질을 먹고 배탈이 **나곤 했어요.** GU14.5

장 기자: 그러다가 마침내 일본이 망했군요.

손 교수: 네. 1945년 8월 15일 낮 12시부터 라디오에서 일본 천황이 "무조건 항복", "무조건 항복" 하는 목소리가 되풀이되고 있었어요. 드디어 한국이 해방된 것이었어요.

장 기자: 정말 고생 많이 하셨네요. 오늘은 시간 관계상 여기까지만 들어야 될 것 같습니다. 좋은 말씀 잘 들었습니다. 바쁘신 중에 귀중한 시간을 내주셔서 다시 한 번 감사드립니다. 다음에 또 뵙겠습니다.

무기 weapon 놋그릇 brassware 수저 spoon and chopsticks 바치다 to give, offer
거머리 leech 모를 심다 to plant rice sprouts 낫 sickle 벼를 베다 to mow rice plants
소나무 뿌리 pine tree root 캐다(=파내다) to dig out 전투기 fighter plane 어린 시절
childhood 겨 chaff 껍질 bark 배탈이 나다 to have a stomachache 망하다 to perish, ruin
무조건 unconditional 되풀이되다 to be repeated 귀중하다 to be important, precious

이해 문제

가... 본문 내용과 맞으면 ○, 틀리면 X에 표시하세요.

    1. 장 기자는 손 교수를 오랜만에 만났다.   ○   X

    2. 손 교수는 제2차 세계 대전을 초등학교에 다니면서 경험했다.   ○   X

    3. 제2차 세계 대전은 독일이 하와이 진주만을 공습해서 일어났다.   ○   X

    4. 일제 강점기에 한국 사람들은 미국, 영국을 적으로 생각했다.   ○   X

    5. 초등학생들은 '황국 신민 맹세'를 외워야 했다.   ○   X

나... 대화를 읽고 다음 질문에 대답해 보세요.

    1. 장 기자가 손 교수와 인터뷰를 한 목적은 무엇입니까?

    2. 태평양 전쟁은 어떻게 일어났습니까?

    3. 태평양 전쟁 때 한국의 초등학생들은 왜 농사를 도왔습니까?

    4. 초등학생들은 전쟁 때 왜 소나무 뿌리를 캤습니까?

    5. 일본 천황이 언제 무조건 항복을 했습니까?

문법과 용법

> ### GU14.1
>
> ## 뵙겠습니다　'Nice to see you; See you (again).'

가: 안녕하세요? 처음 **뵙겠습니다**. 저는 김용석인데요.

　　Hello, nice to meet you. I'm Kim Yongsŏk.

나: 안녕하세요? 어떻게 오셨는지요?

　　Hello. How may I help you?

가: 좀 의논 드릴 일이 있어서요.

　　I'm here because I have something to discuss with you.

나: 아이고! 오늘은 좀 바빠서 지금 나가 봐야겠는데 내일 다시 오시면 안 될까요?

　　Oh no! I was just on my way out to deal with some urgent business. Would it be possible for you to come back tomorrow?

가: 네, 그럼 내일 다시 **뵙겠습니다**.

　　Sure, in that case I will see you again tomorrow.

▶ This expression is used to greet and take leave of a senior or a distant adult, equivalent to 'Nice to see you' and 'I will see you again', respectively. In greeting, it is always preceded by an adverb such as 오랜만에 'after a while' and 처음 'for the first time'. In leave–taking, the adverb attached may be 또 'again', 다시 'again', 내일 'tomorrow', or 곧 'soon'. The verb 뵙다 is a humble form of 보다 'to see'. The suffix –겠 refers to the speaker's conjecture ('think') or intention ('will'). When this suffix is used in interactional situations, it connotes politeness. In greetings, it conveys the speaker's conjecture, as in 처음 뵙겠어요 (lit. 'I think I am meeting you for the first time'). In leave-taking, it conveys the speaker's intentions, as in 또 뵙겠어요 'I will see you again'.

GU14.2

말씀드렸듯이 'as I told you'

가: 아까 **말씀드렸듯이**, 저는 몸이 아파서 일찍 퇴근하겠습니다.

As I told you earlier, I will be leaving early because I am not feeling well.

나: 그렇게 하세요.

Please do so.

▶ The pattern 말씀드렸듯이 is an honorific counterpart of 말했듯이 and is used for a senior or distant adult equal. 말씀 is a polite word for 말 'words' and 드리다 means 'to give something to a senior person' and 듯이 means 'as, like'.

GU14.3

~을/를 중심으로 'centering around (a thing), focusing on'

가: 제 논문은 일본의 한국 침략을 **중심으로 (해서)** 쓸까 해요.

I am thinking of writing my paper about the Japanese invasion of Korea.

나: 저는 태평양 전쟁을 **중심으로** 쓸래요.

I am going to write mine focusing on the Pacific War.

▶ This pattern is a contraction of ~을 중심으로 해서 'by taking something as the central topic or focus', with the omission of 해서 (< 하여서). The Sino–Korean noun 중심 means 'center, middle, focus, core'.

GU14.4

어떻게 되세요? 'May I ask what is …?' (to a senior person or distant adult)

가: 너는 몇 살이니?

How old are you?

나: 저는 13살입니다.

I am thirteen years old.

가: 실례지만 어르신 연세가 **어떻게 되십니까**?

Excuse me, but may I ask how old you are, sir/madam?

나: 일흔 살인데요.

(I am) Seventy.

▶ When a senior person's age, name, occupation, etc., are asked, indirect speech acts are required. Instead of 무엇이에요 'what is …?', one must use 어떻게 되세요? 'how does it become?'. Thus, 이름이 무엇이에요? 'What is your name?' to a friend or a junior is equivalent to 성함이 어떻게 되세요? to a senior or distant adult.

GU14.5

~곤 하다 'do … habitually'

가: 나는 머리가 아플 때마다 바닷가에 가서 쉬**곤 해요**.

Whenever I have a headache, out of habit, I go to the beach to rest.

나: 나는 가슴이 답답할 때마다 산에 올라가**곤 했어요**.

I used to always head up the mountain whenever I felt frustrated and under pressure.

▶ This pattern occurs with a verb to indicate the habituality of the action denoted by the verb. It is a contraction of ~고는 하다, which is composed of the conjunctive suffix –고 'and', the topic/contrast particle –는, and the 'do' verb 하다. ~고는 하다 or ~곤 하다 has been idiomatized to refer to 'to do habitually'.

활동

가... 다음 문장을 한국어로 바꿔 보세요. 'ㄴ'은 주어진 표현을 사용하여 해 보세요.

> 말씀드렸듯이, 뵙겠습니다, 어떻게 되세요?, 여쭈어 보다

1. Hello, long time no see.

    ㄱ: _____ (to a friend/junior)

    ㄴ: _____ (to a senior)

2. See you again.

    ㄱ: _____ (to a friend/junior)

    ㄴ: _____ (to a senior)

3. How old are you?

    ㄱ: _____ (to a friend/junior)

    ㄴ: _____ (to a senior)

4. As I told you earlier by phone, I will not be able to go to school today.

    ㄱ: _____ (to a friend/junior)

    ㄴ: _____ (to a senior)

5. May I ask what your name is?

    ㄱ: _____ (to a friend/junior)

    ㄴ: _____ (to a senior)

나... 빈 칸에 알맞은 표현을 골라 넣으세요.

1. 1935년생이니까 2020년에는 _____ 예요.

    ㄱ. 63세   ㄴ. 77세   ㄷ. 85세   ㄹ. 91세

2. 이번 여름에는 지역별 음식을 _____ 한국 음식을 조사해 보고 싶어요.

    ㄱ. 말씀드렸듯이   ㄴ. 뵙고   ㄷ. 점령하고   ㄹ. 중심으로

3. 전화로 _____ 내일 찾아 뵙겠습니다.

    ㄱ. 경험담에 대해   ㄴ. 죽지 못해서   ㄷ. 말씀드렸듯이   ㄹ. 올해는

4. 시간이 날 때는 카페에 가서 차를 _____.

    ㄱ. 마시곤 했어요   ㄴ. 배탈이 났어요   ㄷ. 망했어요   ㄹ. 중심이에요

5. 지금 살고 계시는 댁의 주소가 _____?

    ㄱ. 외우세요   ㄴ. 바쳐요   ㄷ. 어떻게 되세요   ㄹ. 말할 수 없어요

다... 여러분 주변 사람들이 겪은 가장 인상적인 역사적 사건에 대해 조사해 보세요.

라... 1910–1945년 여러분 나라에서는 어떤 일이 있었는지 조사해서 발표해 보세요.

읽기

일본의 식민 통치와 태평양 전쟁

한반도는 35년 동안 일본의 식민지였다. 일본은 1910년 8월 29일 한반도를 강제로 일본의 식민지로 만들었다. 일본 제국이 한반도를 강제로 점령했기 때문에 이 시기를 일제 강점기라고 한다. 일본의 식민지가 되기 전까지 한반도는 조선 왕조(1392–1910)였는데 그중 1897년부터 1910년까지는 대한제국으로 국호를 바꾸었다.

일본의 조선 침략의 시작은 운요호 사건이었다. 1875년 일본 군함 운요호가 불법으로 조선의 강화도에 들어와서 조선 군대와 전투를 벌였다. 이 사건**을 구실로**^GU14.6 일본은 부산, 인천, 원산을 일본인들에게 개항하게 했다.

개항이 되자 일본인뿐 아니라 청나라, 러시아 등 외국 사람들이 조선에 밀려들어 와서 서로 조선을 지배하려고 전쟁을 했다. 청일 전쟁(1894–1895)과 러일 전쟁(1904–1905)에서 일본이 승리하게 되어 청으로부터는 타이완을 얻었고 러시아로부터는 사할린의 남쪽 반을 얻었다.

강제로 by force 시기 period 조선 왕조 Chosŏn Dynasty 대한제국 Korean Empire
국호 name of a country 침략 invasion 사건 incident 군함 battleship 불법으로 illegally
전투를 벌이다 to fight a battle 구실 excuse 개항하다 to open a port 청나라 Qing Empire of
China 밀려들다 to surge into 지배하다 to control 청일 전쟁 the Sino-Japanese War
러일 전쟁 the Russo-Japanese War 사할린 Sakhalin

일본은 조선을 식민지**화하려는**[GU14.7] 노력을 계속하여 마침내 1910년에 한일 병합 조약을 강제로 맺고 조선을 일본에 병합했다. 이리하여 조선 왕조는 519년 만에 막을 내리**고 말았다.**[GU14.8]

1910년을 전후하여[GU14.9] 70만 명의 일본인이 한반도에 밀려들어왔다. 일본은 서울에 조선 총독부를 설치하고 일본인 총독이 한반도를 통치했다. 한반도는 착취와 차별에 시달렸다. 일본은 한민족의 문화재, 자원, 재산은 물론, 역사, 언어 등도 빼앗았다. 학교나 모든 공공 기관에서 한국어 사용이 금지되었다. 한국 사람들의 이름도 모두 일본식으로 바꾸게 했다.

일본은 1941년 12월 7일 미국 하와이의 진주만에 있던 미국 함대를 공습하고 미국에 선전 포고를 했다. 3년 9개월간의 태평양 전쟁이 시작된 것이다. 태평양 전쟁 중 한민족의 생활은 더욱 힘들었다. "내선일체"라는 이름 아래 한민족의 젊은이들은 군인으로, 노무자로, 위안부로 동원됐다.

제2차 세계 대전이 끝나 **갈 무렵**인[GU14.10] 1945년 미국은 일본의 67개 도시를 폭격했다. 1945년 7월 26일 미국, 영국, 중화민국이 포츠담 선언을 발표했다. 소련도 참전**과 동시에**[GU14.11] 이 선언에 서명했다. 이 선언의 요지는 일본이 항복하지 않으면 "즉각적이고 완전한

한일 병합 조약 Korea-Japan Annexation Treaty 맺다 to conclude 이리하여 in this way
막을 내리다 to come to an end 총독부 governor-general's office 설치하다 to establish
착취 exploitation 차별 discrimination ~에 시달리다 to suffer from 문화재 cultural assets
자원 resources 재산 property 빼앗다 to rob 공공 기관 public institutions 금지되다 to be
prohibited 선전 포고 declaration of war 내선일체 Japan-Korea one body 노무자 laborer
위안부 comfort women 동원되다 to be mobilized 무렵 around the time when 폭격하다 to
bombard 동시에 simultaneously 서명하다 to sign 요지 gist 즉각적 immediate

파멸"을 당한다[GU14.12]는 것과 일본의 주권은 혼슈, 홋카이도, 규슈, 시코쿠와 연합군이 결정하는 작은 섬들에 국한된다는 것이다.

일본이 이 선언을 무시하자, 미국은 8월 6일에는 히로시마 시에, 그리고 8월 9일에는 나가사키 시에 원자 폭탄을 투하했다. 이어 소련도 일본에 선전 포고를 하고 일본이 세운 만주국과 북한의 청진에서 전투를 벌이자, 일본의 히로히토 천황은 1945년 8월 15일 무조건 항복을 선언했다.

한반도의 주권은 다시 한민족에게 돌아왔다. 한국은 일본에서 해방된 8월 15일을 광복절(빛을 되찾은 날)로 기념하고 있다. 그러나 미국은 소련이 한반도 전체를 점령하는 것을 막기 위해 북위 38도 선(삼팔선) 북쪽은 소련군이 주둔하고, 남쪽은 미군이 주둔하기로 소련과 합의했다. 그 결과 한반도는 남북으로 분단되었다. 한반도에 살던 일본인은 거의 모두 일본으로 돌아갔으나 일본의 식민 지배는 한민족이 감당하기 어려울 만큼 큰 상처를 남겼다.

파멸 destruction ~에 국한되다 to be limited to 무시하다 to ignore 세우다 to erect
전투 battle 주권 sovereignty 한민족 Korean people 광복절 National Liberation Day
빛 light 되찾다 to recover 날 day 기념하다 to commemorate 북위 north latitude
주둔하다 to be stationed 감당하다 to cope with 상처 wound 남기다 to leave

이해 문제

가... 본문 내용과 맞으면 ○, 다르면 X에 표시하세요.

1. 일본의 조선 침략의 시작은 일본 군함이   ○   X
   부산항에 들어올 때부터이다.

2. 일본은 1868년부터 한반도를 식민지로 점령했다.   ○   X

3. 일제 시대 학교에서 한국어가 계속 사용됐다.   ○   X

4. 일본은 한국 사람의 이름을 일본식으로 바꾸게 했다.   ○   X

5. 한국의 젊은이들은 일본 군인으로 동원됐다.   ○   X

6. 일본은 미국에 선전 포고를 한 후 미국 하와이 진주만을 공습했다. ○   X

7. 일본은 포츠담 선언을 따랐다.   ○   X

8. 한국은 8월 15일을 광복절로 기념하고 있다.   ○   X

나... 본문을 읽고 다음 질문에 대답해 보세요.

1. 일본이 한반도를 35년간 강제로 점령한 시기를 뭐라고 합니까?

2. 일본은 언제부터 언제까지 한반도를 식민지로 점령했습니까?

3. 일본의 식민지가 되기 전에 한반도는 어떤 나라였습니까?

4. 한일 병합 조약은 어떤 조약이었습니까?

5. 일제 강점기 동안 한민족의 생활은 어땠습니까?

6. 포츠담 선언은 무엇입니까? 무슨 내용입니까?

7. 미국은 일본에 왜 원자 폭탄을 투하했습니까?

8. 소련은 언제 태평양 전쟁에 참전했습니까?

9. 한반도는 왜 남북으로 분단되었습니까?

10. 광복절은 무슨 뜻입니까?

문법과 용법

GU14.6

~을/를 구실로 'under the excuse of, using the excuse of'

가: 일본은 무엇을 **구실로** 한국을 개항하게 했지요?

What excuse did Japan use to force Korea to open its ports?

나: 강화도 사건을 **구실로** 개항하게 했어요.

Japan forced Korea to open its ports using the Kanghwa

incident as an excuse.

▶ This pattern is a contraction of ~을/를 구실로 해서 'using as an excuse', where the Sino–Korean noun 구실 literally means 'pretext' and 로 해서 means 'by taking (something) as'. For example, 병을 구실로 (해서) 결석했다 means '(He) did not come to school under the excuse of illness'.

The expression 구실로 also follows a quotative clause in the form of –다는/라는 (contraction of –다고 하는 and –라고 하는). For example, 아프다는 구실로 회의에 참석하지 않았다 'He didn't attend the meeting with the excuse of being sick', 환자라는 구실로 훈련을 빠졌다 'He did not join the training with the excuse that he is a patient'.

GU14.7

~화하다 '-ize'

가: 한국은 어느 대통령 때부터 현대**화했**어요?

Korea has been modernized since which president?

나: 아마 박정희 대통령 때부터인 것 같아요.

It's probably been since President Chung Hee Park.

▶ The Sino–Korean causativizer –화 'make, change, transform' makes a Sino–Korean noun into a causative verbal noun, as in 근대 'modern age' vs. 근대화 modernization; 식민지 'colony' vs. 식민지화 'colonization'; and 산업 'industry' vs. 산업화 'industrialization'. The native 'do' verb makes the verbal noun (noun + –화) into a transitive verb, as in 한국을 근대화하다 'modernize Korea' and 북한을 공산화했다 'communized North Korea'. The native verb 되다 'become' makes the verbal noun into an intransitive verb, as in 근대화되었다 'became modernized'.

GU14.8

~고 말다 'to end up with'

가: 이번 수능 시험 잘 봤니?

Did you do well on your SAT this time?

나: 너무 어려워서 완전히 망치**고 말**았어.

It was so difficult that I ended up completely failing.

▶ The auxiliary verb 말다 'to end up' is derived from the main verb 말다 'stop (doing)'. It takes the conjunctive suffix –고 'and' (instead of the usual suffix –아/어), as in 망하고 말았다 'ended up being ruined' and 완전히 죽고 말았다 'ended up completely dead'.

GU14.9

~을/를 전후하여 'before and after (a time), around'

가: 일본 사람들이 언제 한국으로 밀려들어 왔어요?

　　When did Japanese people flood into Korea?

나: 1910년**을 전후하여** 많이 들어왔어요.

　　Many arrived around 1910.

▶ This pattern occurs after a time word to indicate that an event occurs before and after the denoted time, as in 작년 말을 전후하여 'before and after (or around) the end of last year'. It is a contraction of ~을/를 전후로 하여 'taking the time as before and after', where the Sino–Korean 전 means 'front, before' and 후 'back, after' while the 'instrument' particle 로 means 'as'.

GU14.10

~(으)ㄹ 무렵(에) 'around the time when'

가: 이번 동해안 여행 재미있었어요?

　　Was your trip to the (Korean) East Coast fun?

나: 네, 그런데 집에 도착**할 무렵**에는 굉장히 피곤했어요.

Yes, but by the time we got home we were so exhausted.

▶ This pattern is composed of the 'prospective' modifier suffix –(으)ㄹ and the time noun 무렵 'an approximate time (when)' followed by the particle 에 'at, on, in, by'. It is also used without 에, as in 우리들은 해질 무렵(에) 집에 돌아왔다 'We came back home toward sunset'.

GU14.11

~와/과 동시에 'at the same time with; as soon as; upon'

가: 제 동생은 대학 입학**과 동시에** 군대에 갔어요.

My younger brother joined the military at the same time he enrolled in college.

나: 우리 형은 대학 졸업**과 동시에** 취직했어요.

My older brother got a job right upon graduating from college.

▶ The Sino–Korean noun 동시 means 'the same time'. It follows the particle 와/과 'with' to indicate 'simultaneously with' another event and precedes the 'location' particle 에 'at' to indicate the time point.

GU14.12

~(을/를) 당하다 'to suffer, undergo'

가: 스티브가 교통사고**를 당해서** 병원에 입원했어요.

Steve got in a traffic accident so he has been hospitalized.

나: 어머, 스티브는 제가 어려움**을 당할** 때 많이 도와준 친구예요. 병원에 가 봐야겠네요.

Oh my goodness, Steve is a friend of mine who helped me a lot when I was in a lot of trouble. I need to go to the hospital to check in on him.

▶ The Sino–Korean verbal noun 당 and the native verb 하다 form the compound 당하다 to mean 'suffer, undergo, encounter'. This compound verb occurs with an adversarial noun such as 거절 'refusal', 체포 'arrest', 파괴 'destruction', 파멸 'ruin', 창피 'humiliation', 불행 'disaster', 괴로움 'suffering', and 어려움 'difficulty'. The compound 당하다 is used as both a transitive verb, as in 거절을 당하다 'be rejected' (*lit*. 'encounter rejection') and an adversarial passive suffix, as in 거절당하다 'be rejected', without any difference in the meaning. When the adversarial noun is a native word or a modified Sino–Korean word, it must be used as a transitive verb, as in 나는 어려움을 당했다 'I suffered from a difficulty' and 나는 세 번째의 거절을 당했다 'I was rejected for the third time'. Otherwise, it is usually used as a suffix, as in 체포당하다 'be arrested', 파멸당하다 'be destroyed', and 창피당하다 'be humiliated'.

활동

가... 빈 칸에 알맞은 표현을 골라 넣으세요.

> 금지되다, 동원되다, 무시하다, 시달리다, 통치하다, 투하하다

1. 일본은 서울에 조선총독부를 설치하고 일본인 총독이 조선을 _____.

2. 한국의 젊은이들은 군인으로, 노무자로, 위안부로 _____.

3. 일제 식민지 기간 동안 학교나 모든 공공 기관에서 한국어 사용이 _____.

4. 일본이 포츠담 선언을 _____ 미국은 일본에 두 개의 원자 폭탄을

   _____.

5. 한국 국민은 착취와 차별에 _____.

나... 주어진 표현을 사용해서 다음 문장을 완성하세요.

1. ~을/를 구실로

스티브는 _____ 매일 집에 늦게 왔다.

2. ~고 말다

한국에서 모르는 곳에 갔다가 _____.

3. ~을/를 전후하여

_____ 많은 사람들이 한국에 관심이 많아졌다.

4. ~(으)ㄹ 무렵(에)

여행을 갔다가 _____ 집으로 돌아왔다.

5. ~와/과 동시에

한국 축구팀은 _____ 한 골을 넣었다.

6. ~을/를 당하다

친구에게 100달러를 빌려 달라고 했지만 _____.

다... 영어 문장의 의미와 같아지도록 맞는 표현을 골라서 밑줄을 그으세요.

> 한국이 일본보다 더 늦게 근대화했다 / <u>근대화됐다</u>.
> Korea became modernized later compared to Japan.

1. 정부가 조약을 무효화됐다 / 무효화했다.

The government nullified the agreement.

2. 국가가 민주화되려면 / 민주화하려면 정부는 선거를 해야 된다.

In order for a nation to become democratized, the government should hold elections.

3. 일본은 조선을 식민지화됐다 / 식민지화했다.

Japan colonized Chosŏn.

4. 수입이 드디어 자유화됐다 / 자유화했다.

The import has finally become liberalized.

5. 한국의 발전을 위해서는 기술이 현대화돼야 합니다 / 현대화해야 합니다.

For Korea's development, technology needs to be modernized.

라... 다음 단어 중 '~을/를 당하다' 형태로 쓸 수 있는 단어와 쓸 수 없는 단어를 나눠 보고 어떤 차이가 있는지 알아보세요.

		~을/를 당하다
공격	attack	○
경험	experience	×
구타	hitting	
보이콧	boycott	
사기	fraud	
사랑	love	
소개	introduction	
여행	trip	
운동	exercise	
이용	use; exploitation	
인사	greeting	
입학	admission to school	
죽음	death	
차별	discrimination	
취직	employment	
퇴학	expulsion from school	
파면	dismissal	
폭격	bombing	
프로포즈	proposal	
행복	happiness	

3·1운동

일제 강점기에 한국인은 일
본의 식민 통치에 반대하는
운동을 일으켰다. 국내에서는 물론, 일본, 중국, 미국, 러시아 등 해
외로 나간 한국인들은 독립운동을 계속했다. 가장 큰 독립운동은 고
종 황제의 장례 날인 1919년 3월 1일에 일어난 3·1 독립운동이었다.

　3·1운동은 독립선언서의 발표를 시작으로 약 2개월간 전국적으
로 약 200만 명이 참가했다. 3·1운동은 한일 병합 조약의 무효와 한
국의 독립을 선언했다. 일본은 한국인 7,500명의 사망자를 내면서 강
제로 3·1운동을 진압했다.

　그러나 해외로 나간 애국자들은 1919년 4월 13일 중국 상하이에
임시 정부를 수립했다. 이 임시 정부는 한국이 일본에서 해방될 때까
지 활동을 계속했다. 1919년부터 1925년까지 상하이 임시 정부의 대
통령이었던 이승만은 주로 미국에서 외교 중심의 독립운동을 벌였
다. 광복이 되자 이승만은 한국으로 돌아가 1948년 대한민국 정부의
초대 대통령이 되었다. 한국은 1919년 3월 1일에 일어난 독립 운동을
기념하기 위하여 3·1절을 국경일로 정하고 있다.

3·1운동 March First Movement 일으키다 to stir up 고종 황제 Emperor Kojong
장례 funeral 독립선언서 declaration of independence 전국적으로 nationally
참가하다 to participate 무효 nullity 사망자 the dead 진압하다 to suppress
애국자 patriot 상하이 Shanghai 임시 정부 provisional government 외교 diplomacy
수립하다 to establish 초대 the first 대통령 president 3·1절 Day of the March First
Movement 국경일 national holiday

한국어에 남아 있는 일본어 영향

일제 강점기에 일본은 한국 사회와 문화를 일본화하려고 했다. 일본 말을 쓰게 하고 이름도 일본식으로 바꾸게 했다. 일제 강점기는 한국의 전통 문화의 암흑 시대였다. 다른 한편으로는 한국은 일본을 통해 많은 서양 문화와 일본 문화를 받아들였다.

1. 영어나 다른 서양 말에서 들어온 단어의 예:
   (일제 강점기에는 일본식으로 발음됐으나 광복 후에는 영어식으로 바뀌었다.)

[일본식 발음]	→	[영어식 발음]	
고뿌	→	컵	cup
네꾸다이	→	넥타이	necktie
도나쓰	→	도넛	doughnut
라지오	→	라디오	radio
바께쓰	→	버킷	bucket
밧떼리	→	배터리	battery
빵꾸	→	펑크	puncture
뽐뿌	→	펌프	pump
비니루	→	비닐	vinyl
샤쓰	→	셔츠	shirt
세타	→	스웨터	sweater
아이스께끼	→	아이스 케이크	ice cake (ice pop)

2. 일본어에서 들어온 단어의 예:

가방	bag
나시	sleeveless shirt
구두	leather shoes
스시	sushi (Japanese delicacy)
오뎅	fishcake
우동	Japanese noodle dish
라면	ramen

3. 한국에서 쓰고 있는 한자어는 과반수(majority)가 일본에서 들어온 것이다. 일본은 많은 서양어를 한자어로 번역했고 그렇게 만든 한자어는 한국에 들어와 한국식으로 읽혔다. "학교, 중학교, 고등학교, 대학교, 대학원, 교장 'principal', 총장 'university president', 학년, 박사 'PhD', 석사 'MA', 학사 'BA, BS', 시험, 국어, 영어, 외국어, 수학, 과학 'science', 공학 'engineering', 정치학 'political science', 경제학, 음악, 미술" 등은 모두 일본에서 들어온 교육에 관한 단어들이다.

4. 일본은 또 많은 일본말을 한자어로 바꾸었다. 그러한 일본말 한자어는 일본에서는 일본말로 읽지만 한국에 들어와서는 한자음으로 발음한다. 예:

[한자어]	[일본어 발음]	
건물 建物	tate-mono	building
견습 見習	mi-narai	internship
시합 試合	shi-ai	contest, match

엽서 葉書	ha-gaki	postcard
입구 入口	iri-kuchi	entrance
입장 立場	tachi-ba	standpoint
추월 追越	oi-koshi	passing (another car)
출구 出口	de-guchi	exit
취급 取扱	tori-atsukai	handling
할인 割引	wari-biki	discount

▮▮ 번역문 ▮▮

CONVERSATION:
Life of Koreans during the Japanese Colonial Period

Chang, a reporter from *Sahoe Ilbo*, is interviewing Professor Sohn, a Han'guk University professor

Reporter Chang: How are you, Professor? It has been a long time since I saw you.

Professor Sohn: Yes, it really has been a long time. You are still busy these days, right?

Reporter: Yes. I have been busy reporting every day. And, as I briefly told you earlier by phone, our newspaper is preparing an Independence Day special report. We are planning to write an article centered around the stories of the elderly people's experiences during the Japanese occupation.

Professor: It's been so long now, I don't know how much I'll remember.

Reporter: Excuse me, but may I ask how old you are this year?

Professor: I was born in 1933.

Reporter: Then you must have been in elementary school during the period of the Japanese occupation, right?

Professor: Yes. When Korea was liberated from Japan in 1945, I was in sixth grade in elementary school.

Reporter: Then you must have experienced World War II all during the time when you were in elementary school.

Professor: Right. When I was in first grade of elementary school, Hitler's German army invaded Poland, and World War II broke out.

Reporter: It must have been the Pacific War that made life difficult for Korean people.

Professor: That's right. The Pacific War began on December 8th, 1941, which was the 7th in the U.S., when Japan attacked an American fleet at Pearl Harbor in Hawaii. The hardship that Korean people had to bear because of the three years and nine months of war was unspeakable.

Reporter: Can you tell me about an experience that comes to your mind when you think of your war experiences?

Professor: We believed that we were Japanese citizens, then. When we entered elementary school, we had to memorize the "Oath of Subjects of the Japanese Empire." So, we thought of the U.S. and Britain as our enemies; therefore, we made all sorts of sacrifices for Japan's war victory.

Reporter: I heard that they did not allow the use of Korean in school during the Japanese colonial era.

Professor: If we spoke Korean at school, we were punished. During that time, at every morning assembly we bowed down facing in the direction of Tokyo, where the Japanese emperor lived.

Reporter: I heard that Korean people had to change their names.

Professor: Yes. They made us change our names to Japanese names. I too, of course had to change my name to a Japanese name. That wasn't all. Whenever Korean young men left for the war, we went out with Japanese flags to send them off. We dedicated a lot of rice to the Japanese military. Also, we even gave brassware and spoon-and-chopsticks sets to make weapons.

Reporter: Then, how was school work during the war?

Professor: We were hardly able to have classes when I was in fifth and sixth grade.

Reporter: Why was that?

Professor: Since the young men were away at war, we elementary school students helped with farming. In the spring we planted rice, getting bitten by leeches. In the fall, we cut rice crops with sickles. Then, we went to the mountain and dug up the roots of pine trees.

Reporter: Pine tree roots? Why pine tree roots?

Professor: They said they used the oil from pine tree roots as fuel for fighter jets.

Reporter: You had a very hard time as a child.

Professor: Now that I think back, we had nothing to live for (lit., lived because we could not die). We lived on bread made with chaff, ate pine bark, and had stomachaches.

Reporter: Then, Japan finally fell.

Professor: Yes. On August 15th, 1945 starting at 12 noon, the words from the Japanese emperor's voice repeating "unconditional surrender" came from the radio. It meant that Korea was finally liberated.

Reporter: You truly suffered greatly. Today, because of a time constraint, I should probably stop here. Thank you for your wonderful input. Thank you again for taking the time out of your busy schedule. I'll see you again next time.

READING: Colonial Rule of the Japanese Empire and the Pacific War

Korea was a Japanese colony for 35 years. On August 29th, 1910, Japan forced Korea (Chosŏn) to become a Japanese colony. Since the Japanese Empire forcefully invaded the Korean Peninsula, this period is called the period of colonial (*lit.* forced) occupation by the Japanese imperialism. Until it became a Japanese colony, the Korean Peninsula was the Chosŏn Dynasty.

Japan's invasion of Korea began with the Unyo incident. In 1875, the Japanese warship, the Unyo, illegally entered Ganghwa Island, and fought in a war with Chosŏn troops. Using this incident as an excuse, Japan forced Korea to open the ports of Busan, Incheon, and Wonsan to the Japanese.

When the ports opened, not only the Japanese, but foreigners of the Chinese Qing Dynasty, Russia, etc., also surged into Chosŏn. The surrounding countries of China's Qing Dynasty, Japan, and Russia fought to control Korea. Japan won in the Sino-Japanese War (1894–1895) and Russo-Japanese War (1904–1905). As a result, Japan gained Taiwan from Qing and the southern half of Sakhalin from Russia.

Japan continued its efforts to colonize Korea, finally annexing the Korean Empire into Japan, forcing the Korea-Japan Annexation Treaty in 1910. As such, the Chosŏn Dynasty fell after 519 years.

Around 1910, 700,000 Japanese rushed into Korea. Japan established a Chosŏn governor-general's office in Seoul, and the Japanese governor-general ruled Chosŏn. The Korean people suffered exploitation and discrimination. Japan took away not only Korean cultural assets, resources, and property, but also history and language, etc. Use of the Korean language was forbidden in all public institutions, including schools. They had all Korean people change names to a Japanese one.

Japan attacked an American fleet in Pearl Harbor, Hawaii on December 7th, 1941

and declared war on the United States. The Pacific War of 3 years and 9 months began. During the Pacific War, life was more difficult for Koreans. Under the name of
"Korea and Japan are One" Policy, young Koreans were mobilized as soldiers, labor-
ers, and comfort women.

Around the time of the end of World War II, the United States had bombed 67
Japanese cities in 1945. On July 26th, 1945, the United States, Great Britain, and the
Republic of China announced the Potsdam Declaration. The Soviet Union signed the
Declaration at the same time of entering the war. The gist of the Declaration is that
Japan would face "prompt and utter destruction" if Japan did not surrender, and Jap-
anese sovereignty shall be limited to the islands of Honshu, Hokkaido, Kyushu, and
such minor islands as the Allies determine.

As Japan ignored the Declaration, the United States dropped two atomic bombs
in Japan. One was on the city of Hiroshima on August 6th, and the other was on the
city of Nagasaki on August 9th. Subsequently, the Soviet Union declared war on Japan and began to fight in a war in the Manchurian country that Japan established
and Cheongjin in North Korea. As a result, Emperor Hirohito declared unconditional
surrender on August 15th, 1945.

Sovereignty on the Korean Peninsula has returned to the Korean people. Ko-
rea celebrates August 15th as National Liberation Day (*lit*. The Day of Regaining the
Light) when Korea was liberated from Japan. However, in order to prevent the Soviet
Union from occupying the entire Korean Peninsula, the U.S. agreed with the Soviet
Union to have Soviet military stationed north of the 38th degree parallel line of latitude (*samp'al-sŏn*) and U.S. military stationed to the south. As a result, the Korean
Peninsula was divided into two Koreas. Almost all of Japanese who lived in Korea
returned to Japan, but the colonial rule by Japan has left Korea with a wound that is
too difficult for Korea to cope with.

FURTHER READING: March First Movement

During the period of Japanese colonial occupation of Korea, Koreans launched cam-
paigns against the Japanese colonial rule. Not only at home but Koreans abroad,
including those in Japan, China, the United States, Russia, etc., continued indepen-

dence movements. The largest independence movement was Samil Undong or the March First Movement of March 1st, 1919, the day of Emperor Kojong's funeral.

Starting with a declaration of independence, approximately 2 million people nationwide participated in the March First Movement for about two months. The March First Movement declared the Korea-Japan Annexation Treaty invalid and Korea's independence. Japan forcefully suppressed the March First Movement causing 7,500 deaths. However, patriots who went abroad set up the Provisional Government of the Republic of Korea in Shanghai, China on April 13th, 1919. The interim government was established on the basis of the March First Declaration of Independence and continued to be active until Korea was liberated from Japan.

Syngman Rhee, who was president of the Provisional Government of the Republic of Korea in Shanghai from 1919 to 1925, was engaged in the independence movement chiefly through diplomacy in the United States. Upon Korea's liberation from Japan, Syngman Rhee returned to Korea and was elected the first president of the Republic of Korea. Korea legislated March 1st as a holiday to commemorate the independence movement that took place on March 1st, 1919.

CULTURE:
The Influence of Japanese that Remains on the Korean Language

During the Japanese colonial occupation of Korea, Japan tried to Japanize Korean society and culture. Japan forced Koreans to use Japanese and change names to the Japanese style. The period of Japanese occupation was a dark age of Korean culture. On the other hand, Korea imported through Japan, many aspects of Western and Japanese culture.

1. Examples of cultural words from English and other Western languages (during the Japanese occupation, they were pronounced in the Japanese style, but, since the liberation, they have been pronounced in the English style) as in the following:

Japanese-style pronunciation → **English-style pronunciation**

koppu	→	khŏp	'cup'
nekkutai	→	nekt'ai	'necktie'
toonassu	→	tonŏt	'doughnut'
rajio	→	ratio	'radio'
pakkessŭ	→	pŏk'it	'bucket'
pattterii	→	paet'ŏri	'battery'
ppangkku	→	p'ŏngk'ŭ	'puncture' (as in tires)
ppomppu	→	p'ŏmp'ŭ	'pump'
piniru	→	pinil	'vinyl'
syassŭ	→	syŏch'ŭ	'shirt'
seettaa	→	swet'ŏ	'sweater'
aisŭkeikki	→	aisŭk'eik'ŭ	'ice cake' (ice pop)

2. Examples of culture words from Japan:

kabang	'bag'
nasi	'sleeveless shirt'
kudu	'leather shoes'
sŭsi	'sushi'
odeng	'fishcake'
udong	'Japanese noodle dish'
ramyen	'ramen'

3. The majority of Sino-Korean words were imported from Japan. Many Western cultural words were translated into Sino-Japanese in Japan. Such Sino-Japanese words came into Korea and were pronounced in Sino-Korean. Examples of education-related culture words imported from Japan include school, intermediate school, high school, university, graduate school, principal, university president, grade, PhD, MA, BA/BS, exam, national language, English, foreign language, math, science, engineering, political science, economics, music, and art.

4. Many Japanese native words were written in Sino-Japanese in Japan. Such Sino-Japanese words are read in Japanese as native words, but in Korean, they are read like any other Sino-Korean words. Examples include:

Sino-Korean	Native Japanese	
건물 (建物)	*tate-mono*	'building'
견습 (見習)	*mi-narai*	'internship'
시합 (試合)	*si-ai*	'contest, match'
엽서 (葉書)	*ha-gaki*	'postcard'
입구 (入口)	*iri-kuchi*	'entrance'
입장 (立場)	*tatchi-ba*	'standpoint'
추월 (追越)	*oi-kkosi*	'passing'
출구 (出口)	*de-kutchi*	'exit'
취급 (取扱)	*tori-assukai*	'handling'
할인 (割引)	*wari-bikki*	'discount'

▦ 단어 ▦

3·1운동	March First Movement	낫	sickle
3·1절	Day of the March First Movement	내선일체	Japan-Korea one body
		노무자	laborer
감당하다	to cope with	놋그릇	brassware
강제로	by force	당시	those days
개항하다	to open a port	대통령	president
거머리	leech	대한제국	Korean Empire
겨	chaff	독립선언서	declaration of independence
겪다	to experience	독일	Germany
경험담	story of one's personal experiences	동시에	simultaneously
		동원되다	to be mobilized
경험하다	to experience	되찾다	to recover
고종 황제	Emperor Kojong	되풀이되다	to be repeated
공공 기관	public institutions	러일 전쟁	Russo-Japanese War
공습하다	to make an air raid	막을 내리다	to come to an end
광복	restoration of independence	말할 수 없다	to be beyond description
광복절	National Liberation Day	망하다	to perish, ruin
구실	excuse	맹세	oath
국경일	national holiday	맺다	to conclude
국기	national flag	모를 심다	to plant rice sprouts
국민	citizen	무기	weapon
국호	name of a country	무렵	around the time when
군함	battleship	무시하다	to ignore
귀중하다	to be important, precious	무조건	unconditional
금지되다	to be prohibited	무효	nullity
기념하다	to commemorate	문화재	cultural assets
기사	news (article)	밀려들다	to surge into
껍질	bark	바치다	to give, offer
날	day	배탈이 나다	to have a stomachache
남기다	to leave	벌을 받다	to be punished

벼를 베다	to mow rice plants	원자 폭탄	atomic bomb
북위	north latitude	위안부	comfort women
불법으로	illegally	이리하여	in this way
빛	light	일으키다	to stir up
빼앗다	to rob	일제 (= 일본 제국)	Japanese occupation
사건	incident	강점기	period
사망자	the dead	임시 정부	provisional government
사할린	Sakhalin	자원	resources
상처	wound	장례	funeral
상하이	Shanghai	재산	property
사회일보	*Sahoe Ilbo*	적	enemy
서명하다	to sign	전국적으로	nationally
선전 포고	declaration of war	전쟁터	battlefield
설치하다	to establish	전투	battle
세우다	to erect	전투기	fighter plane
소나무 뿌리	pine-tree root	전투를 벌이다	to fight a battle
수립하다	to establish	제2차 세계 대전	World War II
수저	spoon and chopsticks	조선 왕조	Chosŏn Dynasty
승리	victory	조회	morning assembly
시기	period	주권	sovereignty
식민 통치	colonial rule	주둔하다	to be stationed
암흑 시대	dark age	즉각적	immediate
애국자	patriot	지배하다	to control
어르신	esteemed elder	진압하다	to suppress
어린 시절	childhood	진주만	Pearl Harbor
~에 국한되다	to be limited to	차별	discrimination
~에 시달리다	to suffer from	착취	exploitation
여쭈다	to say, ask (to a senior)	참가하다	to participate
온갖	all kinds of	천황	emperor
올해	this year	청나라	Qing Empire of China
외교	diplomacy	청일 전쟁	the Sino-Japanese War
외우다	to recite	초대	the first
요지	gist	총독부	governor-general's office

취재하다	to collect news data	한민족	Korean people
침공하다	to invade, attack	한일 병합 조약	Korea-Japan Annexation
침략	invasion		Treaty
캐다(=파내다)	to dig out	함대	fleet
태평양 전쟁	the Pacific War	항복	surrender
투하되다	to be air-dropped	해방되다	to be liberated
특집	special edition	환송하다	to give a hearty send-off
파멸	destruction	황국 신민	royal subject of
포츠담 선언	the Potsdam Declaration		Japanese Empire
폭격	bombing	훑어보다	to look through
폭격하다	to bombard	희생	sacrifice

▓ Grammar and Usages Index ▓

Item	Meaning	GU
~게도	indeed, enough	GU10.9
~고 말다	to end up with	GU14.8
~곤 하다	habitually does, used to	GU14.5
그건 그렇고	by the way; now; on a different note; so that's that	GU9.5
그런 줄도 모르고	without knowing it was the case; being unaware of such a fact	GU12.10
그런가 하면	whereas; on the other hand	GU12.11
그렇다고 ~(으)/ㄹ 수도 없다	even so, it is not right to; even so, (one) cannot	GU12.8
그렇잖아도	as a matter of fact, in fact	GU13.3
~기가 무섭게	as soon as	GU12.5
기왕이면	if that is the case anyway	GU11.9
~끼리	among/by ourselves/themselves; in groups (of)	GU9.4
끼치다	to cause, exert	GU11.7
~느니 (차라리)	would rather … than'	GU10.3
~는/(으)ㄴ 데다가	not only … but also; additionally	GU13.10
~는/(으)ㄴ 거겠지(요)	it may be that, I guess that	GU11.5
~는/(으)ㄴ걸요	indeed, despite anticipations or reservations to the contrary	GU11.3
~는/(으)ㄴ 바람에	because of, as a result of (an unexpected cause)	GU13.2
~다 못해	unable to	GU10.1
~다 보니(까)	while doing … (one realizes that)	GU9.8
~다가는	do … and then; if … (with negative consequence)	GU11.12
~다고 되는 일이 아니다	it wouldn't work even though; just because …, it would be all right	GU12.9
~다고/라고 해서	be called (entitled; known as) … and (so/then)	GU11.11
~다니까(요)	I told you that	GU10.7
~다시피	(just) as	GU9.1
~단/란 말이다	(I) mean	GU12.7

▪▪ Korean-English Glossary ▪▪

3·1운동	March First Movement	건조하다	to be dry
3·1절	Day of the March First Movement	건축물	building, structure
		걸리다	to be caught
38선(삼팔선)	38th parallel	겨	chaff
–가량	about, almost	겨우내	throughout the winter
가로지르다	to cut across	격언	maxim
가슴(이) 아프다	to be heartbroken	겪다	to experience
가입하다	to join	견디다	to endure
각각	each	겸하다	to combine
각종	various kinds	–경	around …, about …
감다	to wind up, coil up	경계선	line of demarcation
감당하다	to cope with	경기	game, match
감동하다	to be impressed	경제력	economic power
감성적	to be emotional	경험담	story of one's personal experiences
감정	emotion		
강제로	by force	경험하다	to experience
강조	emphasis	계약하다	to contract
갚다	to repay	계획을 세우다	to make a plan
갚아 주다	to pay back	고궁	ancient palace
개강	beginning of semester in college	고급	high-level; advanced
		고르다	to choose, select
개방되다	to be open to	고시원	small studios mostly for government test takers
개선문	triumphal arch		
개성	individuality	고약하다	to be nasty
개항하다	to open a port	고종 황제	Emperor Kojong
거머리	leech	고층 빌딩	skyscraper
거북	turtle	고치다	to fix
거실	living room	곤란하다	to be awkward
건국하다	to found a country	공간	space
건설사	construction firm	공공 기관	public institutions

공공장소	public place or area	국경 지대	national border area
공동	common; public	국경선	national border line
공동체	community	국경일	national holiday
공무원	public official, public servant	국기	national flag
		국민	citizen
공습하다	to make an air raid	국제전	international war
공유	sharing	국호	name of a country
공화국	republic	국화	chrysanthemum
과거¹	old government official exam	군대	military
		군복무	military service
과거²	past	군사 분계선	Military Demarcation Line
과학적 근거	scientific basis	군사	military
관계	relationship	군인	soldier
관리하다	to supervise	군함	battleship
관습	custom; convention	군	military
광복	restoration of independence	굳세다	strong and firm
		굳이	particularly
광복절	National Liberation Day	궁금하다	to be curious
괴로워하다	to be in agony	권위	authority
교내	on campus	귀신	ghost
교육 환경	educational environment	귀중하다	to be important, precious
교환	exchange	규모	scale, size
교훈	lesson	그 외에도	in addition
구	district (of a city)	그대로	as it is
구박하다	to mistreat	그릇	bowl
구분되다	to be categorized	그리하여	therefore
구성	composition	극복하다	to overcome
구성원	member	근거	basis
구실	excuse	금물	taboo
구전	oral tradition handed down verbally	금액	amount of money
		금전적	monetary
구하다¹	to obtain	금지 사항	prohibited matters
구하다²	to rescue	금지되다	to be prohibited

급속하게	rapidly	낫	sickle
기관	organization, institution, agency	내용물	content items
		냉전	the Cold War
기념하다	to commemorate	넘다	to cross over
기둥	pillar	넘쳐 나다	to overflow
기러기	wild geese	네 잎 클로버	four-leaf clover
기사	news (article)	노동력	manpower
기온	air temperature	노무자	laborer
기왕이면	if that is the case anyway	노선	line, route
기원하다	to pray, wish	노인	elderly person
기후	climate	노크하다	to knock
김매기	weeding	녹아 있다	to be steeped
김장	kimchi making for the winter		(*lit.*, melted) in
		놈	dude
까다롭다	particular	놋그릇	brassware
까치	magpie	농업	farming
껍질	bark	농촌 봉사 활동	volunteer service in farming communities
꼼꼼하다	to be meticulous, precise		
꽂다	to stick into	놓치고 말다	to end up losing
꽃다발	bouquet	눈물	tears
꿈을 꾸다	to dream	눈을 뜨다	to open one's eyes
꿩	pheasant	눈치 보이다	to care about what others think
–끼리	among or by ourselves or themselves		
		다가가다	to go near
끼치다	to cause	다들	everyone
나뉘다	to be divided	다리를 떨다	to shake one's leg
나무꾼	lumberjack	다행	luck, fortune
낙후되다	to lag behind	단과대(=단과대학)	college or school of a university
날	day		
날카롭다	to be sharp	단기간	short term
남기다	to leave	단독 주택	single-unit house
남북 관계	South Korea-North Korea relations	단둘이	just the two persons (adv.)
		단위	units

단지	complex	동²	neighborhood
단체	group	동경하다	to yearn
단풍	autumn foliage	동기	classmate
달아나다	to run away	동시에	at the same time,
담그다	to make fermented food		simultaneously
당	political party	동아리	club
당시¹	at that time	동아리명	club name
당시²	then, in those days	동원되다	to be mobilized
당연히	naturally	돼지	pig
당첨되다	to win (a prize)	되찾다	to recover
닿다	to touch, reach	되풀이되다	to be repeated
대가족	large family	두드리다	to tap
대담하다	to be bold, daring	두려움	fear
대동제	college festival	둘러싸이다	to be surrounded
대부분	most of, mostly (=거의)	둘레	perimeter
대상	object	드나들다	to come in and go out
대중문화	popular culture	든든하다	to feel secure
대치하다	to confront	들다	to enter
대통령	president of a country	들키다	to get caught
대하다	to deal with	등장인물	character (in book, story)
대한제국	Korean Empire	등장하다	to appear
대회	contest	등재되다	to be registered
더하다	to add	따라가다	to follow
도망가다	to escape	딸리다	to run short
도망치다	to run away	땅	land
도시	city	떨어지다	to drop
도움을 받다	to receive help	뛰어나다	to be outstanding
도저히	utterly; absolutely	러일 전쟁	Russo-Japanese War
독립선언서	declaration of independence	로또	lotto
독일	Germany	리더십	leadership
돌아가다	to go around and take turns	마련	owning; preparation
돌아오다	to return	마을	village
동¹	counter for building	–마저	even, as well

막막하다	to feel lost and gloomy
막을 내리다	to come to an end
막히다	to be jammed
만료	expiration
말을 걸다	to initiate a conversation
말투	one's way of speaking
말할 수 없다	to be beyond description
망하다	to perish, ruin
매료시키다	to attract
맹세	oath
맺다	to conclude
머지않아	in a short time, soon
며느리	daughter-in-law
면접일	interview date
모내기	rice planting
모를 심다	to plant rice sprouts
모습	appearance, looks, figure
목돈	lump sum of money
목숨을 건지다	to escape death
목숨을 잃다	to lose one's life
목적	aim
몰래	secretly
못지않다	to be just as good as
무기	weapon
무덤	grave, tomb
무덥다	to be humid and hot, to be muggy
무렵	around the time when
무사하다	to be safe
무슬림	Muslim
무시하다	to ignore
무조건	unconditional
무지	really, very

무표정하다	to be expressionless
무효	nullity
묵다	to stay, put up
문자	text message
문지방	threshold
문화 시설	cultural facilities
문화재	cultural assets
물가	cost of living
물대기	irrigation
미덕	virtue
미신	superstition
밀려들다	to surge into
밀접하다	to be closely related
밀집	to be concentrated
밉다	to hate
바치다	to give, offer
바탕	base
반복되다	to be repeated
발발하다	to break out
발음	pronunciation
발전하다	to develop
밤새	all night long
밥상	dining table
방음	soundproof
방지하다	to prevent
방향	direction
–배	-fold
배려	consideration
배탈이 나다	to have a stomachache
뱀	snake
버릇	habit
벌을 받다	to be punished
법	law

벗어나다	to deviate, get out of	비판	criticism
벼를 베다	to mow rice plants	빌려 쓰다	to borrow (and use)
변덕스럽다	to be unpredictable	빌리다	to borrow
변화하다	to change	빛	light
병역 의무	compulsory duty of	빼앗다	to rob
	military service	사건	incident
보증금	deposit	사고방식	way of thinking
보편화	generalization	사교적이다	to be sociable
복	luck	사다리	ladder
복원되다	to be restored	사대문	the four main gates of old
볼 만하다	to be worth seeing		Seoul
봉황	phoenix	사라져 가다	to evanesce
봐주다	to help	사망자	the dead
부	richness	사망하다	to die
부각되다	to stand out	사상	thought, idea
부동산	real estate (agent)	사은회	teacher-appreciation
부러워하다	to be envious		banquet
부족하다	to be lacking	사할린	Sakhalin
부채	fan	사회자	emcee
부탁하다	to make a request	산업 시설	industrial facilities
북위	north latitude	살려 주다	to save one's life
북쪽	northern side	상가	household in mourning
분단	division	상대방	the other party
분량	amount	상류층	the upper class
분리되다	to be separated	상상	imagination
분수	fountain	상승	increase
분위기	atmosphere	상점	store, shop
불가능하다	to be impossible	상처	wound
불리다	to be called	상품	product
불법으로	illegally	상하이	Shanghai
불운	bad luck	사회일보	*Sahoe Ilbo*
불행하다	to be unlucky	새	bird
비무장지대	Demilitarized Zone (DMZ)	새내기 배움터	college orientation

새옹지마	the irony of fate	수강 신청 변경	change of course
생활용품	daily necessities		registration
생활하다	to live	수도	capital city of a country
서명하다	to sign	수도권	metropolitan area
서서히	gradually	수도세	water bills
석가탄신일	Buddha's Birthday	수립하다	to establish
선녀	fairy	수시	early college exam
선선하다	(weather) to be cool and	수여식	conferment ceremony
	refreshing	수입	income
선악	good and evil	수저	spoon and chopsticks
선전 포고	declaration of war	수준	level, standard
선풍기	electric fan	수학여행	school or class trip
선호하다	to prefer	술잔	glass for alcohol
설치하다	to establish	숨을 쉬다	to breathe
설화	folktales, fairy tales	스님	monk
섭씨	Celsius	스승	teacher, mentor
성	castle	승리	victory
성실하다	to be faithful, sincere	시간(이) 되다	to have time
성장하다	to grow	시기	period
성형 수술	plastic surgery	시대적	time period; periodic
세대	generation	시설	facilities
세련되다	to be sophisticated	시어머니	mother-in-law
세우다	to erect	시켜 주다	to let or allow someone/
소가죽	cowhide		something
소나무 뿌리	pine tree root	식료품	groceries
소련	the Soviet Union	식문화	eating culture
소속감	sense of belonging	식민 통치	colonial rule
소식	news	신성하다	to be sacred
소심하다	to be timid	신중하다	to be cautious
손수건	handkerchief	신체	body
손실	loss	실내	interior
손톱/발톱을 깎다	to clip one's fingernail/	실용성	practicality
	toenail	심지어	even; what is more

싸우다	to fight	~에 시달리다	to suffer from
쌍	pair of	여겨지다	to be considered, regarded
쓰이다	to be written	여기다	to consider
쏘다	to shoot	여쭈다	to say, ask (to a senior)
아내	one's wife	역사 유적	remains of history
아마(도)	maybe	연결하다	to connect
아예	to begin with	연상시키다	to remind
안전	safety	연예인	celebrity
안정	stability	연합	alliance
안타깝다	to be pitiful	연합군	the Allied Forces
알려지다	to become known	열대야	tropical night
암흑 시대	dark age	열망	desire
애국자	patriot	엿	Korean-style sticky taffy
애정운	being lucky in love	영상	video
약화되다	to be weakened	영향	effect
양	sheep	예술	arts
양식	style, way	예술적	artistic
어느	one	예의에 어긋나다	to go against etiquette
어르신	esteemed elder	예전	former days; the old days
어린 시절	childhood	오해하다	to misunderstand
어린이날	Children's Day	온갖	all kinds of
어민	fisherman	온순하다	to be gentle, docile
어버이날	Parents' Day	올해	this year
어색하다	to be awkward	옮기다	to move
어여쁘다	to be pretty	왕래하다	to come and go
어쩐지	no wonder; somehow	외교	diplomacy
어항	fish tank	외래어	loan word
어휘	vocabulary	외우다	to recite
얼른	quickly	요지	gist
엄격하다	to be strict	욕실	bathroom
엄청	awfully, very	용	dragon
업무	business	용맹함	brevity
~에 국한되다	to be limited to	우유부단하다	to be indecisive

운동회	sports day	이리하여	in this way
운이 좋다	to be lucky	이별	farewell
원래	originally	이산가족	separated families
원룸	studio	이야기를 나누다	to talk (with)
원자 폭탄	atomic bomb	이어주다	to connect
월세	monthly rent	이웃	neighbor
위로하다	to comfort	이전	previous
위안부	comfort women	익숙하다	to be familiar
위치하고 있다	to be located	인구	population
위험하다	to be dangerous	인생	life
유난히	especially, exceptionally	인절미	Korean traditional rice cake
유네스코 인류무형	UNESCO Intangible		coated with bean flour
문화유산 대표목록	Cultural Heritage	일단	first of all
	Representative List	일반적인	usual, general
유용하다	to be useful	일상	daily routine
유익하다	to be helpful;	일상생활	daily life
	to be instructive	일손	worker, hand
유일한	only, sole	일어나다	to occur, break out
유치원	kindergarten	일으키다	to stir up
유형	type	일정	fixed, set
육각형	hexagon	일제 (= 일본 제국)	Japanese occupation
~(으)ㄹ 비롯한	including …	강점기	period
은혜	kindness	잃다	to lose
은혜를 입다	to be indebted to	임대	rented; leased
의리	loyalty	임대료	rental fee
의식	consciousness	임시 정부	provisional government
의약품	medicine and medical	입학식	entrance ceremony
	supplies		of school
이기적	selfish	입학식장	entrance to ceremony hall
이끌다	to lead	자리잡다	to settle
이동하다	to move, travel	자신	oneself
이루어 내다	to pull something off	자원	resources
이르다	to reach	자유롭게	freely

작업	work	전투를 벌이다	to have a fight
장기 자랑	talent show	전해지다	to go down
장기간	long term	절벽	cliff
장례	funeral	젊은이	young person
장례를 치르다	to hold a funeral	점쟁이	fortune teller
장례식	funeral	접속사	conjunction
장마	rainy season	정부	government
장수	longevity	정상	top, summit
장애인	handicapped person	정서	emotion; sentiment
재물운	being fortunate in property	정성껏	with one's utmost sincerity
재산	property	정해 주다	to decide (something for
재수(가) 없다	to be unlucky		someone)
저렴하다	to be cheap	제2차 세계 대전	World War II
저축하다	to save money	제도	system
적	enemy	제한되다	to be limited
적극적이다	to be active	조마조마하다	to be anxious
적용하다	to apply	조선 왕조	Chosŏn Dynasty
적응	adaptation	–조차	even
적응하다	to adjust	조회	morning assembly
전 재산	one's entire assets	종교	religion
전국적으로	nationally	종료	end
전기세	electricity bill	종소리	peal or sound of bells
전달되다	to be delivered	종을 울리다	to ring a bell
전달하다	to deliver	종을 치다	to hit a bell
전설	legend	주거	residence
전세	long-term lease with large	주권	sovereignty
	sum deposit as a rental	주둔하다	to be stationed
전액	total amount	주방	kitchen
전쟁기념관	The War Memorial of Korea	주변	surroundings, vicinity
전쟁	war	주요	major, main
전쟁터	battlefield	주의하다	to be careful
전투	battle	줄이다	to shorten
전투기	fighter plane	중간시험	midterm examination

중순	middle ten days of a month	찹쌀떡	sticky rice cake
중심	center	창호지	traditional Korean paper
중심지	center, hub	천황	emperor
중요시되다	to be considered to be important	철거되다	to be torn down
		청나라	Qing Empire of China
쥐	mice	청바지	jeans
즉각적	immediate	청일 전쟁	the Sino-Japanese War
즐겨 먹다	to enjoy eating (frequently)	체육	sports, physical education
		체험	experience
지갑	wallet	초	beginning (of)
지경	situation	초대	the first
지나다	to pass	초중고	elementary, middle, and high schools
지리	geography		
지배하다	to control	초청	invitation
지어지다	to be built	총독부	governor-general's office
지역	area, region	최대	biggest
지형	geographical features	추측하다	to guess
지혜	wisdom	축제	festival
진압하다	to suppress	충고하다	to advise
진주만	Pearl Harbor	취급하다	to handle
집단주의	collectivism, groupism	취재하다	to collect news data
집세	house rent	침공하다	to invade, attack
집주인	landlord	침략	invasion
징크스	jinx	칭찬	compliment
차라리	rather	칸	cell
차별	discrimination	칼	knife, blade
차이	difference	캐다(=파내다)	to dig out
차차	gradually	키우다	to raise
착취	exploitation	타다	to burn
참가하다	to participate	탈북하다	to escape from North Korea
참다못해	beyond one's endurance	탈출하다	to escape
참여하다	to participate	태평양 전쟁	the Pacific War
참전하다	to enter a war	털털하다	to be easygoing

템플스테이	experiencing temple life ("temple stay")	품앗이	communal sharing of labor
토끼	rabbit	품질	quality
토산품	local product	풍수	feng shui, geomancy
통일	unification	풍습	custom
통치하다	to rule, govern	피를 흘리다	to shed blood
통행증	pass (card)	피하다	to avoid
퇴학당하다	to be expelled from a school	피해를 입다	to be damaged
투하되다	to be air-dropped	필	a counter for horses and large animals meaning 'head'
뛰다	to stand out		
특별하다	to be special	필수적	necessary
특집	special edition	하루빨리	as soon as possible
파괴되다	to be destroyed	하순	last ten days of a month
파내다	to dig out	학	crane
파멸	destruction	학생회관	student center
판단하다	to judge	학술	academics
팔각형	octagon	학위	degree
팔짱을 끼다	to link arms	한국 전쟁	the Korean War
패션	fashion	한꺼번에	at once all together
펴다	to unfold, spread	한눈에	at one sight
편의	convenience	한민족	Korean people
평	units to measure space in Korea, about 35.5 square feet	한반도	Korean Peninsula
		한여름	midsummer
		한일 병합 조약	Korea-Japan Annexation Treaty
평가되다	to be evaluated		
평가하다	to evaluate	한자	Chinese character
평균	average	함대	fleet
평화	peace	합리적이다	to be rational
포츠담 선언	the Potsdam Declaration	합의하다	to agree
포함되다	to be included	항복	surrender
폭격	bombing	해결되다	to resolve
폭격하다	to bombard	해결하다	to resolve
표지판	sign, notice	해내다	to accomplish

해당하다	correspond; applicable to	화산 작용	volcanic action
해방되다	to be liberated	화살	arrow
해태	*haetae* (a unicorn lion)	화재	fire (disaster)
핵심 계층	the core social class of North Korea	화합하다	to unite in harmony
		화해	reconciliation
햇살	sunlight	확인하다	to check
행동	behavior	환송하다	to give a hearty send-off
행사	event	활	bow
행운	good luck	활발하다	to be outgoing
행정구역	administrative district	활용하다	to utilize; apply
현대식	modern style	황국 신민	royal subject of Japanese Empire
현실적	realistic		
현재	present	황사	yellow dust
혈액형	blood type	횡재	unexpected fortune
협동심	cooperative attitude	훌륭하다	to be magnificent
협력	cooperation	훑어보다	to look through
형성되다	to be formed	휘장	insignia
형태	form; format	휘파람을 불다	to whistle
호	counter for unit	휴강	lecture cancellation
호랑이	tiger	휴식 공간	rest area
호응	positive response	휴일	holiday
혼란	confusion, chaos	휴전 협정	armistice agreement
혼자	alone	흐르다	to flow
홍수	flood	흔히	commonly, often
화려하다	to be fancy	희생	sacrifice
화병	emotional disorder from suppressed anger	힌두교도	Hindu

■■ English-Korean Glossary ■■

38th parallel	38선(삼팔선)	at the same time, simultaneously	동시에
about, almost	–가량	atmosphere	분위기
academics	학술	atomic bomb	원자 폭탄
adaptation	적응	authority	권위
administrative district	행정구역	autumn foliage	단풍
aim	목적	average	평균
air temperature	기온	awfully, very	엄청
all kinds of	온갖	bad luck	불운
all night long	밤새	bark	껍질
alliance	연합	base	바탕
the Allied Forces	연합군	basis	근거
alone	혼자	bathroom	욕실
among or by ourselves or themselves	–끼리	battle	전투
amount	분량	battlefield	전쟁터
amount of money	금액	battleship	군함
ancient palace	고궁	beginning (of)	초
appearance, looks, figure	모습	beginning of semester in college	개강
area, region	지역		
armistice agreement	휴전 협정	behavior	행동
around …, about …	–경	being fortunate in property	재물운
around the time when	무렵	being lucky in love	애정운
arrow	화살	beyond one's endurance	참다못해
artistic	예술적	biggest	최대
arts	예술	bird	새
as it is	그대로	blood type	혈액형
as soon as possible	하루빨리	body	신체
at once all together	한꺼번에	bombing	폭격
at one sight	한눈에	bouquet	꽃다발
at that time	당시	bow	활

bowl	그릇	college festival	대동제
brassware	놋그릇	college or school of	단과대
brevity	용맹함	a university	(=단과대학)
Buddha's Birthday	석가탄신일	college orientation	새내기 배움터
building, structure	건축물	colonial rule	식민 통치
business	업무	comfort women	위안부
by force	강제로	common; public	공동
capital city of a country	수도	commonly, often	흔히
castle	성	communal sharing of labor	품앗이
celebrity	연예인	community	공동체
cell	칸	complex	단지
Celsius	섭씨	compliment	칭찬
center	중심	composition	구성
center, hub	중심지	compulsory duty of military	병역 의무
chaff	겨	service	
change of course registration	수강 신청 변경	conferment ceremony	수여식
character (in book, story)	등장인물	confusion, chaos	혼란
to be cheap	저렴하다	conjunction	접속사
childhood	어린 시절	consciousness	의식
Children's Day	어린이날	consideration	배려
Chinese character	한자	construction firm	건설사
Chosŏn Dynasty	조선 왕조	content items	내용물
chrysanthemum	국화	contest	대회
circumference	둘레	convenience	편의
citizen	국민	cooperation	협력
city	도시	cooperative attitude	협동심
classmate	동기	the core social class of	핵심 계층
cliff	절벽	North Korea	
climate	기후	correspond; applicable to	해당하다
club	동아리	cost of living	물가
club name	동아리명	counter for building	동
the Cold War	냉전	counter for horses and large	필
collectivism, groupism	집단주의	animals meaning 'head'	

counter for unit	호	each	각각
cowhide	소가죽	early college exam	수시
crane	학	eating culture	식문화
criticism	비판	economic power	경제력
cultural assets	문화재	educational environment	교육 환경
cultural facilities	문화 시설	effect	영향
custom	풍습	elderly person	노인
custom; convention	관습	electric fan	선풍기
daily life	일상생활	electricity bill	전기세
daily necessities	생활용품	elementary, middle, and	초·중·고
daily routine	일상	high schools	
dark age	암흑 시대	emcee	사회자
daughter-in-law	며느리	emotion	감정
day	날	emotion; sentiment	정서
Day of the March First	3·1절	emotional	감성적
Movement		emotional disorder from	화병
the dead	사망자	suppressed anger	
declaration of independence	독립선언서	emperor	천황
declaration of war	선전 포고	Emperor Kojong	고종 황제
degree	학위	emphasis	강조
Demilitarized Zone (DMZ)	비무장지대	end	종료
deposit	보증금	enemy	적
desire	열망	entrance to ceremony hall	입학식장
destruction	파멸	entrance ceremony of school	입학식
difference	차이	especially, exceptionally	유난히
dining table	밥상	esteemed elder	어르신
diplomacy	외교	even	–조차
direction	방향	even, as well	–마저
discrimination	차별	even; what is more	심지어
district (of a city)	구	event	행사
division	분단	everyone	다들
dragon	용	exchange	교환
dude	놈	excuse	구실

experience	체험	funeral	장례
experiencing temple life ("temple stay")	템플스테이	funeral	장례식
		game, match	경기
expiration	만료	generalization	보편화
exploitation	착취	generation	세대
facilities	시설	geographical features	지형
fairy	선녀	geography	지리
fan	부채	Germany	독일
farewell	이별	ghost	귀신
farming	농업	gist	요지
fashion	패션	glass for alcohol	술잔
fear	두려움	to go down	전해지다
feng shui, geomancy	풍수	good and evil	선악
festival	축제	good luck	행운
fighter plane	전투기	government	정부
fire (disaster)	화재	governor-general's office	총독부
the first	초대	gradually	서서히
first of all	일단	gradually	차차
fish tank	어항	grave, tomb	무덤
fisherman	어민	groceries	식료품
fixed, set	일정	group	단체
fleet	함대	habit	버릇
flood	홍수	haetae (a unicorn lion)	해태
-fold	–배	handicapped person	장애인
folktales, fairy tales	설화	handkerchief	손수건
form; format	형태	hexagon	육각형
former days; the old days	예전	high-level; advanced	고급
fortune teller	점쟁이	Hindu	힌두교도
fountain	분수	holiday	휴일
four-leaf clover	네 잎 클로버	house rent	집세
the four main gates of old Seoul	사대문	household in mourning	상가
		if that is the case anyway	기왕이면
freely	자유롭게	illegally	불법으로

imagination	상상	Korean-style sticky taffy	엿
immediate	즉각적	Korean traditional rice cake	인절미
in a short time, soon	머지않아	coated with bean flour	
in addition	그 외에도	the Korean War	한국 전쟁
in this way	이리하여	laborer	노무자
incident	사건	ladder	사다리
including …	~(으)ㄹ 비롯한	land	땅
income	수입	landlord	집주인
increase	상승	large family	대가족
individuality	개성	last ten days of a month	하순
industrial facilities	산업 시설	law	법
insignia	휘장	leadership	리더십
interior	실내	lecture cancellation	휴강
international war	국제전	leech	거머리
interview date	면접일	legend	전설
invasion	침략	lesson	교훈
invitation	초청	level, standard	수준
the irony of fate	새옹지마	life	인생
irrigation	물대기	light	빛
Japanese occupation period	일제 강점기	line, route	노선
jeans	청바지	line of demarcation	경계선
jinx	징크스	living room	거실
just the two persons (adv.)	단둘이	loan word	외래어
kimchi making for the winter	김장	local product	토산품
kindergarten	유치원	long term	장기간
kindness	은혜	long-term lease with large	전세
kitchen	주방	sum deposit as a rental	
knife, blade	칼	longevity	장수
Korea-Japan Annexation	한일 병합 조약	loss	손실
Treaty		lotto	로또
Korean Empire	대한제국	loyalty	의리
Korean Peninsula	한반도	luck	복
Korean people	한민족	luck, fortune	다행

lumberjack	나무꾼	naturally	당연히
lump sum of money	목돈	necessary	필수적
magpie	까치	neighbor	이웃
major, main	주요	neighborhood	동
manpower	노동력	news	소식
March First Movement	3·1운동	news (article)	기사
maxim	격언	no wonder; somehow	어쩐지
maybe	아마(도)	north latitude	북위
medicine and medical supplies	의약품	northern side	북쪽
member	구성원	nullity	무효
metropolitan area	수도권	oath	맹세
mice	쥐	object	대상
middle ten days of a month	중순	octagon	팔각형
midsummer	한여름	old government official exam	과거
midterm examination	중간시험	on campus	교내
Military Demarcation Line	군사분계선	one's way of speaking	말투
military	군, 군대; 군사	one's entire assets	전 재산
military service	군복무	one's wife	아내
modern style	현대식	oneself	자신
monetary	금전적	only, sole	유일한
monk	스님	open one's eyes	눈을 뜨다
monthly rent	월세	oral tradition, handed down verbally	구전
morning assembly	조회		
most of, mostly	대부분	organization, institution, agency	기관
mother-in-law	시어머니		
Muslim	무슬림	originally	원래
name of a country	국호	the other party	상대방
national border area	국경지대	owning; preparation	마련
national border line	국경선	the Pacific War	태평양 전쟁
national flag	국기	pair of	쌍
national holiday	국경일	Parents' Day	어버이날
National Liberation Day	광복절	particularly	굳이
nationally	전국적으로	pass (card)	통행증

past	과거	rainy season	장마
patriot	애국자	rapidly	급속하게
peace	평화	rather	차라리
peal or sound of bells	종소리	real estate (agent)	부동산
Pearl Harbor	진주만	realistic	현실적
period	시기	really, very	무지
pheasant	꿩	reconciliation	화해
phoenix	봉황	relationship	관계
pig	돼지	religion	종교
pillar	기둥	remains of history	역사 유적
pine tree root	소나무 뿌리	rental fee	임대료
plastic surgery	성형 수술	rented; leased	임대
political party	당	republic	공화국
popular culture	대중문화	residence	주거
population	인구	resources	자원
positive response	호응	rest area	휴식 공간
the Potsdam Declaration	포츠담 선언	restoration of independence	광복
practicality	실용성	rice planting	모내기
present	현재	richness	부
president	대통령	royal subject of Japanese	황국 신민
previous	이전	Empire	
product	상품	Russo-Japanese War	러일 전쟁
prohibited matters	금지 사항	sacrifice	희생
pronunciation	발음	safety	안전
property	재산	Sahoe Ilbo	사회일보
provisional government	임시 정부	Sakhalin	사할린
public institutions	공공 기관	to save one's life	살려 주다
public official, public servant	공무원	scale, size	규모
public place or area	공공장소	school or class trip	수학여행
Qing Empire of China	청나라	scientific basis	과학적 근거
quality	품질	secretly	몰래
quickly	얼른	selfish	이기적
rabbit	토끼	sense of belonging	소속감

separated families	이산가족	studio	원룸
Shanghai	상하이	style, way	양식
sharing	공유	sunlight	햇살
sheep	양	superstition	미신
short term	단기간	surrender	항복
sickle	낫	surroundings, vicinity	주변
sign, notice	표지판	system	제도
single-unit house	단독 주택	taboo	금물
the Sino-Japanese War	청일 전쟁	talent show	장기 자랑
situation	지경	teacher-appreciation banquet	사은회
skyscraper	고층 빌딩	teacher, mentor	스승
small studios mostly for	고시원	tears	눈물
government test takers		text message	문자
snake	뱀	then, in those days	당시
soldier	군인	therefore	그리하여
soundproof	방음	this year	올해
South Korea–North Korea	남북 관계	thought, idea	사상
relations		threshold	문지방
sovereignty	주권	throughout the winter	겨우내
the Soviet Union	소련	tiger	호랑이
space	공간	time period; periodic	시대적
special edition	특집	to accomplish	해내다
spoon and chopsticks	수저	to add	더하다
sports, physical education	체육	to adjust	적응하다
sports day	운동회	to advise	충고하다
stability	안정	to agree	합의하다
sticky rice cake	찹쌀떡	to appear	등장하다
store, shop	상점	to apply	적용하다
story of one's personal	경험담	to attract	매료시키다
experiences		to avoid	피하다
strong and firm	굳세다	to be active	적극적이다
student center	학생회관	to be air-dropped	투하되다

English	Korean	English	Korean
to be anxious	조마조마하다	to be formed	형성되다
to be awkward	곤란하다;	to be gentle, docile	온순하다
	어색하다	to be heartbroken	가슴(이) 아프다
to be beyond description	말할 수 없다	to be helpful; to be instructive	유익하다
to be bold, daring	대담하다	to be humid and hot, to be	무덥다
to be built	지어지다	muggy	
to be called	불리다	to be important, precious	귀중하다
to be careful	주의하다	to be impossible	불가능하다
to be categorized	구분되다	to be impressed	감동하다
to be caught	걸리다	to be in agony	괴로워하다
to be cautious	신중하다	to be included	포함되다
to be closely related	밀접하다	to be indebted to	은혜를 입다
to be concentrated	밀집	to be indecisive	우유부단하다
to be considered, regarded	여겨지다	to be jammed	막히다
to be considered to be	중요시되다	to be just as good as	못지않다
important		to be lacking	부족하다
to be cool and refreshing	선선하다	to be liberated	해방되다
(weather)		to be limited	제한되다
to be curious	궁금하다	to be limited to	~에 국한되다
to be damaged	피해를 입다	to be located	위치하고 있다
to be dangerous	위험하다	to be lucky	운이 좋다
to be delivered	전달되다	to be magnificent	훌륭하다
to be destroyed	파괴되다	to be meticulous, precise	꼼꼼하다
to be dry	건조하다	to be mobilized	동원되다
to be easygoing	털털하다	to be nasty	고약하다
to be envious	부러워하다	to be open to	개방되다
to be evaluated	평가되다	to be outgoing	활발하다
to be expelled from a school	퇴학당하다	to be outstanding	뛰어나다
to be expressionless	무표정하다	to be particular	까다롭다
to be faithful, sincere	성실하다	to be pitiful	안타깝다
to be familiar	익숙하다	to be pretty	어여쁘다
to be fancy	화려하다	to be prohibited	금지되다

to be punished	벌을 받다	to burn	타다
to be rational	합리적이다	to care about what others	눈치 보이다
to be registered	등재되다	think	
to be repeated	반복되다,	to cause	끼치다
	되풀이되다	to change	변화하다
to be restored	복원되다	to check	확인하다
to be sacred	신성하다	to choose, select	고르다
to be safe	무사하다	to clip one's fingernail/toenail	손톱/발톱을
to be separated	분리되다		깎다
to be sharp	날카롭다	to collect news data	취재하다
to be sociable	사교적이다	to combine	겸하다
to be sophisticated	세련되다	to come and go	왕래하다
to be special	특별하다	to come in and go out	드나들다
to be stationed	주둔하다	to come to an end	막을 내리다
to be steeped (lit., melted) in	녹아 있다	to comfort	위로하다
to be strict	엄격하다	to commemorate	기념하다
to be surrounded	둘러싸이다	to conclude	맺다
to be timid	소심하다	to confront	대치하다
to be torn down	철거되다	to connect	연결하다,
to be unlucky	불행하다,		이어 주다
	재수(가) 없다	to consider	여기다
to be unpredictable	변덕스럽다	to contract	계약하다
to be useful	유용하다	to control	지배하다
to be weakened	약화되다	to cope with	감당하다
to be worth seeing	볼 만하다	to cross over	넘다
to be written	쓰이다	to cut across	가로지르다
to become known	알려지다	to deal with	대하다
to begin with	아예	to decide (something for	정해 주다
to bombard	폭격하다	someone)	
to borrow	빌리다	to deliver	전달하다
to borrow (and use)	빌려 쓰다	to develop	발전하다
to break out	발발하다	to deviate, get out of	벗어나다
to breathe	숨을 쉬다	to die	사망하다

to dig out	캐다(=파내다)	to go near	다가가다
to divide, share	나누다	to grow	성장하다
to dream	꿈을 꾸다	to guess	추측하다
to drop	떨어지다	to handle	취급하다
to end up losing	놓치고 말다	to hate	밉다
to endure	견디다	to have a fight	전투를 벌이다
to enjoy eating (frequently)	즐겨 먹다	to have a stomachache	배탈이 나다
to enter	들다	to have time	시간(이) 되다
to enter a war	참전하다	to help	봐주다
to erect	세우다	to hit a bell	종을 치다
to escape	도망가다	to hold a funeral	장례를 치르다
to escape	탈출하다	to ignore	무시하다
to escape death	목숨을 건지다	to initiate a conversation	말을 걸다
to escape from North Korea	탈북하다	to invade, attack	침공하다
to establish	설치하다,	to join	가입하다
	수립하다	to judge	판단하다
to evaluate	평가하다	to knock	노크하다
to evanesce	사라져 가다	to lag behind	낙후되다
to experience	경험하다	to lead	이끌다
to experience	겪다	to leave	남기다
to face, head to	향하다	to let or allow someone/	시켜 주다
to feel lost and gloomy	막막하다	something	
to feel secure	든든하다	to link arms	팔짱을 끼다
to fight	싸우다	to live	생활하다
to fix	고치다	to look through	훑어보다
to flow	흐르다	to lose	잃다
to follow	따라가다	to lose one's life	목숨을 잃다
to found a country	건국하다	to make a plan	계획을 세우다
to get caught	들키다	to make a request	부탁하다
to give, offer	바치다	to make an air raid	공습하다
to give a hearty send-off	환송하다	to make fermented food	담그다
to go against etiquette	예의에 어긋나다	to mistreat	구박하다
to go around and take turns	돌아가다	to misunderstand	오해하다

to move	옮기다	to run away	달아나다,
to move, travel	이동하다		도망치다
to mow rice plants	벼를 베다	to run short	딸리다
to obtain	구하다	to save money	저축하다
to occur, break out	일어나다	to say, ask (to a senior)	여쭈다
to open a port	개항하다	to settle	자리잡다
to overcome	극복하다	to shake one's leg	다리를 떨다
to overflow	넘쳐 나다	to shed blood	피를 흘리다
to participate	참가하다,	to shoot	쏘다
	참여하다	to shorten	줄이다
to pass	지나다	to sign	서명하다
to pay back	갚아 주다	to stand out	부각되다, 튀다
to perish, ruin	망하다	to stay, put up	묵다
to plant rice sprouts	모를 심다	to stick into	꽂다
to pray, wish	기원하다	to stir up	일으키다
to prefer	선호하다	to suffer from	~에 시달리다
to prevent	방지하다	to supervise	관리하다
to pull something off	이루어 내다	to suppress	진압하다
to raise	키우다	to surge into	밀려들다
to reach	이르다	to talk (with)	이야기를 나누다
to receive help	도움을 받다	to tap	두드리다
to recite	외우다	to touch, reach	닿다
to recover	되찾다	to unfold, spread	펴다
to remind	연상시키다	to unite in harmony	화합하다
to repay	갚다	to utilize; apply	활용하다
to rescue	구하다	to whistle	휘파람을 불다
to resolve	해결되다;	to win (a prize)	당첨되다
	해결하다	to wind up, coil up	감다
to return	돌아오다	to yearn	동경하다
to ring a bell	종을 울리다	top, summit	정상
to rob	빼앗다	total amount	전액
to rule, govern	통치하다	traditional Korean paper	창호지

triumphal arch	개선문	vocabulary	어휘
tropical night	열대야	volcanic action	화산 작용
turtle	거북	volunteer service in farming communities	농촌 봉사 활동
type	유형		
unconditional	무조건	wallet	지갑
UNESCO Intangible Cultural Heritage Representative List	유네스코 인류 무형문화유산 대표목록	war	전쟁
		The War Memorial of Korea	전쟁 기념관
		water bills	수도세
unexpected fortune	횡재	way of thinking	사고방식
unification	통일	weapon	무기
units	단위	weeding	김매기
units to measure space in Korea, about 35.5 square feet	평	wild geese	기러기
		wisdom	지혜
the upper class	상류층	with one's utmost sincerity	정성껏
usual, general	일반적인	work	작업
utterly; absolutely	도저히	worker, hand	일손
various kinds	각종	World War II	제2차 세계 대전
victory	승리	wound	상처
video	영상	yellow dust	황사
village	마을	young person	젊은이
virtue	미덕		

CREDITS

All illustrations, except p. 199: Han Sejin, Circus Image Works Co., Ltd.

P. 31: "Geographical Atlas of Seoul 2013," The Seoul Institute of Seoul Metropolitan Government, 2000. http://data.si.re.kr/map-seoul-2013

P. 75: "Seoul 2005 Urban Form and Landscape," The Seoul Institute of Seoul Metropolitan Government, 2005. http://data.si.re.kr/seoulphoto

P. 199: An illustration of a dining get-together, Jungmin Son

Pp. 208–209: "*Kimjang,* Making and Sharing Kimchi in the Republic of Korea," Representative List of the Intangible Cultural Heritage of Humanity of the United Nations Educational, Scientific and Cultural Organization (UNESCO) Cultural Heritage Administration, 2013